Praise for David Hill's other

1788

'Brings to life the events and the major characters of this extraordinary journey.'—*Sydney Morning Herald*

'A must for your bookshelf' . . . the best book I have read all year.' —*News Mail*

The Gold Rush

'A big, sprawling tale of adventure that really shines.'—*The Sun-Herald*

'An exhaustive, compelling and crisply written account of Australia's gold fever and its enduring effects.'—*Daily Telegraph*

The Great Race

'An epic tale told concisely and confidently by Hill.'—*The Times*

'The story of Flinders is fascinating, and Hill's narration of his expeditions is compelling . . . The author's sensitive portraits of Flinders and other historical figures are one of the book's strengths.' —*The Australian*

The Making of Australia

'David Hill captures Australia's past in a very readable way. It is a history book that is a fascinatingly told story. Sometimes colonial politics can be a little dry. Not here.'—*The Weekly Times*

The Forgotten Children

'This book is a heartbreaker you can't put down, a calmly narrated and impeccably researched tale of children from poor British families transported to Australia not in the eighteenth but in the twentieth century . . . For Hill to be able to detail the story in such clinical detail is itself a triumph of spirit and craft and humane forgiveness.' —*Thomas Keneally*

DAVID HILL

CONVICT COLONY

The remarkable story of the fledgling settlement that survived against the odds

ALLEN&UNWIN
SYDNEY • MELBOURNE • AUCKLAND • LONDON

First published in 2019

Allen & Unwin
83 Alexander Street
Crows Nest NSW 2065
Australia
Phone: (61 2) 8425 0100
Email: info@allenandunwin.com
Web: www.allenandunwin.com

NATIONAL LIBRARY OF AUSTRALIA

A catalogue record for this book is available from the National Library of Australia

ISBN 978 1 76052 866 9

Index by Puddingburn
Set in 12/16 pt Adobe Garamond by Midland Typesetters, Australia
Printed and bound in Australia by Griffin Press, part of Ovato

10 9 8 7 6 5 4 3 2 1

FSC www.fsc.org MIX Paper from responsible sources FSC® C009448

The paper in this book is FSC® certified. FSC® promotes environmentally responsible, socially beneficial and economically viable management of the world's forests.

To my son Damian and his godmother Katerina Koulaki.
Σας αγαπώ πολύ

Contents

Introduction

Twenty-five-year-old Ruth Bowyer was living with an aunt and working as a kitchen maid at the Bush Hotel in Staines west of London when she was arrested and charged with stealing five silver spoons valued at 30 shillings.

After spending three weeks in London's Newgate prison she was brought to trial at the Old Bailey on 25 October 1786. The four prosecution witnesses included an ironmonger and his assistant, who both alleged that Bowyer had tried to sell them the stolen spoons, plus a policeman and a local publican. The court records show that Bowyer had no legal representation, offered no evidence and presented no defence. The only words she uttered at her trial were: 'I am not guilty of the crime. I have no witnesses.'[1]

After being found guilty she was sentenced to seven years' 'penal transportation' and sent back to Newgate. Six months later on 30 April 1787 she and 36 other women from Newgate and ten from prison hulks on the Thames were taken in chains on carts to Portsmouth and loaded onto the *Prince of Wales*, which was one of the eleven ships that made up the fleet that would take nearly 800 convicts to form a new settlement at Botany Bay on the other side of the world.

Barely three months after arriving in Sydney on 5 June 1788 Ruth became ill and died. She was buried in an unmarked grave. She was one of hundreds of convicts who died either during the voyage to New South Wales or during the early years of the settlement.

Ruth's death reminds us of the risks and the dangers associated with the early European settlements in far-flung and remote locations around the globe. By the time the first fleet of British convicts was sent to Botany Bay in 1787, a number of European powers, including Spain, Portugal, the Netherlands, Britain and France, had for two centuries already been trying to establish colonial settlements in North and South America, Africa and Asia. In the process, thousands of people had died prematurely, and so many fledging communities had collapsed before ever becoming viable.

With small and leaky ships setting out on voyages that would last months or years many expeditions simply sank without trace, never to be heard of again. And many of those that did reach their destinations failed to survive the inhospitality of the country, the extreme and volatile climates, the hostile natives, the disease and the shortages of food.

The British convict settlement in Australia faced numerous threats, and battled for many years before its future was secure. From the very start, the destination of Botany Bay proved incapable of supporting human settlement and was abandoned only days after the arrival of the First Fleet. One of the major challenges of establishing the new settlement in Sydney was that many of the convicts—men, women and children—were totally unsuited to building a new life in the harsh Australian bush.

In Sydney the early harvests repeatedly failed, hoped-for ships with fresh supplies did not arrive, and the colony only narrowly avoided starvation. For many years the hungry settlers lived in crude shacks with no chairs to sit on, no table to sit at and no bed to sleep in. More than ten years after their arrival, hundreds of convicts were working in the fields naked because they had run out of clothing.

In its first turbulent and uncertain decades the colony also had to survive a corrupt local military dictatorship, increasingly violent conflict with the local Aboriginal people, the threat of invasion from other European powers, an armed convict uprising and an overthrow of the colonial government. In many respects it is truly remarkable that the colony survived to become the nation of Australia.

1

Bound for Botany Bay

> '. . . measures should immediately be pursued for sending out of this kingdom such of the convicts as are under sentence or order of transportation . . . His Majesty has thought it advisable to fix upon Botany Bay.'
>
> Lord Sydney

The British plan to settle Australia proved to be a high-risk venture and involved years of struggle to survive. For a start, very little was known about the original destination of Botany Bay, which had to be abandoned by the First Fleet as totally unsuitable for settlement only a few days after arriving in 1788.

The only Europeans to have visited this part of the southern landmass were members of the expedition led by Captain James Cook on HMS *Endeavour*, which had spent less than a week there a decade and a half earlier, in late April and early May of 1770.

Cook was far from the first foreigner to 'discover' Australia as more than 50 European ships had seen or landed on the continent over the preceding 200 years. The first recorded sighting of Australia by Europeans was believed to be in 1606, when both Dutch and Spanish seafarers separately reached the north-east extremities of what is now known as the Cape York Peninsula, although there may have been others before them. Around 1300, Marco Polo had mentioned the existence of a great southern continent but offered no firsthand knowledge of the place. Some archaeological evidence suggests that, from 1500 or so, Portuguese, Dutch and Spanish ships may have touched on the western and southern coasts.

It has been argued that the Chinese explorer Admiral Zheng He reached part of the west coast in 1421.[1] There is also evidence of other Asian ships regularly visiting the north of Australia from around 1600, including Indonesian and Malay traders who harvested bêche-de-mer, or sea slugs, which were regarded as a delicacy and an aphrodisiac by many in China.

The first Englishman known to have reached Australia was the pirate William Dampier, who landed on the north-west coast in 1688. When Cook charted a large part of the east coast more than 80 years later it was not known for sure that it was part of the same continent. Not until the explorer Matthew Flinders charted the remaining 'unknown coast' of what he would later name Australia more than 30 years after Cook in 1803 was it confirmed that there was no strait or sea separating the east and west coasts.

The British decision to establish a convict colony was largely because it needed a solution to the huge increase in the number of prisoners in its gaols in the second half of the eighteenth century. This was the Georgian era, the start of the Industrial Revolution, and the British Empire was expanding at a time when the earlier European powers of Spain, Portugal and the Netherlands were in decline. In 1774 the British government took over the administration and control of India from the British East India Company and thus began 150 years of British rule over the subcontinent. In 1768 James Cook began his remarkable voyages of discovery in the Pacific, which resulted in more British possessions.

It was also the age known as the Enlightenment, which questioned traditional beliefs and authority and embraced the idea that humanity could be advanced through rational change. The Church was slipping from its central role in cultural and intellectual life and science was becoming increasingly emancipated from the restraints of theology. It was also a period that saw the flourishing of music, theatre, literature and art.

Britain's king at the time was George III. He was to sit on the throne for 50 years from 1760—at the time the longest reign of any British monarch. He had come to the throne on the death of his grandfather George II and was the third German to become the British monarch but the first of those to be born in England and to speak English as his native language. The first two Georges took little interest in the politics of their realm and were quite content to let Britain's ministers govern on their behalf but George III became far more involved in the running of his governments. When the British established the convict colony in New South Wales, George took a strong interest in its progress and read each of the sixteen dispatches sent back in the first years of the colony by Governor Arthur Phillip.[2]

George was first believed to have gone mad in 1788, the year the First Fleet arrived in Australia, and at that point the parliament debated whether he should continue as king but he then appeared to recover. However, in 1811, with a recurrence of his illness his son ruled as Prince Regent, later becoming King George IV when his father died in 1820.

George III typified the enlightenment of the era. He founded and paid for the establishment of the Royal Academy of Arts, started a collection of royal books and later gave the 65,000 volumes to the British Museum. He was keenly interested in agriculture, which earned him the nickname 'Farmer George', and was an enthusiastic student of science. Many of his scientific instruments survive and are now in the British Science Museum.

The remarkable advances of the age did not benefit everyone of course. While the rich got richer the overwhelming majority of people continued to live and die poor. The industrial changes brought a huge number of people from the country into the increasingly overcrowded towns and cities. This overcrowding was compounded by the 'enclosures' of the commons, whereby landowners fenced off land that had previously been used by everyone. Hand in hand with the growing numbers of displaced and out-of-work citizens came an increase in crime as many resorted to stealing to survive.

By the second half of the eighteenth century crime rates had spiralled as the number of property thefts increased and it was estimated that in London 115,000, or one in eight, people were living off crime.[3] Historian and politician Horace Walpole said at the time that robbery in broad daylight had become so common that 'one is forced to travel, even at noon, as if one was going into battle'.[4]

To combat the rise in crime, the British Parliament increased the number of laws protecting property. At the beginning of the 1700s criminal offences that attracted the death penalty had been limited to the most serious acts such as murder or treason. By the end of the century more than 100 additional crimes—almost all of them involving offences against property—had been made capital offences. Thirty-three were added during the reign of George II and a further 63 during the first decades of the reign of George III.

The new crimes that warranted execution included smuggling, selling a forged stamp, burglary, extortion, blackmail, larceny by servants, arson, wilful destruction of property, petty theft and stealing horses. Most of the new capital offences were created by a 'placid and uninterested' parliament, where in nine cases out of ten there was 'no debate or opposition'.[5] So great was the increase in the number of capital offences that by 1800 Sir Samuel Riley could observe that 'there is probably no other country in the world in which so many and so great a variety of human actions are punishable by loss of life than in England'.[6]

However, despite the dramatic rise in the number of convicts sentenced to death, fewer were actually being executed. The judges in the courts of England were increasingly reluctant to send offenders to the gallows and more and more death sentences were being commuted to transportation to America—even after such shipments had been suspended.[7] As a consequence of this judicial leniency the proportion of those executed fell dramatically over the second half of the eighteenth century. In the 1750s about 70 per cent of those convicted were actually hanged but, by the time the First Fleet set sail, barely a quarter of the condemned reached the gallows. By the end of the century the figure would drop to less than 20 per cent.[8] Accordingly, throughout the last quarter of the eighteenth century, the gaols and the prison hulks overflowed as the prison population increased by more than a thousand people every year.

James Hardy Vaux was eighteen years old when he was convicted at the Old Bailey for stealing a handkerchief valued at eleven pence and sentenced to seven years' transportation. Before being sent to New South Wales he spent time both at Newgate and on the prison hulk *Retribution* on the Thames. At Newgate, he later wrote, he was lucky to survive an outbreak of contagious disease that killed many others:

> . . . being unusually crowded with prisoners, a most dreadful contagion, called the gaol fever, made its appearance, and spread so universally, throughout every ward and division of the prison, that very few escaped its attack. I was one of the first to contract it, and was immediately carried to the infirmary, or sick-ward of the prison, where I only remember having my irons taken off . . . I became delirious, and was so dreadfully affected, as to continue insensible for three weeks, during which time, I had no knowledge of my parents, or of any other person who approached me; and the fever raged to such a degree, that I was obliged to be bound in my bed.[9]

Vaux described his time on the hulk as 'miserable', 'distressing' and 'shocking':

> There were confined in this floating dungeon nearly six hundred men, most of them double-ironed; and the reader may conceive the horrible effects arising from the continual rattling of chains, the filth and vermin naturally produced by such a crowd of miserable inhabitants . . . All former friendships or connexions are dissolved, and a man here will rob his best benefactor, or even mess-mate, of an article worth one halfpenny.[10]

Vaux wrote of how each day the men would be taken ashore to work supervised by brutal overseers:

> Every morning, at seven o'clock, all the convicts capable of work, or, in fact, all who are capable of getting into the boats, are taken ashore . . . and are there employed at various kinds of labour, some of them very fatiguing; and while so employed, each gang of sixteen, or twenty men, is watched and directed by a fellow called a guard. These guards are most commonly of the lowest class of human beings; wretches devoid of all feeling; ignorant in the extreme, brutal by nature, and rendered tyrannical and cruel by the consciousness of the power they possess . . . They invariably carry a large and ponderous stick, with which, without the smallest provocation, they will fell an unfortunate convict to the ground, and frequently repeat their blows long after the poor sufferer is insensible.[11]

In another written account of life on prison ships and hulks, Thomas Watling, convict and artist, said they were worse than the French Bastille or the Spanish dungeons during the Inquisition:

> When I have seen so much wanton cruelty practised on board the English hulks, on poor wretches, without the least colour of justice, what may I not reasonably infer?—French Bastille, nor Spanish Inquisition, could not centre more of horrors.[12]

There was also at this time growing pressure from prison reformers who were campaigning against the appalling conditions in the gaols and the prison hulks. Foremost among them was John Howard, the wealthy son of a successful merchant, who became a well-known advocate and campaigner. In 1777, after studying incarceration in England, he wrote a book that painted a devastating picture of the reality of prisons and brought into the open much of what for those in genteel society had been out of sight and thus out of mind. Howard wrote that healthy men who entered the system were often reduced to illness and death. He said that disease was so rife that more prisoners were killed by ill health than 'were put to death by all public executions in the kingdom'.[13]

In some prisons, he wrote, there was no food allowance, and in others no fresh water and no sewerage. In most gaols there was a shortage of fresh air and ventilation, and of beds and bedding, with the result that many prisoners were forced to sleep 'upon rags, others on bare floors'.[14]

Largely as a result of the agitation of Howard and other reformers legislation was passed in parliament for the building of two new prisons but funding was not made available and construction never began. To reduce the numbers of prisoners incarcerated in England parliament legislated in 1777 for the reintroduction of the overseas transportation of convicts, although the bill did not prescribe to which countries the prisoners would be sent.

The idea of transporting convicts to some faraway country was not new. Legislation had been introduced in Elizabethan England to banish certain criminals to 'lands beyond the seas', but the practice took on a new dimension in the eighteenth century.[15]

It was during the early 1700s that the British began sending significant numbers of felons to America. In 1717 parliament had passed the *Act for the Further Preventing Robbery, Burglary, and Other Felonies and for the More Effective Transportation of Felons and Unlawful Exporters of Wool; and For the Declaring the Law upon Some Points Relating to Pirates*—better known as the *Transportation Act*. This marked the beginning of the large-scale removal of criminals to foreign shores. Over the next 60 years or so about 40,000 convicts were sent to America.

Unlike the later transportation to Australia the transporting of convicts to America was privately run. Convicts were sold by their gaolers to shipping contractors, who took them across the Atlantic and sold them to plantation owners for the duration of their sentences.

America ceased to be a convenient dumping ground for convicts following the War of Independence. The revolt that began in the 1760s turned into a full-blown war, triggered by resentment in the colonies about the unfair taxes the British government was extracting from them. In December 1773 a number of Boston radicals dumped a large quantity of British-owned tea into the harbour in what became known as the Boston Tea Party. During the following years a number of colonial delegates, including George Washington and John Adams, met in Philadelphia and famously denounced 'taxation without representation'. The year 1775 saw the first serious outbreak of hostilities, at the Battle of Bunker Hill, in Massachusetts, which the British won, but they also incurred heavy losses. In 1776 the American colonies issued their Declaration of Independence and the British dispatched their biggest ever force to fight overseas.

A number of major battles were won by either side. The Americans were supported by France, which joined the war on their side in 1777.

The decisive battle was the Battle of Yorktown in Virginia in May 1781, where British General Cornwallis surrendered and more than 6000 of his soldiers were taken prisoner.

When news of Yorktown reached London, the parliament moved to end the war, despite the opposition of George III, who wanted to continue the British military commitment until the insurrection was crushed. His prime minister Lord North duly continued fighting but was forced to resign in March 1782, in the face of declining parliamentary support for the war. After three short-lived prime ministerships, 24-year-old William Pitt ('the Younger') came to power in December 1783, and it was he who was head of the government when the decision was made to establish a convict colony in Australia.

The loss of the American colonies was a crushing blow to the prestige of the British Empire, and meant that the British no longer had a convenient dumping ground for their surplus convicts. The selection of the site to establish the new convict colony took many years, and Botany Bay was only chosen as a last resort when all the other options had been eliminated.

In 1779 the House of Commons had established a committee to find a workable solution to the escalating prison problem. The committee heard from a number of witnesses who argued for the establishment of a convict colony in a number of overseas locations, including Gibraltar and sites along the west African coast. The committee noted that because of the American War of Independence it 'was not in the power of the executive government at present to dispose of convicted felons in North America'.[16]

When asked by the parliamentary committee which location he thought was best for the establishment of a penal colony eminent botanist Sir Joseph Banks, who had sailed with Cook on the *Endeavour* a decade before, praised Botany Bay's fertile soil and plentiful water and food.

> Joseph Banks Esq. being requested, in the case it should be thought expedient to establish a colony of convicted felons in any distant part of the Globe, from whence escape might be difficult. And where, from the fertility of the soil, they might be able to maintain themselves, after the fifth year, with little or no aid from the mother country, to give his opinion what place would be the most eligible for such settlement, informed your committee that the place that appeared to him adapted for such purpose, was Botany Bay.[17]

Banks went on to tell the committee that he thought the local people would not offer resistance; there were also no 'beasts of prey' and 'plenty of fish'. He added that much of the soil was barren but enough of it was sufficiently rich 'to support a very large number of people'. The grass 'was long and luxuriant' and the country 'well supplied with water'. It was also well supplied with wild vegetables and there was an 'abundance' of timber for any number of buildings.[18] Banks's evidence finished on the optimistic note that after a while the settlers might 'undoubtedly maintain themselves without any assistance from England'.[19]

Banks was not the first to argue for the establishment of a penal colony in the Pacific. Nearly a quarter of a century earlier, French writer and statesman Charles de Brosses had suggested that France settle a penal colony on the island of New Britain, where felons could be purged from society.[20] Englishman John Callander proposed the same solution for Britain in 1776. In his three-volume *Terra Australis Cognita* he argued that Britain should found a convict colony on New Britain and explore the possibility of annexing New Holland, New Zealand and Van Diemen's Land (Tasmania).

Banks's report to the parliamentary committee was strangely at odds with his own far less enthusiastic journal entries at the time of his voyage. On 1 May 1770, the second day after the arrival of the *Endeavour*, Banks recorded that he had gone on a long walk with his botanist colleague Daniel Solander:

> We . . . walked till we completely tired ourselves, which was in the evening . . . the soil wherever we saw it consisted of either swamps or light sandy soil on which grew very few species of trees.[21]

Three days later he had ventured further inland:

> Where we went a good way into the country which in this place is very sandy and resembles something of our moors in England, and no trees grow on it but everything is covered with a thin brush of plants about as high as the knees.[22]

At the time the committee was hearing its evidence the commander of the 1770 *Endeavour* expedition, James Cook, was on his third great voyage in the Pacific Ocean. And when Banks was giving his evidence to the House of Commons in April 1779 it was not yet known in London that Captain Cook had been killed. In February Cook had been searching for a passage linking the Pacific and Atlantic oceans when he was murdered in Hawaii.

Back in 1770 Cook had recorded his own assessment of Botany Bay. He noted that the soil was 'generally sandy' and otherwise made no enthusiastic assessment as Banks had done.[23]

But even if Cook had been available to give evidence in London he had far less sway than Joseph Banks. While Cook had been the commander of the *Endeavour* expedition, the aristocratic Banks was far more influential in England, where he had the ear of the government, the Admiralty and the King. He would be a hugely prominent figure in England over the first twenty years of British settlement in New South Wales, the person everyone turned to for advice about the colony. Even though he had only spent six days there eighteen years before the arrival of the First Fleet he was regularly consulted on a wide range of matters, including botany, earthquakes, sheep breeding and exploration. Over many years he corresponded with the colony's governors and the commanders of British exploration ships whose captains regularly returned with more botanical samples for his analysis.

Banks was the only son of a wealthy landowner and retained a lifelong interest in the family estates at Revesby Abbey in Lincolnshire. Both his father and grandfather had been members of parliament. He had first travelled as a botanist to Newfoundland and Labrador in 1766, when he was 23 years old, and was soon afterwards elected as a member of the Royal Society.

When he boarded Cook's *Endeavour* as a 'gentleman of fortune', he had taken aboard with him his two pet greyhounds and a suite of eight staff, including the noted naturalist Daniel Solander. Of the party, only Banks, Solander and two tenants from his family estates survived the expedition.

Banks was made president of the Royal Society at the relatively young age of 35 and was heavily involved in the development of Kew Gardens. He became a trustee of the British Museum and a member of many London gentlemen's clubs, including the Society of Dilettanti. In later years he became a well-known spectacle in London where he lived in New Burlington Street—overweight and crippled by gout, he presided over the Royal Society in a wheeled chair in full court dress, wearing the Order of the Bath.

It has never been clear why Banks was so enthusiastic about Botany Bay as a site for the convict colony but it is worth noting that he stood to gain personally from a settlement on the east coast of Australia. He had collected many botanical samples during his short stay at Botany Bay and for many years would benefit from ships returning with more specimens. In the event, the settlers in New South Wales would struggle for many years to survive in an environment that was far harsher than Banks had suggested to the House of Commons.

Despite the House of Commons report and Banks's strong recommendation, the decision of where to send the surplus convicts was deferred for several years. It seems that some of the British ruling elite were still hopeful that the American insurrection could be put down and the transportation of convicts to the American colonies resumed. As late as 1783 George III was adamant that 'unworthy' British convicts should be sent there.[24]

As the issue dragged on unresolved the community concern at the ever-increasing prison population increased. In 1784 the House of Commons debated and passed a bill titled *An Act for the Effectual Transportation of Felons and Other Offenders*, which, like its predecessor in 1777, urged the reintroduction of transportation but did not specify any sites to which they would be sent.

A petition delivered to the government on 5 March 1785 by the high sheriff and grand jury of the county of Wiltshire typified the widespread and growing concern about the overcrowded prisons and hulks:

> To His Majesty's Secretaries of State.
>
> The country is overburdened with such a number of transports [hulks] which have been increasing since the last two assizes and is continuing to increase by the addition of many more sentenced to the same punishment. We apprehend from the physicians employed for the purpose of inspecting the state of the gaols by the justices of the said county that there is a great danger of an epidemic distemper being the consequence of the close confinement of so many prisoners. We therefore humbly entreat that the [prisoners] may be removed from the said gaol with the utmost expedition.[25]

In April 1785 an increasingly frustrated House of Commons set up another committee to look at how its *Transportation Bill* of the year before might be given effect.[26] The committee heard that the hulks were failing to address the convict problem and how being confined on a hulk was *more* likely, and not less likely, to corrupt newcomers and commit them to a life of crime. The usual destinations were again presented, including Africa, but these were rejected largely because of evidence that convict settlements there were unlikely to be able to sustain themselves.

Earlier in the year attorney-general Richard Arden had sent to his colleague Lord Sydney a detailed proposal for the transportation of convicts to Botany Bay. Arden had been sent the idea by Sir George Young, an admiral in the Royal Navy, who had added his own highly qualified recommendation:

> I profess myself totally ignorant of the probability of the success of such a scheme, but it appears upon a cursory view of the subject, to be the most likely method of effectively disposing of convicts, the number of which requires the immediate interference of the government.[27]

Young's elaborate plan to send convicts to Botany Bay took up many of the proposals that had been suggested over a number of years and it would become the basis of the plan eventually adopted by the government.

> Botany Bay, or its vicinity . . . with a fair open navigation . . . there is no doubt . . . that a lucrative trade would soon be opened . . . I think . . . that a territory so happily situated must be superior to all others.[28]

By 1785 the public clamour for a decision about the overcrowded gaols increased and there were 56 separate petitions from sheriffs, judges, mayors, town clerks or gaolers calling for the removal of prisoners from the gaols and hulks. In March 1786 the country was shaken by the news of a riot by prisoners on a hulk at Plymouth, which resulted in 44 people being shot, eight fatally. For months the government procrastinated, while 'parliament, press, pamphlet and pulpit' were all demanding that something be done.[29]

Finally, Lord Sydney announced that the government had reached a decision. According to Sydney, the King had approved a plan for the convicts to be sent to establish a colony in New South Wales.

Born in 1733, the aristocratic Thomas Townshend began his political career in the House of Commons at the age of 21 and was elevated to the House of Lords in 1783 as Lord Sydney, where he served as home secretary and colonial secretary for six years in the government of Pitt the Younger. There is considerable argument about Sydney, who has been variously described as an enlightened and progressive politician and a person who 'scarcely rose above mediocrity'.[30]

In his letter to the Treasury outlining the decision, Sydney's main argument concerned the overcrowding of England's gaols:

> The several Gaols and places for confinement of felons in this kingdom being so crowded a state that the greatest danger is to be apprehended, not only from their escape, but for infectious distempers, which may hourly be expected to break out among them, his Majesty, desirous of preventing by every possible means the ill consequences which might happen from either of these causes, has been pleased to signify to me his royal commands that measures should immediately be pursued for sending out of this kingdom such of the convicts as are under sentence or order of transportation . . . His Majesty has thought it advisable to fix upon Botany Bay.[31]

Sydney's letter instructed the Treasury to provide the necessary shipping to transport 750 convicts, 'together with such provisions to last two years'.[32] The fleet would sail via the Cape Verde Islands in the Atlantic and Cape Town, where it would be authorised to take on fresh supplies as well as cattle and other farm animals for the new settlement in New South Wales. The orders also called for the provision of the necessary officers and assistants and would be accompanied by three companies of marines, who would stay in Botany Bay 'so long as it is found necessary'.[33]

Responsibility for the detailed planning of the expedition fell to Lord Sydney's deputy, Evan Nepean. Thirty-three-year-old Nepean worked as the under-secretary in the Home Office responsible for the administration of Britain's overseas colonies and organising the details of the First Fleet was his first major appointment.

Nepean came from Saltash in Cornwall and began his naval career working as a purser on British ships along the American east coast during the American War of Independence. In 1782 he became secretary to Admiral Lord Molyneux Shuldham, before being promoted a year later to work in London as Lord Sydney's under-secretary. He was regarded as an excellent administrator and proved a valuable friend of the First Fleet and its commander, Arthur Phillip, particularly in the early years of the settlement. He later became chief secretary for Ireland, a Lord of the Admiralty and a member of parliament.

The Times newspaper came out in favour of the Botany Bay decision, arguing—erroneously, as it turned out—that transportation would cost less than other schemes to deal with the growing number of convicts:

> There is one circumstance to be alleged in favour of the Botany Bay scheme in which it surpasses every other mode of punishment of felons which has hitherto been carried into execution. In every former scheme, whether of confinement and hard labour, ballast heaving on the Thames etc., etc., there was a constant and growing expense on the public, which could not be reduced so long as the punishment continued. In the present instant the consequence is quite reversed for after the second year it is to be presumed that the convicts will be in the habit of providing for themselves and the expense to the public will be trifling.[34]

It had taken years, but now that the decision had finally been made the British civil service and the Royal Navy began the challenging task of organising the world's biggest overseas migration fleet at Portsmouth. In a little over nine months it would be ready to sail.

2

An Unpromising Commander

'I cannot say the little knowledge I have of the Captain Phillip would have led me to select him for a service of this complicated nature.'

Admiral Richard Howe, First Lord of the Admiralty

The man chosen to lead the expedition to Botany Bay and become the first governor of New South Wales was 48-year-old naval captain Arthur Phillip. Like James Cook before him Phillip was an example of how men of relatively modest backgrounds could progress through the ranks of the Royal Navy in a way that was far less likely at the time in the army, where class and connections were all-important. When Phillip was plucked from semi-retirement at his Hampshire farm there was nothing particularly outstanding in his career to recommend him but he would prove a good choice.

Phillip was born in Bread Street, London on 11 October 1738, the son of a German language teacher from Frankfurt who had come to England for work. Phillip's mother had previously been married to Captain John Herbert of the Royal Navy and this helped Phillip gain entrance to the Greenwich Royal Naval School at the age of twelve. The school had been established in the early eighteenth century for the sons of naval men who had died or been killed at sea. Not only had Captain Herbert been a naval man but he was related to Lord Pembroke, who was to become an MP, a privy councillor, a major general in the army and a Knight of the Garter. It is unlikely that Phillip would have been enrolled at Greenwich but for this connection.

At fifteen, Phillip went to sea on the merchant ship *Fortune*, transferring two years later, before the start of the Seven Years War, to the Royal Navy ship the *Buckingham* as the captain's servant. Phillip was progressively promoted to able seaman then yeoman-corporal in 1756. His early career involved sailing to the West Indies and to the Mediterranean, where he was involved in a battle with French ships off the island of Majorca. Three of his colleagues were killed and another eight injured in the conflict. The commander of the British fleet Vice Admiral the Honourable John Byng was accused of mismanaging the British effort. He was court-martialled, found guilty and shot.

In 1760 and aged 22 Phillip was made master's mate and began the steady climb up the Navy promotional ladder. In 1762, while serving on the *Stirling Castle* in Barbados, he was part of the fleet that successfully took Havana, which was a significant event in Spain's decline as a dominant European power. Between 1763 and 1775, and with the ending of the Seven Years War, Phillip spent most of his time in semi-retirement on half-pay farming near Lyndhurst, in Hampshire.

In 1763 Phillip married Margaret Denison, the widow of a successful London merchant. Not much is known about the marriage except that the couple had separated within five years. Over the next 40 years there was an almost total absence in his reports and correspondence of any reference to his marriage or his wife.

Phillip resumed active service at 37 years old, in 1775—as a captain in the Portuguese Navy. At the time, hostilities had again broken out between Portugal and its colonial rival, Spain, and Portugal sought experienced leadership for its navy from its ally Britain. Phillip would serve in the Portuguese Navy for three and a half years before leaving in 1778 with high praise. He was particularly remembered for protecting the Portuguese port of Colonia do Sacramento on the River Plate with only his ship the *Pillar* to restrain a Spanish assault. In 1778 he returned to the British Navy.

After only a year as commander of the *Basilisk* in the English Channel fleet, and another spell on his Hampshire farm, Phillip was captain of a number of British naval ships until 1784 when he was again laid off. After this date we know little about what he did until he was appointed governor of New South Wales two years later except that he took leave for about a year to visit the south of France.

The circumstances surrounding his appointment are somewhat mysterious. While he was not totally unqualified—Phillip was an experienced farmer and few others among the First Fleet settlers had any background in working the land—there was nothing in his career that suggested he stood out as the most suitable candidate for the post. The appointment did not impress the First Lord of the Admiralty Lord Howe, who made it clear in a dispatch to Lord Sydney that although Phillip was a naval man, he was not the choice of the Admiralty:

> I cannot say the little knowledge I have of the Captain Phillip would have led me to select him for a service of this complicated nature.[1]

In reply, Lord Sydney noted that 'presumably . . . he was appointed on his merits, as he appears to have no private influence with his superiors'.[2]

Could this have been the case? There is some indication that Sir George Rose, the under-secretary of the Treasury, was the minister responsible for making the decision. Rose's estates were near Phillip's farm in Hampshire; later in New South Wales, Phillip would name the rich farming land 20 kilometres west of Sydney 'Rose Hill' in honour of Sir George. Evan Nepean, Lord Sydney's deputy, may also have had some say in the appointment. Nepean knew Phillip well from his time with the Portuguese Navy. Perhaps Phillip did have a certain amount of influence with the right people after all.

After confirmation of his appointment in October 1786 Phillip had many months to study all of the information about Botany Bay, including Cook's journal and maps and the extensive reports of Sir Joseph Banks. Much of his time was spent in a small office at the Admiralty in London where he wrote on small sheets of paper his 'views on the conduct of the expedition and the treatment of convicts'.[3] While there is no date on these documents, which are now in the safekeeping of the UK Public Records Office, it is believed they were written in January or February 1787, three months before the First Fleet sailed. Much of what he wrote was included in the official instructions he was given several months later, which suggests Phillip may have been involved in designing his own role as governor.

Phillip wrote that he wanted an advance party to build huts and other buildings in the new settlement before the bulk of the convicts arrived. He planned to pick up plants and animals in Rio de Janeiro but did not want any food or grog loaded onto the convict ships where it could be stolen. During the voyage he said he wanted to regularly inspect the convict transports to 'see they are kept clean and receive the allowance ordered by the Government'. He was aware of the health risks of crowding so many people below decks and saw a need to protect the women convicts from abuse by the seamen:

> The women in general I should suppose possess neither virtue nor honesty . . . But there are some who still retain some degree of virtue, and these should be permitted to keep together, and strict orders to the master of the transport should be given that they are not abused and insulted by the ship's company.[4]

Phillip believed marriage between the convict women and men should be encouraged. He also suggested the men might marry Aboriginal women, who should be protected from ill-treatment:

> The natives may, it is probable, permit their women to marry and live with the men after a certain time. In which case I should think it necessary to punish with severity the men who use the women ill, and I know of no punishment likely to answer the purpose of deterring so well as exiling them to a distant spot, or an island, where they would be obliged to work hard to gain their daily subsistence, and for which they would have the necessary tools, but no two to be together.[5]

To help address the shortage of women in the new settlement Phillip argued that some of the convict women should become prostitutes in government-organised brothels, as he said had been the case at London's Millbank prison:

> It may be best if the most abandoned are permitted to receive the visits of the convicts in the limits allotted them at certain hours, and under certain restrictions; something of this kind was the case in Millbank formerly.[6]

For the 250 marines at the new settlement, Phillip promoted the novel idea of sending ships to various Pacific islands to bring back women:

> Women may be brought from the Friendly and other islands, a proper place to receive them, and where they will be supported for a time, and lots of land assigned to such as marry with soldiers of the garrison.[7]

Curiously, Phillip did not believe the convicts should be allowed to become part of the new colony even at the end of their sentences:

> As I would not wish convicts to lay the foundations of an empire, I think they should ever remain separated from the garrison, and other settlers that may come from Europe, and not be allowed to mix with them even after the seven or fourteen years for which they may be transported.[8]

With regard to punishing the convicts, Phillip's vision was surprisingly tolerant, or perhaps naive, when he suggested that the death penalty 'should never be necessary. In fact I doubt if the fear of death ever prevented a man of no principle from committing a bad act.'[9] He believed only two crimes warranted the death penalty—murder and sodomy—even though he must have been aware of the widespread homosexuality among seamen, who were often away at sea for years at a time with few or no encounters with women.

> For either of these crimes I would wish to confine the criminals till an opportunity offered of delivering him as a prisoner to the natives of New Zealand, and let them eat him. The dread of this will operate much stronger than the threat of death.[10]

While Phillip was working in London, preparations were proceeding at Portsmouth for a fleet of ships to take almost 1500 people, with food for two years and all the tools and equipment they would need, to the other side of the world. The people to be carried on eleven tiny and leaky wooden sailing ships included nearly 800 convicts (which was more than the 750 originally planned), 250 marines, military officers and civil officials, about 50 wives and children and several hundred of the ships' crews.

The British planning was meticulous. The preparation for the voyage would take nine months and would include the provision of ships, the appointment of officials and marines, and the loading of convicts, supplies and equipment.

The organisation started when home secretary Lord Sydney wrote to the Lords of the Treasury on 18 August 1786 asking that the necessary arrangements be made for the shipping of the convicts:

> My Lords, I am . . . commanded to signify to your Lordships his Majesty's pleasure that you do forthwith take such measures as may be necessary for providing a proper number of vessels for the conveyance of seven hundred and fifty convicts to Botany Bay, together with such provisions, necessaries and implements for agriculture as may be necessary for their use after arrival.[11]

Two weeks later Lord Sydney wrote to the Admiralty with a specific request for the organising of the ships necessary for the transport of the fleet:

> My Lords, the King having been pleased to signify his Royal Commands that seven hundred and fifty of the convicts now in his kingdom under sentence of transportation should be sent to Botany Bay, on the coast of New South Wales . . . at which place it is intended the said convicts should form a settlement, and that the Lords of the Treasury should forthwith provide a sufficient number of vessels for their conveyance thither, together with provisions and other supplies, as well as tools to enable them to erect habitations, and also implements for agriculture.[12]

Of the eleven ships of the First Fleet only two were supplied by the Navy: the *Sirius* and the *Supply*. The other nine were privately owned and chartered by the Navy on behalf of the government. Six of these were to transport the convicts, some marines and some officers and, in a few cases, their families. The remaining three carried supplies and equipment for the settlement.

On 14 September 1786 *The Times* reported that 'the Government is now about settling a colony in New Holland in the Indian seas and the commissioners for the Navy are now advertising for 1500 tons of transports'. To attract tenders for the supply of the ships the government posted advertisements in its offices, on public noticeboards and at Lloyd's coffee house in London.[13]

The British government paid 10 shillings per ton per month for the privately contracted ships.[14] The charges would be applied until the ships returned to England except for three that would be released from service when they unloaded in New South Wales and would then go on to China to pick up a cargo of tea for the British East India Company.[15]

The contract stipulated that the shipowner provide the captain and crew for the ship, which would operate under the instruction of the fleet commander Captain Arthur Phillip. The Admiralty had a great deal of experience contracting ships for the movement of British troops overseas and was thorough with the details of the contract. The contractor had to fit out the ship with bunks and bedding for the convicts, provide adequate food rations and ensure their quarters were adequately ventilated and regularly cleaned and fumigated. They also had to provide space for a small infirmary and regularly take the prisoners on deck for exercise.

By today's standards the ships were tiny. The largest was less than 35 metres long and less than 10 metres wide. They all had three masts, except the supply ship *Friendship* and the Navy ship *Supply*, which only had two masts. The flagship was the *Sirius*. It was a six-year-old 500-ton converted merchant ship that was 33.7 metres long and 9.98 metres wide. It carried over 140 people including crew, Commander Arthur Phillip, other senior officers and marines, and some wives and children. The *Sirius* was fitted with extra guns, with the intention that these would be taken ashore in the new settlement if fortifications were required.

The second Navy vessel, the *Supply,* was the smallest and fastest ship in the fleet. Weighing only 170 tons, and only about a third of the size of the *Sirius,* it was to carry 50 people and a limited amount of supplies. Twenty-nine-year-old Royal Navy lieutenant Philip Gidley King, who sailed with the First Fleet and later became governor of New South Wales, believed the *Supply* was a poor choice for the voyage:

> Her size is much too small for a long voyage which added to her not being able to carry any quantity of her provisions and her sailing very ill renders her a very improper vessel for this service.[16]

Six of the nine chartered ships transported convicts. The largest was the *Alexander,* which at 35 metres long was of a similar size to the *Sirius.* It left Portsmouth with 198 male convicts, 37 marines, the wife of one marine and the ship's crew of about 100.[17] The next-largest transport was the *Scarborough,* which was 34 metres long and carried 208 male convicts, 34 marines and the ship's crew. The *Charlotte* carried both male and female convicts. In addition to its crew it carried a total of 160 people, including 88 male and twenty female convicts, with two of their children, 44 marines, six marines' wives and one child. The *Lady Penrhyn* and the *Prince of Wales* were smaller and almost identical in size at a little over 31 metres long and a little over 9 metres wide. The *Lady Penrhyn* carried 102 women convicts with their five children, six marines and the ship's crew. The *Prince of Wales* carried almost all the families of the marines, 49 male and female convicts and its crew. The *Friendship* was the smallest of the transports at 23 metres long and it carried 97 male and female convicts, 45 marines and a number of officials and their families. The remaining three ships of the fleet were the *Golden Grove,* the *Fishburn* and the *Borrowdale,* which carried food and supplies.

The details for the equipment taken to build the new settlement were elaborate. They included 300 chisels, 175 handsaws and hammers ('one for every four men'), 140 drawing knives and augers (large drills), 100 wood planes, broad axes and adzes (an arched axe with the blade at right angles to the handle), 50 pickaxes, 40 crosscut saws, 30 grindstones, 84 razors, twelve ploughs, ten blacksmiths' forges, ten blacksmiths' bellows, ten barrels of nails, 10,000 bricks, 600 fishing lines, several thousand fish hooks and 40 wheelbarrows.

It was envisioned that the settlers would build their own homes. For initial accommodation, they took 500 tents for the convicts and 160 tents for the marines, and 36 larger 'marquees' for the married officers and their wives.[18]

For Phillip, the Navy Board commissioned a 'Mr Smith in Knightsbridge' to make a special timber-and-canvas prefabricated government house. The structure, which was initially the largest building in the settlement, was 45 feet (13.7 metres) long, 17 feet 6 inches (5.3 metres) wide, and 8 feet (2.4 metres) high, with five windows on each side.[19] Notwithstanding that Phillip had accommodation that was superior to that of anyone else in the settlement he still complained to Lord Sydney five months after it was erected that his house was 'neither wind nor water proof'.[20]

For the construction of more permanent dwellings, official buildings and storehouses, the ships were loaded with 1000 small squares of glass, 200 pairs of door hinges and 100 iron locks with keys.

As part of the plan the fleet was 'to take on board . . . a sufficient quantity [of food] for two years consumption'.[21] The basic diet for the sailors and the marines was salted meat, dried peas, rice, oatmeal and hardtack bread—and a grog ration of half a pint of spirits per man each day. The convicts were rationed about three-quarters of the food given to the sailors and marines but without the grog ration.

The grog ration was an important part of the Royal Navy seaman's diet for nearly 300 years and was also issued to marines serving overseas, including those who went to guard the convicts in New South Wales.

The widespread and corrupt trading of 'rum', which was the colloquial term for all fortified wine and spirits, would become a prominent feature of the early decades of the new colony.

The meat ration was either pork or beef that had been dried, salted and stored in barrels. The notorious hardtack bread, the basis of the seafarer's diet for hundreds of years, was made from wheat or barley baked brick-hard and devoid of moisture, like a tough biscuit. Normal bread would only be edible for a week if stored in cool and dry conditions and even less if it was damp or hot. Hardtack bread could last almost indefinitely but was less palatable, very hard to chew and often infested with weevils.

For cooking and eating, the fleet carried with it 330 iron pots and a dozen tin saucepans, six large butcher's knives, 40 camp kettles, 700 wooden bowls, 700 platters and 500 tin plates, as well as thousands of wooden spoons.

In addition to taking some seeds and plants from England, the fleet was also ordered to buy vegetable and fruit plants and grain seeds en route as well as farm animals that they could breed at the new colony:

> These vessels should touch at the Cape of Good Hope, or any other places that may be convenient, for any seed that may be requisite to be taken from thence, and for such live stock as they can possibly contain . . . which can be procured . . . and at the most reasonable rates, for the use of the settlement at large.[22]

The animals included chickens, geese, ducks, pigs, goats, horses, pigeons and cows, as well as a number of pet cats and dogs, including Captain Arthur Phillip's two greyhounds. Some farm animals were taken aboard at Portsmouth, but most were bought at the ports of call along the way—and most at Cape Town, the last stop before the long haul across the Southern Ocean to New South Wales.

While the plan for the first settlement did not include rabbits, Phillip included a number of them in his first inventory of animal stocks in May 1788, which suggests they were taken to the new settlement aboard the First Fleet.[23] By the twentieth century, of course, rabbits were causing terrible devastation to Australia's pastoral industries until largely eradicated, first by myxomatosis and later the calicivirus.

The plan provided for clothing for the male convicts. Each was issued two jackets, four pairs of woollen drawers, one hat, three shirts and four pairs of worsted stockings, three frocks, three trousers and three pairs of shoes. The plan did not elaborate on the items of clothing for the women other than saying a 'like sum' of money should be allocated to ensure they were adequately provided for. When the fleet eventually sailed from Portsmouth nine months later, however, it left without enough clothing for many of the women.

There was little official discussion of why women should be included in the First Fleet and how their number was calculated.

> I am therefore commanded to signify to you Lordships his Majesty's pleasure that you do forthwith take such measures as may be necessary for providing a proper number of vessels for the conveyance of 750 convicts to Botany Bay . . . and perhaps 200 females.[24]

The plan echoed Phillip's own simple solution to the anticipated shortage of women in the new colony:

> After arrival of the ships which are intended to convey the convicts . . . [a] ship . . . if it should be thought most advisable, may be employed in conveying to the new settlement a further number of women from the Friendly Isles, New Caledonia, etc., and from whence any number may be procured.[25]

This proposed large-scale removal of women to another country was wholly a pragmatic measure as it was felt that otherwise 'it would be impossible to preserve the settlement from gross irregularities and disorders'.[26]

In instructions issued to Phillip a few weeks before the fleet sailed he was told that if he did go looking for women they could not be abducted:

> Whenever [the ship] shall touch on any of the islands in those seas . . . you are . . . to instruct [your commanders] to take on board any of the women who may be disposed to accompany them to the said settlement. You will, however, take special care that the officers who may be employed upon the service do not, upon any account, exercise any compulsive measures, or make any fallacious pretences, for bringing away any of the said women from the places of their present residence.[27]

The convicts loaded onto the transports of the First Fleet were not chosen with any regard to their fitness for the long voyage, or to their ability to build a new colony once they reached Botany Bay.

Nearly all of the close to 600 men and almost 200 women prisoners had been convicted of theft—and almost 60 per cent of the First Fleet's convicts had been sentenced for stealing food or other goods of relatively low value. Thirteen per cent were guilty of burglary or breaking and entering, and a further 15 per cent had been convicted of highway robbery, robbery with violence or grand larceny. The remainder had been found guilty of living off the proceeds of stolen goods (fencing), swindling, forgery or some other stealing offence. Many had been sentenced to death but had had their sentences commuted to transportation. Typically, the terms were for seven years, fourteen years or life imprisonment; in many cases any sentence effectively became a life sentence because of the difficulty of returning to England once a term had expired.

Over 80 per cent of the convicts were sentenced to seven years, and many of these had already served at least half of their term in British gaols or hulks by the time they reached New South Wales. Remarkably, it appears that no consideration was given to how much of their sentences the convicts had left to serve when they were put on the fleet. In addition to being unjust to the prisoners, this was a major headache for Phillip, who sailed without the convicts' records and had no way of confirming whether prisoners who complained that they had completed their sentences were telling the truth.

A number of convicts had been destined for transportation to America or Africa and had been for some years in gaols or hulks already. For example, 43-year-old Thomas Eccles had been sentenced in Guildford, Surrey, in March 1782 to be hanged for stealing bacon and bread but 'reprieved for service in Africa for life'.[28] Eccles had served five years in gaol before being assigned to the *Scarborough.*

The average age of the First Fleet convicts was around 27. Nearly 50 per cent were under 25 and only 5 per cent were older than 45.[29] The oldest male was believed to be Joseph Owen, who was in his early 60s, and the youngest was John Hudson, who was just nine years old when convicted and sentenced.

The youngest female is believed to have been thirteen-year-old Elizabeth Hayward (or Haywood). Born on 30 July 1773, she was a clog maker who had stolen a linen dress and a silk bonnet.[30] She was charged in 1786, and convicted and sentenced at the Old Bailey to seven years' transportation in January 1787 barely four months before the departure of the fleet. The oldest woman is thought to have been Dorothy Handland, who sailed on the *Lady Penrhyn* and was recorded by the ship's surgeon as being 82, although other prison records say she was 60 or 65. Many of the women on the First Fleet had relationships and children with military and naval officers. In a few cases the relationships lasted, but in most the women were abandoned, along with their children.

Twenty-three-year-old Rebecca Boulton was found guilty of stealing a cotton gown and a silk handkerchief in July 1784 and sentenced to seven years' transportation. For the next three years she was held in a filthy Lincoln gaol, before being loaded on the convict ship the *Prince of Wales*, which carried 47 convict women and two convict men. In April 1787, the month before the departure of the fleet, she gave birth to a daughter she named Rebecca, who was allowed to go with her to New South Wales. Possibly from spending three years in squalid conditions, Boulton died at the age of 26, within two months of reaching Sydney. Her one-year-old daughter died a week later.

John Hudson's case provides a good example of how the British legal situation took no regard of the age of offenders. He was just nine years old when brought before Justice Hall at the Old Bailey two weeks before Christmas 1783 and sentenced to seven years' transportation. He had been found guilty of 'feloniously breaking into' the house of William Holdsworth in East Smithfield at one o'clock in the morning the previous October and stealing a linen shirt, five silk stockings, a pistol and two aprons, which had a total value of £1.2s. In evidence, the court was told that the boy had entered the house by breaking a windowpane. He had later been seen by a woman, Sarah Baynes, washing himself near a boarding house in East Smithfield, with the stolen goods near him. A pawnbroker, John Saddler, told the court that on 17 October Hudson had tried to sell him the stolen shirt saying it belonged to his father. John Hudson did not have a father, or a mother, as the proceedings of the Old Bailey record:

COURT TO PRISONER: How old are you?
PRISONER: Going on nine.

COURT: What business were you brought up in?
PRISONER: None, sometimes chimneysweep.
COURT: Have you any father or mother?
PRISONER: Dead.
COURT: How long ago?
PRISONER: I don't know.

After his conviction, Hudson was loaded on the convict transport *Mercury* bound for America in April 1784, but the convicts rose up and overpowered the crew when the ship passed the Isles of Scilly off the south-west coast of England. However, severely bad weather forced them back towards Torquay. Many of the convicts made land and disappeared but over 100 were eventually recaptured, some later in London. Hudson and another boy, thirteen-year-old James Grace, were in one of the *Mercury*'s small boats off Torquay when they were recaptured. Grace had also been convicted and sentenced at the Old Bailey to seven years' transportation, for stealing cloth.

The fact that the two boys were able to escape the death penalty had nothing to do with their young age: they and a number of other escaped convicts successfully argued that they were technically still at sea when they were apprehended. After their recapture both Grace and the now ten-year-old Hudson were tried for returning from transportation 'before their term had expired'. They were convicted, sentenced again and sent to Exeter prison in Devon, and then to the *Dunkirk*, a de-masted former warship that had been converted to a prison hulk in Plymouth harbour. There they waited till they were sent on the First Fleet to New South Wales.

Hudson's trial took place more than 50 years before Charles Dickens wrote *Oliver Twist.*[31] The boy was one of thousands of abandoned or orphaned children trying to survive in the recesses of urban England. Many died young—of malnutrition, cold, exhaustion, neglect, cruelty or any of a range of ugly infections and diseases.

Hudson was initially sent to Newgate in London and survived the prison's 'depravity, profanity, wretchedness and degradation'[32] probably because the conditions there were little different to those he had been used to before going to prison. For many of the convicts, young or old, life in prison was no worse than on the outside; in some respects it was better. John Nicol, who sailed as a steward on the all-women Second Fleet convict ship the *Lady Juliana*, believed that many convicts were hardened and indifferent to prison life:

> Numbers of them . . . were thankful for their present situation . . . when I enquired their reason they answered . . . we have good victuals and a warm bed. We are not ill-treated, or at the mercy of every drunken ruffian, as we were before. When we rose in the morning we knew not where we would lay our heads in the evening, or if we would break our fast in the course of the day.[33]

Thirty-five-year-old George Barrington, who had given his occupation to the Middlesex court in 1791 as 'gentleman', was one of London's most notorious pickpockets. He was convicted and sentenced to seven years' transportation. Later, he wrote to his wife describing how the convicts had been taken from prison to the ships for transportation to New South Wales:

> Our departure from Newgate was so sudden it was utterly impossible to leave you even a single word. We had not the least notice of it until four in the morning; and before we could get the better of the shock three hundred and nineteen of us were conveyed to the riverside . . . the unfortunate wretches were all of them loaded with irons and chained together . . . You may be sure I have often pictured to myself the state of your mind upon finding me dragged away without our seeing one another at parting . . . it has . . . given me infinitely more pain and misery than the punishment itself.[34]

Marine Captain Watkin Tench was responsible for censoring the convicts' letters to their families while the fleet was at Portsmouth waiting to sail, and said fear and uncertainty among the convicts was a constant theme. A feature of the letters written by the convicts, he noted, was their apprehension about 'the impracticality of returning home, the dread of a sickly passage and the fearful prospect of a distant and barbarous country'.[35]

The convict quarters below decks on the transport ships were extremely uncomfortable. Typically, each convict was allocated a sleeping space only 18 inches (46 centimetres) wide and on most transports the headroom was usually under 6 feet (183 centimetres) and some as low as 4 feet 5 inches (135 centimetres). Only the shortest convicts would have been able to stand without bending over and the tallest had to bend double to move around. To add to the discomfort the convicts lived in almost total darkness as there were no portholes and lanterns were considered an unacceptable fire risk.

Arthur Phillip's deputy on the First Fleet was 50-year-old bachelor John Hunter, who would eventually succeed Phillip as governor of New South Wales and become another significant figure in the story of the early colony. Hunter was born in Leith, Edinburgh's port, in August 1737 into reasonably comfortable circumstances. His father was a ship's master and his mother Helen was the niece of a lord provost of Edinburgh, a position similar to city mayor. Hunter enjoyed music and Latin, briefly studying at the University of Aberdeen before pursuing a career at sea when he became the captain's servant on HMS *Grampus* at sixteen years old in May 1754.

Over the next six years he was promoted to able seaman and then midshipman. In 1760 he qualified for promotion as a lieutenant but he must not have sufficiently impressed his superiors because he remained without a commission for another twenty years. During this time he served on a number of ships and was involved in several Royal Navy actions, including the assault on the French coast fort of Rochefort in 1757, the capture of Quebec in 1759, and various operations in North America and the West Indies. In 1780 he obtained his first commission as a lieutenant, commanding a number of ships before being appointed captain of the *Sirius* under Commander Arthur Phillip in 1786.

The chaplain for the new colony was 34-year-old Reverend Richard Johnson, who was probably the best-educated member of the First Fleet. Born in Yorkshire, he attended grammar school at Kingston upon Hull before graduating from Magdalene College, Cambridge. He sailed on the store ship *Golden Grove* with his wife Mary and a servant. Distressed by what he regarded as the depravity of the convicts, Johnson went to a lot of trouble to take with him plenty of material that, he hoped, would help straighten their twisted souls. With the help of the Society for the Promotion of Christian Knowledge he loaded aboard the First Fleet 4200 books, including 100 Bibles, 100 Books of Common Prayer, 400 testaments, 500 psalters and 200 church catechisms. In addition, he took a large number of pamphlets on moral guidance, including 110 copies of *Exhortations to Chastity*, 100 copies of *Dissuasions from Stealing*, 200 copies of *Exercises Against Lying* and 50 copies of *Caution to Swearers*. No doubt Johnson hoped the convicts would derive great benefit from all of this but only a small minority of the new settlers—most of whom were officers—could actually read. In Sydney in 1790, Johnson and his wife had their first child, a daughter, to whom they gave the Aboriginal name Milbah. Two years later they had a son.

The first judge in the new colony was 31-year-old David Collins, who sailed with Phillip on the *Sirius*. Collins was born in Ireland and came from a reasonably well-to-do family, his father having been a marine officer who reached the rank of major-general. In 1770 young David had joined his father's division as a fourteen-year-old ensign and five years later fought in the American War of Independence. Later, while stationed at Halifax, Nova Scotia, he married Maria Stuart, the daughter of a British officer. He was retired aged 27 on half-pay in 1783 with the rank of captain. Like a lot of his fellow officers Collins would at this time have been looking for an appointment that would allow him to resume his career on full pay, and it is believed that his father encouraged him to take the position of Judge Advocate in the new colony even though he had no formal legal training.

Unlike some of his officer colleagues, Collins left his wife in England. He would not return for another ten years, and when he did he found her ill. However, Maria recovered sufficiently to help her husband publish his journal in England in 1802. Two years later Collins left her again, to lead an expedition to establish a convict settlement at Port Phillip Bay, near present-day Melbourne. He would never see Maria again.

The commander of the marines was the cantankerous and opinionated 47-year-old veteran Major Robert Ross, who had a tempestuous and unfriendly relationship with Arthur Phillip.[36] Strained relations would continue between the senior officers of the marines and the first four New South Wales governors—Phillip, Hunter, Philip Gidley King and William Bligh—who were all naval men. This would culminate in the army's overthrow of Governor Bligh on the twentieth anniversary of the arrival of the First Fleet, 26 January 1808. Ross was a gruff, larger-than-life character who was disliked even by his own officers and men. Lieutenant Ralph Clark said Ross was 'without exception the most disagreeable commanding officer I ever knew'.[37] Judge Advocate David Collins wrote of his 'inexpressible hatred' of Ross.[38]

Ross was born in Scotland in 1740 and joined the marines as a sixteen-year-old lieutenant in 1756. Over the next 30 years he served in North America and in the war against the French; he was involved in the capture of Quebec and then the American War of

Independence, including the pyrrhic British victory at the Battle of Bunker Hill in Massachusetts in 1775, when the English incurred more than 200 dead and 800 wounded. On his way home to England on the *Ardent*, Ross was captured by the French but subsequently returned as part of an exchange of prisoners. From 1781 he served in the Mediterranean and the West Indies until he was appointed lieutenant-governor, or second in command to Phillip.

When Ross sailed to New South Wales he took with him his eight-year-old son, John, whom he signed up as a volunteer in the marines. Six months after arriving in Sydney, Ross wrote to England seeking permission to appoint his son as a second lieutenant to fill a vacancy: 'As I have ever since arriving here entered my son, John Ross, as a volunteer, serving without pay, may I presume to solicit their Lordships to do me the honour of appointing him to that vacancy in the detachment?'[39] Young John was appointed by his father in February 1789 and served with the Major in Sydney and later on Norfolk Island before both returned to England in 1792.

The chief of the twelve surgeons with the fleet was John White, who arrived at Portsmouth in early March 1787 two months before the fleet sailed. He carried with him various dispatches authorising the loading of the convicts onto the ships for transportation. He had travelled overland from London to Plymouth in 'the most incessant rain I can ever remember', only to be greeted by gale-force winds that delayed the loading of convicts from the hulk *Dunkirk* onto the *Charlotte* and the *Friendship*. They then sailed to join the bulk of the fleet at Portsmouth.

Based on the advice he subsequently received from White in Portsmouth, Phillip complained about the wholly unsuitable state of some of the women convicts being loaded for the voyage:

> The situation in which the magistrates sent the women on board the *Lady Penrhyn*, stamps them with infamy—tho' almost naked, and

> so very filthy, that nothing but clothing them could have prevented them from perishing, and which could not be done in time to prevent a fever, which is still on board that ship.[40]

At White's prompting, Phillip proposed a series of measures to improve the health of the convicts, including washing and dressing new arrivals in clean clothes before loading them onto the transports, allowing the sick a little wine, and supplying them all with fresh meat while they were in Portsmouth harbour.

It was not only the convicts who were sick and dying. By early 1787, a number of marines had arrived at Portsmouth and been assigned to the transports to watch over the convicts. After his arrival Major Ross complained about the conditions on the *Alexander* and the other ships in Portsmouth harbour:

> I have to request . . . to inform their Lordships that the sickness that has, and still does prevail among the marine detachment embarked on the *Alexander*, transport, gives me a great deal of concern. Since the time of their first embarkations no less than one sergeant, one drummer and fourteen privates have been sick on shore from her, some of whom, I am informed, are since dead.[41]

Thirty-seven-year-old Arthur Bowes Smyth was the son of a doctor and came from Tolleshunt D'Arcy, Essex. He sailed on the women's convict ship the *Lady Penrhyn* and kept a detailed journal of the voyage beginning with a description of the appalling squalor he found when he boarded the ship at Portsmouth:

> A corpse sew'd up in a hammock floated alongside our ship. The cabin, lately occupied by the third mate Jenkinson, who died of a putrid fever the night before I came on board, and was buried at Ryde, was fresh painted and fumigated for me to sleep in.[42]

While waiting for the fleet to sail Bowes Smyth was able to go on long walks on the mainland and the Isle of Wight, an escape not available to the convicts who were already being loaded and held below decks on the transports. Back on board the *Lady Penrhyn* Bowes Smyth recorded that many of the women convicts who had never been to sea before 'were very sick with the motion of the ship' out in Spithead where they were waiting to sail.[43]

Twenty-nine-year-old marine Captain Watkin Tench said he put the time before sailing to good use by establishing his authority over the convicts:

> Unpleasant as a state of inactivity and delay for many weeks appeared to us, it was not without its advantages, for by means of it we were able to establish regulations among the convicts, and to adapt such a system of defence, as left us to apprehend our own security, in case a spirit of madness and desperation had hurried them on to attempt our destruction . . . an opportunity was taken, immediately on their being embarked to convince them . . . that any attempt . . . to contest the command, or to force their escape, should be punished with instant death.[44]

Thirty-one-year-old naval surgeon George Worgan, the son of a doctor of music, took a small piano with him on the *Sirius.* It would become the centre of what was a very limited range of entertainments for the civil and military officers and their wives in the infant settlement. When Worgan returned to England in 1791 he left the piano to Elizabeth Macarthur, the first educated woman in the colony and wife of the marine Lieutenant John Macarthur, who was destined to become one of the most controversial and divisive characters in the history of early New South Wales.

The ships' officers and the marine officers were from a different world compared to the ordinary seamen and the marine privates. Accordingly, the officers would enjoy a very different voyage from the others, even though their cabins were small by today's standards. Typically these measured 5 feet by 7 feet (1.5 metres by 2.1 metres), so there was barely enough room for a small bed, a desk and chair, and a storage trunk. The more senior officers had their own cabin, while junior officers often shared with another. Some of the senior officers were permitted to take their servants with them, provoking envy in those who were not. Chief Surgeon John White, when he learned that the chaplain Richard Johnson had been given permission to take his servant, wrote to the naval secretary, Evan Nepean, to complain:

> Sir,
> Finding that the Revd. Johnson is to be allowed the privilege of taking with him to Botany Bay a servant, I hope it will not be deemed unreasonable or improper if I should solicit a little indulgence. Being without a servant my situation must be truly uncomfortable . . . you . . . must know and admit the inconveniences I shall be subject to, not only on the passage, but after landing without one . . . I have applied to Captain Phillip, who has no objection.[45]

While at sea, the officers ate and drank better than anyone else. They would usually eat in the great cabin with others, although sometimes they ate privately at the invitation of the captain. As well as port and other wines, they would often share in the eating of a chicken, pig or other animal that had been killed for the occasion.

The officers' uniforms were colourful and impractical. The dress coat was full-skirted with very deep cuffs, and made of heavy wool that would have been extremely uncomfortable in the tropics. The one practicality was that the officers' garb visibly distinguished and distanced those who gave the orders from those who carried them out.

There were around 300 sailors on the First Fleet, although no exact number was ever recorded. Most of the crews of the nine chartered ships were merchant seamen who were expected to return with their ships to England, so they were not included in the total that formed the original settlement in New South Wales. The crews on the two naval ships, the flagship *Sirius* and the smaller *Supply*, were Royal Navy seamen, men who had either volunteered or been pressed into service during wartime. Signing up enough sailors in England at the time of the First Fleet was not difficult because as Lieutenant Philip Gidley King noted, 'a great number of seamen were at that time out of employ and the dockyard was constantly crowded with them'.[46]

The only seaman known to have written a comprehensive account of his experiences on the First Fleet was 25-year-old Jacob Nagle. Born in 1762 in Pennsylvania, Nagle was fifteen years old when he joined his father in the American War of Independence in 1777 to fight against the British. After three years with George Washington's armies, Nagle joined the American Navy before transferring to the privateers, which were privately owned ships that attacked any ships flying English colours. In 1781 he was captured and pressed into service with the Royal Navy along with sixteen other American sailors. At the end of the American War of Independence Nagle found himself discharged in London. Unable to find a passage back to America, he worked for several years on the Royal Navy ship the *Ganges* before signing on to sail on the *Sirius* in the First Fleet. Of this he wrote:

> I was now near four years on the HMS *Ganges* . . . when the *Sirius*, twenty-eight gun freighter came round the downs to Spithead . . . bound for Botany Bay with a fleet of eleven transports . . . full of men and women convicts and soldiers, with provisions and stores. The Governor [Arthur Phillip] having the privilege of taking any men

> that turned out from the men of war . . . took his pick . . . a hundred and sixty in number.[47]

Most of the seamen on the First Fleet would typically have first gone to sea as boys of ten or twelve, beginning work on the deck and the rigging where nimbleness was required. By the age of sixteen, most had become able to work aloft, reefing sails and knotting and splicing ropes. At sea the sailors were divided into watches that shared work and into 'messes' of eight men for catering, including the cooking of food, collecting cooked food and cleaning up. They had no personal space on the ship and would sleep, usually in hammocks, in a common area below deck that had little space for personal effects and no provision for the men to wash or relieve themselves, which was always done up on deck. The clothes worn by ordinary sailors were completely practical. At work they wore long trousers that could be rolled up, short-waisted jackets that kept the torso warm, and in colder weather heavy woollen pullovers. Most worked barefoot for better grip on the ropes while aloft.

Discipline aboard ship in the eighteenth century was enforced with brutal beatings. There was little point imprisoning sailors on the ships, so offenders were typically flogged and then forced to return to work as soon as they were physically able. The whip was usually a cat-o'-nine-tails, which had nine leather strands, each with a small metal stud at the end that would tear the flesh from the back of the man being punished, causing blood to flow down the back of his legs, into his shoes and across the deck. The rest of the crew would be forced to watch this punishment as an example. Sometimes the punishment would be suspended if the person being flogged became unconscious or was thought to be at risk of dying. The balance of the lashes would be applied when he had sufficiently recovered.

The 250 marines who were to maintain order during the voyage of the First Fleet and provide security for the settlement once they reached Botany Bay were largely from a similar lower-class background to the convicts and the seamen. They were also disciplined severely—in fact, they were flogged more frequently for breaches of rules than the convicts, which would become one of a number of sources of resentment among the marines when the fleet reached New South Wales.

During the voyage, the marines and the seamen would be lucky to have a bench on which to sit while they ate their rations. They were entitled to fruit and vegetables for as long as these lasted, and of course to their daily ration of half a pint of foul-smelling rum.

The marines in particular would play a big role in shaping life in early New South Wales. In the absence of free settlers the marines and especially their officers would become leading farmers and merchants and would take almost monopoly control of the colony's economy.

At the end of April 1787 the fleet was ready to sail but first had to confront a series of last-minute problems. The worst was, with only a week to go, the marines discovered they would not be issued a grog ration once they arrived in New South Wales. In protest, the officers argued that a daily grog ration was 'requisite for the preservation of life' in the new colony:

> We the marines . . . who have voluntarily entered on a dangerous expedition replete with numerous difficulties . . . now conceive ourselves sorely aggrieved by finding the intention of the Government to make no allowance of spirituous liquor or wine after our arrival in the intended colony.[48]

Captain Phillip supported the marines and warned the government of 'much discontent in the garrison' and feared 'very disagreeable consequences' unless they were given the allowance they sought. With only days left, the government yielded and Phillip was authorised to spend the vast sum of £200 at either Tenerife or Rio de Janeiro to buy enough grog for the marines' ration.

By early May the fleet was due to leave—more than four months later than originally planned. It was initially envisaged that the fleet would arrive in October or November 1787, the southern hemisphere spring and a good time for planting crops. Now they would arrive in the second half of summer, far too late to sow for a successful harvest.

Finally, on the night of Saturday, 12 May 1787, Phillip ordered the fleet to prepare to leave early the next morning, and at three o'clock the next morning all the ships were ready. At 4 a.m. the signal was given from the flagship *Sirius*, and by 6 a.m. the whole fleet was under sail, beginning its voyage into the great unknown.

3

A Journey to the Other End of the World

'It was natural to indulge at this moment a melancholy reflection . . . The land we left behind us was the abode of civilised people; that before us was the residence of savages. When, if ever, we might again enjoy the commerce of the world, was doubtful and uncertain . . . all communication with families and friends now cut off, [we were] leaving the world behind us, to enter a state of unknown.'

Judge Advocate David Collins

The First Fleet, heavily laden with passengers, supplies and equipment was finally underway on an eight-month journey fraught with dangers to start a new life on a remote spot at the other end of the world.

As the fleet left Portsmouth the crews struggled to familiarise themselves with sailing the heavily loaded ships. American seaman Jacob Nagle complained that his ship, the *Sirius*, was 'so deep with stores . . . we could scarcely steer her'.[1]

The fleet had passed the Isle of Wight by 10 a.m., and Watkin Tench went below decks on the *Charlotte* to register the mood of the convicts. 'A very few excepted, their countenances indicated a high degree of satisfaction,' he wrote, 'though in some the pang of being severed, perhaps forever, from their native land could not be wholly suppressed.'[2] By noon on the first day they were well past the Needles on the west of the Isle of Wight and they headed for Tenerife, three weeks and almost 2000 kilometres to the south in the Canary Islands.

As the fleet made the run down the English Channel there was a rising swell and 'great sea sickness', particularly among the convicts who had never been to sea before. On the second day they could see the Devon coast and on the third many boats off Falmouth; later in the day they passed the Lizard Peninsula on the Cornish coast, which for many on the First Fleet would be the last they would ever see of England.

This was the first time that the whole fleet had sailed together and they found, to the 'mortification' of the officers, that the sailing speeds of the ships varied considerably. Shortly after the start the convict transports the *Lady Penrhyn* and the *Charlotte* sailed 'exceedingly bad' and the *Charlotte* fell so far behind that it had to be towed out of the English Channel by the *Hyena*, a Navy escort vessel.

The first serious accident occurred after three days at sea, when Corporal Baker of the marines accidentally fired off his musket on the *Sirius*. The shot shattered the ankle of his right foot before the ball went through a casket of beef and killed two geese on the other side.[3] After a week, and when the ships were well out to sea, Phillip gave orders 'to release from their irons' those convicts who were still fettered but sufficiently well behaved. Tench recorded that the disposition of the convicts immediately improved and Captain John Hunter also noted that the additional freedom of the prisoners would 'improve their health', as they could 'now wash and keep themselves clean'.[4]

Phillip's enlightenment was not followed by the notorious Second Fleet, where convicts were permanently kept chained and not allowed on deck; hundreds died on the voyage to Sydney. It was on subsequent convict voyages that the Navy Board stipulated that much of what

Phillip had done would become standard practice, and ship's captains were instructed to provide adequate ventilation and exercise, and to air the bedding and fumigate their quarters regularly.

Towards the end of the first week, with the convoy still battling its way in heavy rain westward along the English Channel, the sailors on the convict transport *Friendship* demanded an increase in their meat ration from one and a half to two pounds per day. It seems the sailors wanted the extra food not for themselves but to pay the convict women for sex. While the ship had been fitted with a prison wall below decks to keep the convicts separated from the crew, the sailors had already created a hole in the barrier to reach the women.

Marine Ralph Clark kept a detailed diary of the voyage and was unimpressed by the sailors' actions: 'I never met with a parcel of more discontent fellows in all my life. They only wanted more provisions to give it to the damned whores, the convict women of whom they are very fond since they broke through the bulk head and had connection with them.'[5]

On the eighth day, Navy agent John Shortland began to visit all the transports to collect for Arthur Phillip information about the convicts' 'trades and occupations'. The commander, well aware of the limited number of skilled workers he had, was already planning the building of the new settlement at Botany Bay.

Having cleared the English Channel, the convoy turned southward into the Atlantic and the high seas of the Bay of Biscay. About 200 kilometres west of the Isles of Scilly, the navy escort *Hyena* left the fleet and returned to Portsmouth.

About halfway to Tenerife, the officers and men witnessed an incident that would give them a valuable insight into Arthur Phillip's thinking about the future of New South Wales. It occurred when the duty officer on the *Sirius*, Sergeant Maxwell, ordered the flogging of two seamen who were not on deck during their watch. Jacob Nagle described the incident in his journal:

> The Governor ordered every officer on board the ship to appear in the cabin, even the boatswain's mate, and told them all if he knew any officer to strike a man on board he would break him immediately. He said those men are all we have to depend upon, and if we abuse these men we have to trust the convicts will rise and massacre us all. Those men are our support and if they are ill-treated they will all be dead before the voyage is half out and who is to bring us back again.[6]

On 2 June, after almost three weeks of sailing, the fleet reached Tenerife. By this time eight convicts had died in addition to those who had died before the fleet left Portsmouth. Five of the eight had died on the *Alexander*, the unhealthiest ship in the fleet. One was convict Ismael Coleman, whom Surgeon John White recorded 'resigned his breath without a pang', having been 'worn out by lowness of spirits and debility brought on by long and close confinement'.[7] Sixteen had died on the *Alexander*—mostly of fever, pneumonia or dysentery—even before the ship departed Portsmouth. However, the rate of fatalities on all ships began to fall after Tenerife and John White observed that the convicts were generally in better health than before the fleet set sail.[8]

The Canary Islands were under Spanish control, having become part of the Spanish empire in the late fifteenth century. While Spain's influence as a world power had for a long time been on the wane Tenerife's port of Santa Cruz remained strategically important for Atlantic shipping. For several hundred years ships from many nations stopped at the port to replenish their water and other supplies as they sailed from Europe to the Americas, Africa or the Pacific.

On arriving, the English fleet was met by the Spanish authorities and, as protocol dictated, the following morning Arthur Phillip sent Lieutenant King to wait on the Spanish governor, the Marquess of

Branciforte. A day later the governor sent a 'very polite reply', indicating that the island would be happy to supply all of the 'articles' the English needed and giving his 'assurance that every refreshment the place afforded' would be made available.[9]

Over the next week the fleet was able to acquire some but not all of the supplies it needed. Tenerife's economy depended on being able to sell its fresh produce to the ships that called in. However, the English fleet was of an exceptional size and it is unlikely the port had ever been challenged to provide for so many people at once. The timing of the English was also a problem because they had arrived earlier than much of the food they needed was ripe enough to harvest. According to John White, much of the available food was 'rather scanty, little besides onions being to be got, and still less fruit, it being too early in the season'.[10]

Stocking up on fresh food, particularly fruit, was vital for protection against scurvy, and the fleet was able to take on board large quantities of figs and mulberries, which were then being harvested. The English had no choice but to purchase fresh vegetables, fruit and meat from the Spanish, but Phillip baulked at the cost of the local bread and decided instead to draw on their own supplies of dried hard-tack biscuits. 'Wishing that it could be done with as little expense to Government as possible,' he recorded, 'I have ordered bread to be issued to the marines and convicts from the store ships, for it could not be got here but at very high prices.'[11]

Phillip had intended to stay in Tenerife only a few days but needed to stay longer because of the time it took to load fresh water onto the ships for the next leg of the journey. Captain Hunter noted that the water pipe to the port only allowed two small boats to fill their casks at the same time so it took a very long time to fill up the eleven ships of the fleet.

While in Tenerife a number of the officers took the opportunity to do some sightseeing and to take long walks, knowing they would enjoy no exercise for months on end in the confines of their small ships. The convicts who had already been able to exercise up on deck were largely confined in chains below deck until the fleet was safely out to sea again. The night before they left, convict John Powers on the *Alexander* managed to get up on deck and then lower himself into a small boat and escape. However, he was recaptured the next morning, when a search party of marines found him asleep on a nearby beach.

On 10 June the fleet departed Santa Cruz and headed south for the Cape Verde Islands off the west coast of Senegal (about 1500 kilometres of sailing), where they planned to stop again for more water and supplies, before heading across the Atlantic to Rio de Janeiro, Brazil. Captain Hunter said the reason for the additional stop was to buy fruit and vegetables they had been unable to procure in Santa Cruz. However, when they reached Port Praya, on the island of Santiago, on 19 June, Phillip had misgivings. 'I should have stopped for twenty-four hours at Port Praya,' he wrote, 'but when off that port light airs of wind and a strong current making it probable that some of the ships might not get in, I did not think it prudent to attempt it.'[12]

Even though it meant the imposition of water rationing on the long leg across the Atlantic, Phillip ordered the fleet to head for Rio de Janeiro. Over the next weeks, as the fleet sailed south-west, they occasionally passed other ships, including a Portuguese trader that fell in with the convoy for a week, another from the coast of Guinea that was bound for the West Indies, and an English ship sailing to the Falkland Islands.

The increasingly high temperatures, humidity and heavy tropical rains would have distressed and confused the convicts, who would have been ignorant of geography and climate and would never have experienced weather even remotely like this. Chief Surgeon John White became worried about the health of the convicts:

> The weather became exceedingly dark, warm and close, with heavy rain, a temperature of the atmosphere very common on approaching the equator, and very much to be dreaded, as the health is greatly endangered thereby . . . my first care was to keep the men, as far as was consistent with the regular discharge of their duties, out of the rain, and I never suffered the convicts to come upon deck when it rained, as they had neither the linen nor clothing sufficient to make themselves dry and comfortable after getting wet: a line of conduct which cannot be too strictly observed, and enforced in those latitudes.[13]

To add to their discomfort the fleet had to endure plagues of insects. On the *Prince of Wales*, marine Lieutenant William Faddy complained that he had to kill over a hundred bugs in his small sleeping area before he was able to get any sleep.[14]

When the ships reached the equator and sailed into the southern hemisphere the crews celebrated the 'crossing of the line'. The traditional ceremony paid homage to Neptune, god of the sea, and those sailors crossing for the first time were ritually dunked in water, lathered with tar, greased and shaved.

Living conditions for the convicts became extremely arduous. Many had already spent years in cramped, overcrowded prisons and hulks in Britain, and were now locked in the even more congested bowels of the transports for eight months. Because of the risk to security, there were no portholes in the convicts' quarters and the risk of fire meant no candles below decks, so the convicts were always in the dark as well as having limited fresh air. Rats, parasites, bed bugs, lice, fleas and cockroaches thrived on the ships. Their bilges—the lowest part of the ship, where all the excess liquids tend to drain—became foul, and the smell overwhelming. The convict exercising area in the open air at the front of the ship was only a few metres long, because all the transports had high wooden security walls with large metal spikes installed across the deck next to the mainmast to keep the prisoners from the quarterdeck and the rear of the ship.

On the way to Rio de Janeiro the number of convicts who fell ill jumped dramatically. Reports of a large number of sick convicts on the *Alexander* brought Chief Surgeon John White across from the *Sirius* to investigate. 'The illness complained of was wholly occasioned by the bilge water,' he wrote, 'which had by some means or other risen to so great a height that the panels of the cabin and the buttons on the clothes of the officers were turned nearly black by the noxious effluvia. When the hatches were taken off the stench was so powerful that it was scarcely possible to stand over them.'[15]

The filth below decks was made worse by the disregard for hygiene by some of the convicts. At one point in the tropics, Margaret Hall on the *Friendship* was put in irons for 'shitting between the decks' rather than off the poop deck, as required.[16]

When convicts became ill there was not a great deal the ship's surgeon could do for them and in most cases they were left until they recovered or died. One of the standard remedies was a medicinal measure of rum. Another common form of treatment at the time was bloodletting. While the practice is now widely discredited and believed to have taken more lives than it saved, at the time of the First Fleet it was a standard treatment for almost any serious ailment. The theory went back to the fifth century BC, when ancient Greeks believed that many diseases were caused by an excess of 'humours' in the blood. On the First Fleet every surgeon carried a range of instruments designed to puncture the flesh of the patient and suck out various quantities of blood.

The inevitability of convict deaths on the voyage was an accepted part of the journey. When someone died, there would usually be a burial at sea, which involved a simple funeral ceremony: a prayer would be read and then the body, weighted and wrapped in cloth, would be slid over the side of the ship.

The appalling conditions did nothing to halt the promiscuity. As the heat and humidity increased the normally locked hatches above the convicts were left open at night to allow in more air; however, as John White observed:

> The weather was now so immoderately hot that the female convicts perfectly overcome by it frequently fainted away . . . and yet, notwithstanding the enervating effects of the atmospheric heat . . . so predominant was the warmth of their constitutions, or the depravity of their hearts, that the hatches over the place where they were confined could not be suffered to lay off, during the night, without a promiscuous intercourse immediately taking place between them and the seamen and the marines.[17]

Lieutenant Clark was equally damning of the convict women's sexual conduct during the voyage. 'I never could have thought there were so many abandoned wenches in England,' he wrote. 'They are ten thousand times worse than the men Convicts and I am afraid that we will have a great deal more trouble with them.'[18] So strong was his disgust that he hoped that a 21-year-old convict woman, who was dying, had infected the sailors with venereal disease:

> Sarah McCormick taking very ill this afternoon. The doctor has been obliged to bleed her twice today and says that She will not live the night out—She is now quite speechless[.] I am apt to think (God forgive) if it is not so, that She is eating up with the pox . . . She is one of them that went through the Bulk head to the Seamen—I hope she has given them something to remember her—never was there a Set of greater rascals together than the[y] are.[19]

Clark's low opinion of the convict women and his repeated declarations in his journal of his love and devotion to his 'dear beloved' wife Betsy Alycia did not prevent him, when the fleet reached New South Wales, from striking up a relationship with seventeen-year-old Mary Branham, a convict on the *Lady Penrhyn* who would become his mistress and give birth to his child.

> Two of the convict women that went through the bulkhead to the seamen . . . have informed the doctor they are with child . . . I hope the commodore will make the two seamen that are the fathers of the children marry them and make them stay in Botany Bay.[20]

The crossing of the Atlantic Ocean took almost two months. As a precaution after not having stopped for more water at Cape Verde Islands, a month out of Tenerife the water ration was cut to three pints per day for everyone on the fleet. The decision was made after Phillip called all the masters of the ships over to the *Sirius* to assess how much water was left and how much was being used. With the new ration came the stipulation that the water could only be used for consumption; washing and laundry had to be done in sea water. As Lieutenant Clark recorded, the rationing of water was seriously controlled:

> A lieutenant of marines with a sergeant or corporal and two of the convicts always to be present when the water is served. That part of the hold where the water is kept is never to be opened but in the presence of those appointed to see the water served and the sergeant or corporal and the two convicts are to be changed every day . . . Water . . . served to the people and the quantity Issued daily [is] to be marked in the ship's log book.[21]

Two weeks later, and with the fleet enjoying a firm south-westerly wind, Phillip agreed to lift the water ration and the *Sirius* signalled to the rest of the fleet that each person was now permitted four pints per day.

By the end of July, and 800 kilometres and about a week's sailing from Rio de Janeiro, many of the ships' food supplies began to run low. On the *Lady Penrhyn*, surgeon Arthur Bowes Smyth recorded that the last goose was killed for the officers' table and for the remainder of the trip the ship's crew supplemented their diet with the flying fish that landed on the decks of the ships, along with fish they caught more conventionally.

On this long leg of the voyage Phillip continued to have difficulty keeping the fleet reasonably close together, given their different speeds. The fastest continued to be the *Supply* and the slowest the *Lady Penrhyn*, which constantly struggled to keep up with the others. The winds were generally mild on this leg of the voyage but occasional heavy squalls tore the sails or damaged the masts of more than half the ships, including the *Golden Grove*, the *Borrowdale*, the *Friendship*, the *Alexander*, the *Lady Penrhyn* and the *Supply*.[22]

At last, on 2 August, the *Supply*, which was again sailing ahead of the fleet, sighted land, but the wind died away and it took another four days for the rest of the fleet to reach the harbour.

Rio de Janeiro—or San Sebastian as it was then more commonly known—was an important part of the Portuguese network of strategically positioned ports around the known world that linked its trading empire, which dated back to the early sixteenth century. At the time of the arrival of the First Fleet, Rio was a thriving port even though the Portuguese empire, like the Spanish, had been in decline for more than a century while Britain was still expanding its global influence.

Portugal possessed the earliest and the longest extant modern European empire spanning nearly 600 years from the early fifteenth century to the twentieth century. The Portuguese explorer Bartolomeu Dias rounded the Cape of Good Hope in 1488 and a decade later Vasco da Gama reached India. In 1500 Pedro Álvares Cabral landed in South America, which ultimately led to the establishment of the Portuguese colony of Brazil. Through the 1500s Portugal established a network of ports from Lisbon to Japan, including Goa in south-west India, Mozambique and Angola in southern Africa, Macau in China, Ormus in the Persian Gulf and Nagasaki in Japan.

Rio de Janeiro, with an estimated population of around 40,000 people,[23] was rich in its own right and exported gold, sugar, rice and rum. Its fine harbour well located on the east coast of South America was on the trade winds route not only to the Americas but also to Asia.

As Phillip later wrote, when sailing from the north to the south of the Atlantic, the prevailing winds meant it was quicker to go across to South America rather than along the coast of Africa. 'The calms so frequent on the African side,' he noted, 'are of themselves a sufficient cause to induce a navigator to keep a very westerly course . . . which . . . will carry him within a few degrees of the South American coast.'[24] When the First Fleet eventually reached the Cape of Good Hope it would encounter in Table Bay an American ship bound for India that had taken longer to sail there from the Canary Islands than it had taken Phillip's ships to sail via Rio de Janeiro.

All eleven ships sailed into Rio harbour in relatively good shape considering that they'd been travelling for almost three months and had last taken on board fresh food and water in Tenerife two months before. However, by the time the fleet was anchored in the harbour, between twenty and thirty convicts had come down with the expedition's first outbreak of scurvy.

By the eighteenth century, disease—and most prominently scurvy—was the largest killer of seafarers, causing more deaths than the combined ill-effects of shipwrecks, falling from rigging, fire and explosions, and fighting enemies at sea. It took the European seafaring powers almost 250 years from the first voyages of discovery in the early fifteenth century to find the simple remedy to scurvy, which caused liver spots to appear all over the body, bleeding from every orifice, the loss of teeth, depression and death. Until the mid-eighteenth century, fatalities were accepted as inevitable until it was learned that the disease could be largely avoided with a regularly intake of fresh food, particularly fruit and vegetables—although at the time it was not specifically known that the vitamin C content was the crucial factor.

By the time of Captain Cook's voyages of the 1760s and 1770s there was increasing control of the disease and now, twenty years later, Phillip and his surgeons had learned the lessons well. David Collins described how the arrival of the ships in Rio allowed the scorbutic convicts to be treated and all were strengthened for the long voyage ahead:

> During their stay in this port for refreshment, the convicts were each served daily with a pound of rice and a pound and a half of fresh meat together with a suitable portion of vegetables. Great numbers of oranges were at different times distributed among them, and every possible care was taken to refresh them and put them in to a state of health to resist the attacks of scurvy, should it make its appearance in the long passage over the ocean, which was yet between them and New South Wales.[25]

The benefits of plentiful fresh food delighted the officers. Captain John Hunter was to boast that the general health of the fifteen hundred confined to the fleet's eleven tiny ships was probably better than to be found in any English town with a similar population.

> I may without a probability of being much mistaken, venture to say, that there are few country towns in the island of Great Britain, which

> contain 1500 inhabitants (the number which the ships employed on this service had on board) which have not frequently as many sick as we had.[26]

The English were courteously received at Rio by the Portuguese authorities. Phillip had met the administrator and viceroy of Brazil, Luís de Vasconcelos e Sousa, in 1783, when Phillip had been on an earlier stop in Rio on the Royal Navy ship *Europe.* Also, or so Phillip's colleagues believed, the Portuguese revered Phillip for his heroic service in the Portuguese Navy, and provided royal treatment to the English visitors. Collins wrote:

> [Their treatment of us] could . . . be attributed only to the great esteem in which Captain Phillip was held by all ranks of people during the time of his commanding a ship in the Portuguese service; for on being informed of the employment he now held, the viceroy's guard was directed to pay him the same honours during his stay here, that were paid to himself as the representative of the crown of Portugal.[27]

The courtesy extended to Phillip was taken to extremes. Wherever he went ashore he was attended by palace guards, who would parade at the wharf steps and then escort him and his party around the city. Seaman Jacob Nagle, who was one of the rowers on Phillip's barge, recorded Phillip's embarrassment at this: 'The Governor often landed in different parts of the town . . . because he didn't wish to bother the gurds, but land where we would, we could see the soldiers running to wherever we landed and parade under an arrest for him.'[28]

The Portuguese also permitted the English to pitch a tent on the little island of Enchandos, about 2 kilometres further up the river from where the fleet was anchored, which Phillip could use as a base while in the port. They also allowed 25-year-old marine Lieutenant

William Dawes to use the island for his astrological measurements and calculations.

While the convicts were held on the ships, the seamen and officers were able to enjoy some shore leave. A number of the officers were able to enjoy the exotic birds, butterflies, plants and other wildlife, as well as the coffee houses and markets. Collins described the 'very numerous' African slaves 'of a strong robust appearance' that had been brought from the 'coast of Guinea, forming an extensive article of commerce'.[29]

A number of the officers also noted how colourful they found Rio de Janeiro. 'The country likewise produces, in the most unbounded degree, limes, acid and sweet lemons,' wrote Chief Surgeon John White, 'oranges of an immense size and exquisite flavour, plantains, bananas, yams, cocoa-nuts, cashoo apples and nuts, and some mangos.'[30]

White also described the well-dressed citizens and how the churches were decorated with flowers and 'most brilliantly illuminated'. But he was shocked by the number of well-dressed women who were 'unattended' and who after dark 'had no objection to bestow their favours' on strangers as well as acquaintances.[31]

The surgeon on the *Lady Penrhyn*, Arthur Bowes Smyth, said that he and some of the other officers went for long walks, after which they found themselves 'very much fatigued', having been 'without any exercise for nine weeks aboard ship'.[32]

The marines spent much of their time on board the ships guarding the convicts but were permitted occasional shore leave. While in Rio a number of them were punished for having sexual relations with convict women. Cornelius Connell, a private in the marines, was given 100 lashes after he was caught having sex with female convicts, and Thomas Jones was sentenced to 300 lashes when caught trying to bribe one of the sentries to let him go below decks and among the women.[33]

Despite the security risk Phillip allowed all the well-behaved convicts to spend the daytime and even some of the night on the deck of their ship, 'which has kept them much healthier than could have been expected'.[34] Some of the convicts were able to buy fresh local food and other wares from small boats that came alongside and were caught paying with counterfeit money.

Many of the 'quarter dollar' coins had been very well manufactured by convict Thomas Barrett on the transport *Charlotte* with the help of some other convicts. They were coined from old buckles, buttons from the marines and from pewter spoons during the long voyage from Tenerife. John White said that the fake currency was of a high standard: 'The whole was so inimitably executed that had their metal been a little better the fraud, I am convinced, would have passed undetected . . . the adroitness . . . gave me a high opinion of their ingenuity, cunning, caution and address; and I could not help wishing that these qualities had been employed to more laudable purposes.'[35]

Barrett had already been twice condemned to execution and twice sentenced to transportation. He would eventually be the first convict hanged in New South Wales within a month of the arrival of the First Fleet.

Before leaving Rio the fleet also loaded many plants and seeds for cultivation at Botany Bay. Collins recorded that they took coffee, cocoa, cotton, banana, orange, lemon, guava, tamarind, prickly pear and eugenia, 'or Pommel Rose—a plant bearing a fruit in the shape of an apple, and having the flavour and the odour of a rose'. Collins said they also took some ipecacuanha seedlings, which at the time was used as a stomach-purging syrup, and some jalap seedlings, a vegetable root used to clean out the digestive system and thought to help patients with kidney ailments.[36]

The fleet loaded aboard some farm animals, with more to be purchased and crammed aboard when they reached Cape Town. In addition to the government stores some of the officers bought their own animals intending to use them when they reached New South Wales or else for food during the rest of the voyage.

The biggest single purchase while the fleet was in Rio was 115 pipes (around 60,000 litres) of spirits for the remainder of the voyage and the first three years at the new settlement. This purchase no doubt would have brought great relief to the marines, who had earlier feared they might not have their daily rum ration in the new colony.

Rio's version of 'rum' was *aguardiente*, distilled from sugar cane. According to Arthur Phillip the huge quantity needed by the English sent the local retail price soaring by 'more than five and twenty per cent',[37] and forced the fleet to offset its costs by buying only half the amount of the spirit intended for medicinal purposes. It was felt to be unsafe to store any of the rum on the convict transports and its loading required the reorganisation of the entire fleet. As Phillip reported to London, it was 'necessary that the store ships might receive the spirits to move part of the provisions from them to the transports'.[38]

As things turned out Rio's rum was of poor quality and would attract criticism when the settlers reached their destination and began to drink it. Major Robert Ross later complained in Sydney that 'in taste and smell' it was 'extremely offensive', adding that his marines only drank it out of 'absolute necessity'.[39]

A few days before departing Rio de Janeiro Jane Scott, the wife of marine sergeant James Scott, gave birth to a baby daughter after a 27-hour labour on the *Prince of Wales*. Baby Elizabeth was to be one of nine girls and twelve boys born on the ships of the First Fleet. She would have been more fortunate than the fourteen children born during the voyage to convict women, who would have been wrapped in torn-up rags from adult clothing because there was no provision made for convict babies when the ships were prepared at Portsmouth. This was in spite of many women being obviously pregnant before the fleet set sail. The first child born to a convict was the daughter of Isobel Lawson, who gave birth on 31 May, when the fleet was less than three weeks out of Portsmouth.

At the beginning of September, almost a month after it had arrived, the fleet was nearly ready to resume its journey. The settlers were, recorded White, 'thoroughly recovered and refreshed'.[40] Immediately before sailing, Arthur Phillip spent two days finalising a long dispatch to Lord Sydney, to his deputy, Evan Nepean, and to Navy secretary Alfred Stephens. These letters would be delivered by the next ship leaving Rio heading for England. It was Phillip's last chance to communicate with the British government until the fleet reached the Cape of Good Hope at the southern tip of Africa, which was more than six weeks away.

In his lengthy letters Phillip reported on the hospitality of the Portuguese; the port charges he had paid; the fresh food, rum, plants, animals, clothing and equipment he had bought; the improved health and the lower death rate among the convicts; and the condition of the ships of the fleet as they prepared for the next leg of their journey.

A number of officers who were unable to continue on the voyage were left behind to be put on the next available ship back to England. They included Micah Morton, the master on the *Sirius*, who had been badly injured in an accident when unmooring the ship two months before, when leaving Tenerife. Two midshipmen were also sent home. One had been injured and the other suffered from 'a venereal complaint which, being neglected, is not likely to be cured at sea'.[41] They were put on to a British whaling ship that had called in at Rio for repairs.

At six o'clock on the morning of 4 September, the fleet sailed, 'weighed with a light breeze'. As the ship with Commander Phillip aboard approached the Santa Cruz fort, 'he was saluted from the Portuguese batteries with twenty-one guns', which he returned from the *Sirius* 'with an equal number'.[42] Such a salute was uncommon, and a further indication of the high esteem in which Phillip was held by the Portuguese.[43] By 10 a.m. the eleven English ships were clear of land, steering east with a gentle breeze. Four days after leaving Rio, convict Mary Bryant gave birth to a baby daughter she named after the transport she was carried in, the *Charlotte*. Four years later young

Charlotte would die of fever in a boat off the African coast, following a daring escape attempt from New South Wales by her mother and other convicts.

Out in the Atlantic the ships were finally moving in to cooler latitudes. The winds picked up and thanks to a solid south-westerly the fleet made good progress but in the higher seas many were seasick.

On 19 September a 'very well behaved convict' named William Brown was lost overboard. He was bringing in some washing that had been drying on the bowsprit at the front of the *Charlotte* when he slipped. White described the reaction on board:

> As soon as the alarm was given . . . the ship was instantly hove to, and a boat hoisted out, but to no purpose . . . notwithstanding every excursion, the poor fellow sunk before either the *Supply* or our boat could reach him. The people on the forecastle, who saw him fall, say the ship went directly over him, which . . . must make it impossible for him to keep on the surface long enough to be taken up.[44]

By the end of September, the fleet was battling against a gale that Lieutenant Clark said blew so hard that the large amount of water between the decks of the *Friendship* washed some of the marines who were sleeping with convict women out of their bunks.[45]

The flagship *Sirius* was also struggling in the high seas, and was found to have a number of serious problems below the waterline. Lieutenant King believed that the ship should never have passed its dockyard inspection before leaving England: 'A discovery has also been made which tends to prove the extreme negligence of the dock yard officers . . . On inspection we found that not only were the top timbers rotten but also many of the futtocks were in the same condition.'[46]

About a month out of Rio and with all the stores of fresh food gone the fleet was again back on preserved rations: hardtack biscuits, rice and salted meat. Some of the officers were able to break the monotony of their diet by eating a few of the animals they had privately purchased in Rio. On one occasion a sheep was killed on the *Lady Penrhyn* and shared with the officers on the *Alexander*.

On 29 September Lieutenant Clark recorded in his diary that a doctor was unable to save a convict woman's small son who had been ill almost for the whole journey: 'It departs this life at 2 o'clock this morning. Poor thing. It is much better out of this world than in it . . . After 9 [a.m.] committed the body of Thomas Mason to the deep . . . Henry Lovall, one of the convicts read prayers over it.'[47]

On 6 October, and a week before the fleet was to arrive at the Cape of Good Hope, there was an attempted mutiny on the *Alexander*. With the help of some of the seamen on the ship a number of convicts armed themselves with iron bars and were planning to overpower the marines. But before the mutineers could rise up they were betrayed to the master of the *Alexander*, Duncan Sinclair, who alerted the marines, strengthened the watch and locked all the convicts below decks. The convict ringleaders were captured and taken to the *Sirius*, where they were chained to the deck. The four seamen were flogged and replaced by others from the *Sirius*. The convict who betrayed the mutineers was moved for his own protection to the *Scarborough*.

It took longer than expected to reach Cape Town as the ships were blown to the south and away from the mouth of the port. Finally, at daylight on Saturday, 13 October, they sighted Lion's Head and by nightfall the fleet was safely anchored in Table Bay, where there were already more than twenty American, French, Danish, Portuguese, Dutch and English ships lying at anchor. Captain Phillip was unimpressed that the harbour could not provide sufficient shelter for his eleven ships. 'This bay cannot be properly called a port,' he wrote in his journal, '[as] it is exposed by all the violence of winds, which set into it from the sea . . . The gusts, which descend from the summit of Table Mountain, are sufficient to force ships from their anchors.'[48]

Bowes Smyth was equally unimpressed by what he saw on the shore of the town when the English arrived:

> There are many gallows and other implements of punishment erected along the shore and in front of the town. There were also wheels for breaking felons upon, several of which were at this time occupied by the mangled bodies of the unhappy wretches who suffered upon them; their right hands were cut off and fixed by a large nail to the side of the wheel, the wheel itself elevated upon a post about nine or ten feet high, upon which the body lies to perish.[49]

However, not all the observations of the Dutch inhabitants of Cape Town were negative. Chief Surgeon John White said that the locals treated their slaves well—and better than he had seen in the British-controlled West Indies when serving there with the Royal Navy:

> However severe and cruel the Dutch may be considered in other respects, they certainly treat their slaves with great humanity and kindness, which, I am sorry to say, I scarcely ever saw done in the West Indies, during a residence there of three years, [where] I have frequently been witness to the infliction of the most brutal, cruel, and wanton punishments on these poor creatures . . . At the Cape . . . [they] treat them humanely.[50]

Cape Town at this time was a major port under Dutch control. It had first been reached nearly three hundred years earlier by Portuguese explorer Bartholomew Dias, who sailed round the southern part of Africa in 1488 and was the first European known to have done so. Dias had originally named it Cape of Storms but the name was changed by Portuguese King John II to the Cape of Good Hope. Table Mountain was given its name by another Portuguese explorer, António de Saldanha, fifteen years later.

For the next 150 years the Cape was rarely used. In 1652 Jan van Riebeeck was sent by the Dutch East India Company to establish a station there that could provide fresh food and water to ships sailing to and from the Dutch East Indies.

At the time the Dutch were a major European trading power with ports at New Amsterdam (New York), Suriname and Guyana in South America, and the Antilles in the Caribbean. However, its biggest trading area was in the East Indies, which covered large parts of current-day Indonesia and Malaysia, where the Dutch government had granted extensive powers to the Dutch East India Company.

In the early nineteenth century the Cape region of southern Africa would come under British control but in 1787 the port at Cape Town existed to serve the interests of Dutch shipping first and those of the British and other nations second.

The English very soon found the Dutch reception decidedly cool, in sharp contrast to the generous welcome they had received from the Portuguese authorities in Rio de Janeiro and the Spanish in Tenerife. On Tuesday, 16 October, three days after they arrived, Phillip and a number of his senior officers presented themselves to Governor Cornelis Jacob van de Graaff. A polite exchange took place, before Phillip turned the discussion to the English need to buy food. The governor told the English that they could purchase livestock and wine, but there was a shortage of grain following recent failed harvests. Collins detailed the Dutchman's response:

> [T]he governor expressed his apprehensions of being able to comply, as the Cape had very lately been visited by that worst of scourges—a famine, which had been most severely felt by every family in the town, his own not excepted.[51]

Phillip said that after the meeting, he learned 'that the last year's crops had been very good' and then 'requested by letter to the Governor . . .

permission to purchase what provisions were wanted'. Three days later he 'received a letter from the Governor granting all my demands'.[52]

The fleet had arrived at Cape Town with twenty sick marines and 93 sick convicts. However, Phillip was able to report back to London that, following being 'amply supplied with soft bread, vegetables and fresh meat', it was not necessary to take any of the men ashore to the town's hospital.[53]

There was an element of desperation at the Cape as provisions were hastily loaded aboard the ships of the fleet. As 23-year-old *Sirius* midshipman Daniel Southwell was to write in a letter home, this was the last chance to take what was needed for survival in the new colony.

> It was a time of constant bustle as this being the last port we must take every advantage of it, for the leaving behind of many articles that are requisite and necessary beyond here would be irreparable; and this keeps us constantly employed in getting the ships supplied.[54]

During the month the fleet was anchored at the Cape, some of the officers enjoyed exploring the town and the surrounding countryside. Most were granted shore leave, took up lodgings and shopped for 'comfort and refreshments to be enjoyed on land [before] the last and longest stage of the voyage'.[55]

Cape Town boasted both a Calvinist and a Lutheran church; its impressive Government House, with its adjacent parklands, reminded some of the English officers of St James's Park in London.

In their private journals a number of officers compared aspects of life at Cape Town to what they had experienced in Rio, including Chief Surgeon John White, who said courting between the sexes was much cruder.

> The habits and customs of the women of this place are extremely contrasted to those of the inhabitants of Rio de Janeiro. Among the

> latter a great deal of reserve and modesty is apparent between the sexes in public. Those who are disposed to say tender and civil things to a lady must do so by stealth, or breathe their soft sighs through the latticework of a window, or the grates of a convent. But at the Cape, if you wish to be a favourite with the fair . . . you must . . . *grapple* the lady, and paw her in a manner that does not partake in the least of gentleness. Such a rough and uncouth conduct . . . is not only pleasing to the fair one, but even to her parents . . . in fact the Dutch ladies here . . . admit to liberties that may be thought reprehensible in England.[56]

During the next few weeks the ships of the fleet took on board a variety of plants, including oak, myrtle, fig, quince, apple and pear trees, sugar cane, 'vines of various sorts', strawberries and 'all sorts of grain', including rice, wheat, barley and Indian corn. Judge Advocate David Collins said they also took some bamboo and Spanish reed, which was valued more as a decorative plant.[57]

While still in Table Bay, the ship's carpenters constructed wooden stalls on the already congested upper and lower decks of the *Sirius* and the transports, and more than 500 animals—including cows, bulls, pigs, horses, ducks, chickens, sheep, goats and geese—were crowded on board the already heavily loaded ships. The sight led one of the surgeons on the *Sirius*, George Worgan, to write that each of the ships now looked like a 'Noah's Ark'.[58] In a letter to his mother, young midshipman Daniel Southwell described the scene below decks on the *Sirius*, where plants, provisions and animals had been stored:

> Were you to take a view of our ship below you would be apt to take it for a livery stable . . . for there are a number of partitions all along the below decks, and racks for the provender; nor do we want pig sties, hog troughs . . . among the stock are many of the feathered kind, and

> also plants of various sorts. These all together take up much room, and the ship is lumbered. The people, considering the number are much crowded, for the cattle are now to occupy a deck which till now was theirs. This is a disagreeable part of it . . . but we hope to get over it without much sickness; some must be expected.[59]

Caring for the animals was, understandably, a very high priority. On the decks of the *Sirius* alone there were six cows with calf, two bulls and a number of sheep, goats, pigs and chickens. On the *Friendship* some of the men and women convicts were moved to other ships to make way for 35 sheep. The decks of all the ships were now crowded with penned animals, whose urine and faeces would seep through the deck and onto the convicts below. In addition to the stock taken for the settlement, a number of officers took on board what livestock they could—intended for the remainder of the voyage and for the private farms they planned to establish when they reached New South Wales.

The ships had to be loaded with large amounts of fodder to keep the animals alive for the almost three months it would take to sail to New South Wales. Unfortunately, the hay feed began to run out long before the end of voyage and many of the animals became emaciated and died before reaching Botany Bay.

The long delay in purchasing and then loading the supplies grated on everyone's nerves. The convicts fought among themselves and the marines were regularly drunk and disorderly. On 20 October a brawl broke out between marines on the *Scarborough*; it involved Private Thomas Bullimore, who shortly after arriving in New South Wales would be murdered by other marines. Two days later a marine was flogged for stealing and fighting on the *Alexander* and another for insubordination on the *Charlotte.* On the anchored *Friendship*, second mate Patrick Vallance fell overboard at the front of the ship while drunk and trying to relieve himself; three men jumped overboard but could not save him, for he soon sank 'and has not been seen since'.[60]

Finally, on 12 November, 'with all people clear of scurvy',[61] the heavily laden fleet left the Cape. There was great relief at finally getting away from what had been too long a stay at a decidedly unpleasant port. Yet, as Collins observed, the relief was mixed with anxiety, sadness and fear. Many felt as they headed away from the Cape that they were leaving behind them all connections with the civilised world. It was not just leaving everything that was familiar; they would be the first Europeans to try to live in the great unknown southern continent.

> It was natural to indulge at this moment a melancholy reflection which obtruded itself upon the mind. The land we left behind us was the abode of civilised people; that before us was the residence of savages. When, if ever, we might again enjoy the commerce of the world, was doubtful and uncertain . . . all communication with families and friends now cut off, [we were] leaving the world behind us, to enter a state of unknown.[62]

The route taken by the fleet from the Cape to Botany Bay had only rarely been sailed by Europeans—and part of it they were sailing for the first time. The first leg, of more than 8000 kilometres to the south-west tip of the Australian continent, had first been charted by Dutch explorers in the 1620s. The second leg, of about 4000 kilometres east to Van Diemen's Land, had first been sailed by Abel Tasman in 1642 and not sailed again until James Cook in 1769. The final leg was almost 1500 kilometres northwards from Van Diemen's Land to Botany Bay: the first half of this leg was uncharted, up to Point Hicks, near the current border between New South Wales and Victoria. It was from Point Hicks that Cook in 1770 had begun charting northwards along the east coast of Australia, including Botany Bay, eighteen years before the First Fleet.

The long haul to the east coast of Australia would take more than two months and prove to be the most difficult stage of the voyage. For the first five days after leaving the Cape the ships battled into a strong headwind and made practically no progress. Even this early in the trip Phillip was worried that they might run short of fresh water and rationed everyone to three pints per day.

Soon a number of the livestock began to die. Lieutenant Clark noticed the chickens were beginning to perish on the *Lady Penrhyn*, and recorded in his diary that the *Borrowdale* came alongside to report that they, too, were losing a lot of the birds to disease.

In the middle of November there was an outbreak of dysentery, first among the convicts and then spreading to the marines. Chief Surgeon John White said this occasioned 'violence and obstinacy' until Christmas. No medication seemed to provide effective relief, and the disease was only brought under control through unrelenting attention to cleanliness. Despite the large number brought down by the sickness, only one, marine Daniel Cresswell, died—though he suffered the 'most acute, agonising pain'.[63]

In the middle of the night of 24 November, one of the seamen on the *Prince of Wales* fell from high on the rigging into the sea, but no search was launched to try to save him. 'Indeed it was so dark, and the ship went so fast through the water,' White wrote, 'that all efforts to save him, had any been made, would have proved fruitless.'[64]

Two weeks after leaving, and as the fleet was entering the great Southern Ocean, Phillip decided to split the fleet by taking the four fastest ships ahead and leaving the seven slower ships to follow at their own pace. While his decision may have been a surprise to his fellow officers Phillip had earlier pondered the merits of dispatching such an advance party during the time of his detailed planning in London:

> By arriving at the settlement two or three months before the transports, many and very great advantages would be gained. Huts would

> be ready to receive the convicts who are sick . . . huts would be ready for the women; the stores would be properly lodged and defended from the convicts in such a manner as to prevent their making any attempt on them. The cattle and stock would be likewise properly secured.[65]

There may have also been another reason for Phillip's desire to reach his destination well ahead of the bulk of the fleet. He may have suspected that Botany Bay might be less than suitable as a site for the new settlement and wanted time to explore other possible locations. Joseph Banks's journals would have been available to Phillip, the Navy and the government, so Phillip may well have read Banks's earlier and more negative comments about the bay in his journals, which starkly contrasted with the more fulsome recommendations he later gave to the House of Commons committee.

In March 1787, before he left England, Phillip had sought permission to settle 'in such port as I may find the most convenient and best to answer the intentions of the government', should he find something more suitable than Botany Bay.[66] Within weeks of receiving the letter, Lord Sydney had replied, assuring him that 'there can be no objection to your establishing any part of the territory or islands upon the coast of New South Wales, in the neighbourhood of Botany Bay, which you may consider as more advantageously situated for the principal settlement'.[67]

According to Lieutenant King, who was to join the governor in the advance party, Phillip hoped to explore more than 200 kilometres of the coastline north of Botany Bay. 'The Governor flatters himself that he shall arrive at the place of our destination [Botany Bay] a fortnight before the transports,' King wrote, 'in which time he will be able to make his observations on the place whether it is a proper spot for the settlement or not and in the latter case he will then have time to examine Port Stephens before the arrival of the transports on the coast.'[68]

Over the next two days, Phillip and some of his officers transferred from the *Sirius* to the smaller and faster *Supply* and ordered the three fastest transports—the *Friendship*, the *Scarborough* and the *Alexander*—to leave the rest of the fleet and sail ahead with him. Expecting to reach Botany Bay a few weeks ahead of the slower ships he also took with him some convicts who had gardening and carpentry skills to help prepare the colony before the others arrived. Tonnes of fresh water was transferred in little boats from the *Scarborough* and the *Alexander* to the slower boats as it was anticipated that they would take longer and so be in greater need of supplies. The balance of the fleet was now under the command of Captain John Hunter on the *Sirius*. On 26 November the fleet split and by daylight the next morning Lieutenant King, aboard the *Supply*, recorded in his journal that 'the *Sirius* and her convoys were out of sight'.[69]

Throughout December the four ships of the advance party sailed further into the great Southern Ocean where they encountered what seaman John Easty on the *Scarborough* described as the 'heaviest seas I ever saw'.[70] Lieutenant King wrote that they were experiencing 'the most confused tumbling seas'. 'Had very strong gales of wind from the south south west to the north west with a very strong sea running which keeps the vessel almost constantly under water,' he noted, 'and renders the situation of everyone on board her truly uncomfortable.'[71]

The rough seas and high winds made life even more difficult for the convicts, who were forced to stay cramped, wet and cold below decks. Their hatches were battened down for much of this leg of the journey and they would have had little opportunity of seeing daylight. As Christmas approached, King recorded that it was as cold as an English winter even though they were at the height of the southern hemisphere summer.[72]

On 3 January 1788 the *Supply*'s crew and officers sighted Van Diemen's Land. They then turned around its south-eastern tip and struggled for more than 1000 kilometres up the coast to Botany

Bay, sailing in an adverse current and into a northerly wind. The *Supply* finally entered Botany Bay on the afternoon of 18 January. The *Alexander*, the *Scarborough* and the *Friendship*, which had fallen behind weeks before, caught up and arrived the following day.

The seven vessels of the bigger, slower second division found the going even more difficult. Immediately after the *Supply* and the three fastest ships had sailed ahead, Captain Hunter made his first big independent decision and ordered all the ships under his command to change course to a more southerly route where the winds blew stronger. 'I was at this time of [the] opinion,' he later wrote, 'that we had kept too northerly a parallel to ensure strong and lasting winds, which determined me, as soon as Captain Phillip had left the fleet, to steer to the southward and keep in higher latitude.'[73]

This decision would subject the seven ships to the most dangerous sailing since they had left England but the new route was faster and they would arrive at Botany Bay seven weeks later, only a day or so behind the faster ships.

A few days before Christmas, and with the fresh food from the Cape exhausted, Chief Surgeon John White reported an outbreak of scurvy on the *Prince of Wales* and then the *Charlotte*:

> I found some of the female convicts with evident symptoms of the scurvy, brought on by the damp and cold weather we had lately experienced . . . The scurvy began to show itself in the *Charlotte*, mostly among those who had the dysentery to a violent degree; but I was pretty well able to keep it under by a liberal use of the essence of malt and some good wine, which ought not to be classed among the most indifferent antiscorbutics.[74]

A week before Christmas and running short on fodder, more of the farm animals had begun to die. On 19 December surgeon Arthur Bowes Smyth on the *Lady Penrhyn* recorded in his journal that two cows on the *Sirius* had calved, but the calves had died; 'many' sheep on the *Fishburn* had also died', as had 'the greatest part of the poultry throughout the fleet'. Bowes Smyth was not alone in believing that the English had been sold diseased chickens by the Dutch at the Cape.[75]

On Christmas Day the officers tried to celebrate. On the *Prince of Wales*, Sergeant Scott and his colleagues ate beef, pork with apple sauce, and plum pudding and drank four bottles of rum, which he described as the 'best we veterans could afford'.[76] Over on the *Sirius*, Judge Advocate Collins and his fellow officers tried to celebrate Christmas dinner but the weather was too rough to allow any real enjoyment. By the end of December the seas were 'mountainously high'. On the *Lady Penrhyn* the water was ankle-deep on the quarter-deck, women convicts were being washed out of their berths and the water had to be bailed out from below decks with buckets. On New Year's Day, the sea poured through the hatchway and washed away the bedding from Bowes Smyth's cabin. Lieutenant Newton Fowell, the second-most senior officer on the *Sirius*, described the high winds and threatening seas in a letter to his father, saying they were the worst they had experienced since leaving England.

As the weather worsened the fleet was forced to reduce sail and slow down. 'The rolling and labouring of our ship,' wrote Captain Hunter, 'exceedingly distressed the cattle, which were now in a very weak state, and the great quantities of water which we shipped during the gale, very much aggravated their distress. The poor animals were frequently thrown with such violence off their legs and exceedingly bruised by their falls.'[77]

At the end of the first week of January 1788, the bulk of the fleet passed around the south coast of Tasmania and began the journey north to Botany Bay. On the evening of 6 January and believing Van Diemen's Land to be part of the same coastline as their destination, the officers on the *Lady Penrhyn* toasted 'two bumpers of claret': one to the success of the voyage and the other to a safe anchorage in Botany Bay.[78]

Yet as they sailed northwards they met more bad weather and bad luck. Faced with what Bowes Smyth called the 'greatest swell than at any time during the voyage', they were forced to sail further out to sea. Tubs containing a number of plants for the new colony, including bananas and grapes, were smashed and lost.[79]

> The sky blackened, the wind arose and in half an hour more it blew a perfect hurricane, accompanied by thunder, lightning and rain . . . I never before saw a sea in such a rage . . . every other ship in the fleet except the *Sirius* sustained some damage . . . During the storm the convict women in our ship were so terrified that most of them were down on their knees in prayer.[80]

Finally, on the night of 19 January, the seven ships of the main convoy reached the entrance of Botany Bay; they decided to wait until the next morning to navigate through the heads. By 8 a.m. the following day they were all safely at anchor alongside the four ships that had sailed ahead; they were surprised to discover that the *Sirius* had only arrived on 18 January, and the others the day after. The time between the arrival of the *Sirius* and the last of the ships was barely 40 hours.

Arthur Phillip had entered Botany Bay on the *Supply* a little after 2 p.m. on the afternoon of 18 January followed by the other three ships of the advance fleet the next morning. To their even greater surprise, on the following morning, Sunday, 20 January, they saw 'the *Sirius* and all her convoy coming round Point Solander'.[81]

Remarkably given the dangers of ocean voyages the fleet had reached Botany Bay without losing a ship. What's more, its passengers were in relatively good health—there had been fewer deaths than most convoys bringing convicts to Australia would experience over the next 60 years.

No matter how optimistic they were when they landed, however, the settlers could not know that their problems were just about to begin.

4

A Crisis Looms

> 'Hope is no more, and a new scene of distress and misery opens our view . . . For all the grain of every kind which we have been able to raise in two years and three months would not support us for three weeks.'
>
> Chief Surgeon John White

Having sailed halfway around the world to establish a new colony the British were dismayed to find Botany Bay totally unsuitable for settlement. This was unexpected and posed an immediate threat to the lives of all aboard the fleet. A solution had to be quickly found.

Arthur Phillip first went ashore on the afternoon of Friday 18 January 1788, shortly after the *Supply* had entered the bay and anchored. As was the custom, the Naval officers in their smart uniforms were rowed close to the shore and wading seamen would carry them the last few metres to prevent them from getting wet.

Once ashore, Phillip examined the north of the bay while some of his colleagues were rowed to the south side closer to where Cook had anchored eighteen years before. Within an hour of landing, Phillip, who was unarmed, came across a group of Aboriginal people who had been watching the Europeans from the shore. They were naked and carried spears but according to Lieutenant King, who was with Phillip, proved friendly and 'directed us, by pointing, to a very fine stream of fresh water'.[1]

After less than two days looking for a suitable spot to establish their new town the leaders of the First Fleet were already forming the opinion that Botany Bay was not a good location for their settlement. It had insufficient fresh water and the bay was open to the region's strong southerly and easterly winds, which would not have provided the ships of the fleet with adequate shelter. The only significant fertile soil was found by Phillip's colleagues on the south side of the bay at a spot Cook had named Point Sutherland, after a sailor who had been buried there.

Later, when the first chartered ships of the fleet were returning to England, Phillip sent a dispatch to Lord Sydney explaining why he had ordered the abandonment of Botany Bay:

> I began to examine the bay as soon as we anchored, and found, that though extensive, it did not afford shelter to the ships to the easterly winds; the greater part of the bay being so shoal [shallow] that ships of even a moderate draught of water are obliged to anchor with the entrance of the bay open, and are exposed to a heavy sea that rolls in when it blows heavy from the eastward. Several small runs of fresh water were found in different parts of the bay, but I did not see any situation of which there was not some strong objection.[2]

Phillip's colleagues were equally unimpressed by what they found at Botany Bay. On his first day ashore marine Captain Watkin Tench said they were unable to find a good supply of fresh water or fertile soil:

> We set out to observe the country, on inspection rather disappointed our hopes, being invariably sandy and unpromising for the purposes of cultivation . . . close to us was the spring at which Mr. Cook

> watered but we did not think the water very excellent, nor did it run freely. In the evening we returned on board, not greatly pleased with our discoveries.[3]

Surgeon Arthur Bowes Smyth said that he had quickly realised Botany Bay was not what he had expected:

> Upon first sight one would be induced to think this is a most fertile spot . . . but on nearer inspection, the grass is found long and coarse, the trees very large and in general hollow and the wood itself unfit for no purpose of building, or anything but a fire—the soil to a great depth is nothing but a black sand which . . . is not fit for the vegetation.[4]

Phillip was facing a crisis. He had more than 1400 people aboard the fleet's eleven ships desperate for fresh food. Scurvy had already begun to break out. Even more pressing were the starving animals. The fodder loaded in Cape Town more than ten weeks before had been exhausted, and many animals had died. During the first few days at Botany Bay, men were sent ashore to cut grass but they had difficulty obtaining enough to feed the surviving farm animals.

Phillip was also conscious that he was under instructions not to keep the chartered ships of the fleet any longer than was 'absolutely necessary'; his orders were to unload them as quickly as possible so as to minimise the daily charter cost the British government was paying the East India Company.[5]

After only three days and convinced Botany Bay would fail to support the new colony Phillip set off to search for an alternative. Leaving the fleet anchored in Botany Bay with everyone still aboard he left on Monday, 21 January, in three small boats accompanied by his deputy John Hunter, Judge Advocate David Collins and a number of other officers to examine Port Jackson 12 kilometres to the north.

They had little knowledge as to what to expect there. The only information about it was a passing reference in Cook's journal to what he named Port Jackson from eighteen years before as they sailed past the headland several miles out to sea:

> Having seen everything this place [Botany Bay] afforded we at daylight in the morning weighed with a light breeze . . . and steered along the shore NNE and at noon we were by observation . . . almost two to three miles from the land and abreast of a bay or a harbour wherein there appeared to be safe anchorage, which I called Port Jackson.[6]

Phillip's three small boats reached the mouth of Port Jackson in the early afternoon, and that night they pitched their tents at what is still known as Camp Cove.

One of the oarsmen on Phillip's boat was American sailor Jacob Nagle of the *Sirius*, who recalls on that first day he caught some fish, which attracted the attention of the commander: '[He] observed the fish I had hauled in and asked who had caught that fish. I recollect he said that you are the first white man that ever caught a fish in Sydney Cove.'[7]

Later on the second day and after examining 6 kilometres further up the harbour Phillip discovered a sheltered bay about 800 metres long and 400 metres wide, which had fresh water running into it. It was here, he quickly decided, and not Botany Bay that the settlers would found the new colony. He was to describe Port Jackson as 'the finest harbour in the world, in which a thousand sail of the line may ride in most perfect safety',[8] and named the site Sydney Cove after the home secretary responsible for the First Fleet.

While Phillip was examining Sydney Cove a group of Aboriginal people came to see the Europeans while they were preparing to eat. According to Phillip they appeared friendly and curious and were fascinated at seeing food being cooked in a metal pot.[9]

Back at Botany Bay, as they waited for Phillip to return some of the officers went ashore to see the Aboriginal people who had approached carrying spears and shields. Chief Surgeon John White fired a pistol to frighten them and his shot pierced a shield that was standing in the sand. This, White recorded, had the desired effect because the local people learned 'to know and dread the superiority of our arms'. He said that 'very soon did they make themselves acquainted with the nature of our military dress, that, from the first, they carefully avoided a soldier, or any person wearing a red coat, which they seemed to have marked as fighting vesture'.[10]

Phillip and his party arrived back in Botany Bay on the evening of Wednesday, 23 January, and gave immediate orders for the fleet to sail to Sydney Cove in Port Jackson. But on the morning of 24 January strong headwinds were blowing and the English decided to delay till the following day before trying to sail out of Botany Bay. While they were waiting for more suitable sailing conditions they were shocked to see two strange ships appear outside the bay. Watkin Tench had woken at dawn on the *Sirius* and said he was getting dressed when he heard the news:

> Judge my surprise on hearing from the sergeant, who ran down almost breathless to the cabin where I was dressing, that a ship had been seen off the harbour's mouth. At first I only laughed but knowing the man who spoke to me to be of great veracity and hearing him repeat his information, I flew up on deck, on which I barely set my foot, when a cry 'another sail' struck on my astonished ear.[11]

Tench had every reason to doubt what he was hearing. The only Europeans to have sailed in this part of the world had been on Cook's *Endeavour* eighteen years before. Now, in a remarkable coincidence, two more ships had arrived only days after the First Fleet.

At first it was not known whose ships they were but as surgeon George Worgan noted, 'by noon we could by the help of our glasses discern that they had French colours flying'.[12]

The ships were the *Astrolabe* and the *Boussole* under the command of Captain Jean-François de Galaup La Pérouse. They had been on a remarkable exploration voyage of the Pacific for nearly three years, having left Europe in June 1785—nearly two years before the First Fleet. When the English saw them the French ships were battling to sail into Botany Bay and kept being blown south; this was at the same time as the British were being thwarted by the winds as they tried to sail out.

Throughout Friday, 25 January, the English continued to struggle to sail out of Botany Bay in the face of strong winds. Around midday only the nimble *Supply* was successful, carrying away Arthur Phillip, a number of officers, some marines and about 40 convicts. They passed the French but Phillip decided that dealing with them could wait until another day. The *Supply* sailed that afternoon up to Port Jackson, where it anchored for the night.

Early the next morning, Saturday, 26 January 1788, Phillip and the officers in his party were rowed ashore to the spot he had chosen a few days earlier near the southern side of what would become Sydney's Circular Quay.

Here a flag was planted and a little ceremony took place. Possession was claimed on behalf of His Majesty King George III, whose health was drunk, as were that of the Queen and the Prince of Wales and the success of the new colony. A *feu de joie* (salute) was fired by a party of marines, and the whole group gave three cheers. The events of that day were the basis for 26 January later officially becoming Australia Day. Only a few dozen marines, officers and oarsmen participated in the new country's christening ceremony, while others, including the 40 convicts, witnessed it from the deck of the *Supply*.

Meanwhile, the bulk of the fleet finally sailed out of Botany Bay after three days of trying.[13] According to Lieutenant Clark on the *Friendship* there was a 'great sea rolling into the bay'.[14] The *Charlotte* was blown off course dangerously close to the rocks and the *Friendship* and the *Prince of Wales* became entangled, which resulted in the *Friendship* losing its jib boom and the *Prince of Wales* its mainmast staysail and topsail. Clark later said it was only 'the greatest of good luck' that they were not blown onto rocks where 'the greater part if not the whole on board [would have] drowned'.[15]

Surgeon Arthur Bowes Smyth who witnessed the events blamed the near calamity on Arthur Phillip for insisting the fleet head immediately for Sydney Cove when it was too dangerous to do so:

> Everyone blam[ed] the rashness of the Governor [Phillip] in insisting upon the fleet working out in such weather, and all agreed it was next to a miracle that some of the ships were not lost, the danger was so great.[16]

At around 3 p.m. the fleet had finally cleared Botany Bay and a little more than an hour later it reached the heads of Port Jackson for the 8-kilometre run up to Sydney Cove. Shortly before dark on 26 January the entire fleet anchored at the site where the British would begin their occupation of Australia. Interestingly, though, for the next 60 years the British would refer to the convict settlement in New South Wales as 'Botany Bay' even though no convicts were ever landed or settled there.

The unloading of the ships began in earnest the next morning, a Sunday, when some of the marines and about a hundred convict men began clearing ground and felling trees. For many of the convicts it was the first time they had been on land for more than a year. Judge Advocate David Collins described the scene as hundreds of men began to scramble out of the little rowboats and onto the shore, where the dense vegetation came down almost to the water's edge:

> The confusion that ensued will not be wondered at, when it is considered that every man stepped from the boat literally into the wood. Parties of people were everywhere heard and seen variously employed; some in clearing ground for the different encampments; others pitching tents, or bringing up stores as were immediately wanted.[17]

There was a particular urgency about unloading the surviving but weak farm animals. At Botany Bay the fresh-cut grass had been rowed out to the ships to keep the surviving animals alive; but now the fleet had reached Sydney Cove, the livestock was lowered by ropes into the boats and rowed ashore where they were allowed to graze on the eastern side of Sydney Cove.

Earlier in the day Governor Phillip had 'marked out the lines for the encampment'.[18] He and some of the officers were to be camped on the eastern side of the cove, with most of the marines on the western side, and the convicts further to the west. The western side of the cove was steeper and rockier and would later be known as The Rocks.

It was to be another ten days before the majority of the female convicts were unloaded from the transports and rowed ashore by which time a large number of tents had been pitched for them. A number of the women had somehow managed to keep some good clothing, and were rowed to shore on their first morning in Sydney Cove dressed in colourful dresses and pretty bonnets.

The unloading of the female convicts resulted in wild celebrations that shocked many of the officers. Bowes Smyth described what happened, especially at night after the seamen came ashore during a fierce thunderstorm, bringing grog with them, which was usually denied to the convicts:

> The men convicts got to [the women] very soon after they landed, and it is beyond my abilities to give a just description of the scene of debauchery and riot that ensued during the night . . . the scene . . . beggars description; some swearing, others quarrelling others singing, not in the least regarding the tempest, though so violent that the thunder . . . exceeded anything I ever before had conception of.[19]

Marine Captain Watkin Tench said it was impossible to 'prevent their intercourse': 'licentiousness was the unavoidable consequence' of the men and women having been keep separate for a year or more and 'their old habits of depravity were beginning to recur'.[20]

The day after the orgy, Thursday, 7 February 1788, when just about everyone was ashore, many with hangovers, the battalion under arms was marched on parade to a piece of cleared land with colours flying and pipes playing. The convicts were forced to stand in line during the formal declaration of the colony, while they listened to the lengthy reading of Arthur Phillip's commission by Judge Advocate David Collins. This was followed by a speech from Phillip who promised good treatment for those convicts who deserved it, but threatened severe punishment and execution for any wrongdoers.

After the parade, the officers and senior civilians were invited to the governor's tent for a celebratory dinner at which 'many loyal and public toasts were drank'.[21] Lieutenant Clark recorded the meal was marred by the maggots in the mutton, which had been killed only the day before; 'nothing will keep 24 hours in this country,' he complained.[22]

The most pressing security problem was the theft of food, which was strictly rationed. Initially the provisions were simply put on the ground and covered until secure storehouses could be built but even with a 24-hour guard the theft of food and grog was an immediate problem, which severe punishment and executions failed to prevent.

A week after landing and as the clearing continued and the construction of buildings started, Phillip sent Lieutenant King to call on the French, who were still anchored at Botany Bay. King left Sydney at 2 a.m. on 2 February, rowed in a cutter with Lieutenant William Dawes and a marine escort; he was instructed to offer La Pérouse 'whatever he might have occasion for'. After arriving at around 10 a.m., King recalled, he was received with 'the greatest politeness and attention' by La Pérouse and his officers.[23]

King was told that he was not the first of the English to visit and that a number of convicts had already walked the 12 kilometres overland from Port Jackson and had been refused the opportunity of escaping on the French ships. During their cordial meeting King learned of the remarkable voyage the French had made over the past three years. They had sailed from Brest, the Brittany port near the most westerly tip of France, around Cape Horn and up from Chile to Easter Island, Hawaii, Alaska, California, across the Pacific to Macau, Manila, Korea, Japan and Kamchatka, in eastern Siberia, then south to Samoa, Tonga and Norfolk Island.

When the French ships had been in Kamchatka they had learned that the British intended to establish a colony at Botany Bay and La Pérouse said he'd been surprised to see nothing there when he arrived except the English fleet attempting to leave. King was also told of how a number of French officers and crew—including the captain of the *Astrolabe*, M. De Langle, eight officers and a boy—had been massacred and others injured two months before by natives in the Isles des Navigateurs (the French name for Samoa). La Pérouse also told King of how he'd lost 21 men when two boats had been destroyed in heavy surf on the Alaskan coast eighteen months before, in July 1786.

King was particularly impressed by the French expedition's array of scientists, which included botanists, astronomers and natural historians. He also recorded how the French were equipped with a far more extensive array of astronomical and navigation equipment than the English. On 4 February, after two cordial days with the French, King said his goodbyes and returned to Sydney.

Over the next weeks there was little contact between the English, who were busy trying to establish their new home, and the French, who were preparing for the next leg of their exploration. Before the French left Botany Bay two weeks later Captain Hunter also paid them a visit and the captain of the *Astrolabe*, M. de Clonard, was sent to Sydney by La Pérouse with dispatches that the French asked the English to deliver to the French ambassador in London by the first transports returning to England.

A few weeks later, on 10 March, the French quietly left Botany Bay, with the two commanders, Phillip and La Pérouse, having never met. The *Astrolabe* and the *Boussole* were not seen again; they are believed to have sunk off the coast of Vanikoro north of the New Hebrides (Vanuatu), with loss of all crew.

Despite the friendliness of the encounter, the arrival of La Pérouse—along with a number of other French explorations over the coming years—spooked the British and fuelled fears in Sydney and London of French ambitions to try to colonise the Australian coast for themselves.

Back at Sydney Cove, as the building work continued the English were surprised at the harshness and volatility of the climate. Less than a week after arriving five sheep were killed by lightning and a number of trees caught fire during 'very heavy storms of thunder and lightning'.[24] The surgeon from the *Sirius*, George Worgan, said they were totally unprepared for the local climate:

> The thunder and lightning are astonishingly awful here, and by the heavy gloom that hangs over the woods at the time these elements are in commotion and from the nature and violence done to many trees we have reason to apprehend that much mischief can be done by lightning here.[25]

Marine Captain Watkin Tench described the fierceness and changeability of the hot summer winds, which were 'like a blast from a heated oven':

> It is changeable beyond any other I have ever heard of . . . clouds, storms and sunshine pass in rapid succession . . . thunderstorms in summer are common and very tremendous.[26]

The settlers were having great difficulty clearing the tough Australian bush. They found that many of the tools they had brought from England were not strong enough for the gnarled hardwoods of Australia. Sir Joseph Banks and Captain Cook may have been right in claiming there was abundant timber but, as Phillip was to report, the settlers found it far from ideal for building:

> The timber is well described in Captain Cook's voyage but unfortunately it had one very bad quality, which puts us to great inconvenience; I mean the large gum tree, which splits and warps in such a manner when used green . . .[27]

Chief Surgeon John White said the wood was only good for firewood, but no good for 'the huts for officers, soldiers, and convicts, some storehouses' and a 'good hospital' that needed to be built.[28]

All the settlers lived initially in tents as the building of secure storehouses for the food and grog was the highest priority. Erecting the buildings proved difficult and slow. It took days for a team of men to cut down a single tree, drag it to the saw pit and cut it into usable strips of timber. There were only sixteen ship's carpenters, most of whom were kept busy on their ships and they then returned to England. This left the entire settlement with only twelve convicts who had any carpentry training. It took two years for the bulk of the settlers to graduate from tents to crude shacks, which in any case were ineffective shelters in heavy weather.

In the early years there was no sewerage system and no established roads; during heavy rain the paths would become fast-running filthy streams that would undermine and flood the little dwellings. More than two years after arriving, Collins observed how rain 'came down in torrents, filling up every trench and cavity' and 'causing much damage to the miserable mud tenements, which were occupied by the convicts'.[29]

It was envisaged that religion would play a big role in the colony, but more than five years would pass before a temporary church was built with wooden posts and wattle-and-daub walls. In the meantime the Reverend Richard Johnson was one of the busiest men in the colony, working in the open air or temporarily using one of the storehouses, performing all the services of the church—baptisms, marriages, burials—while also attending the executions of condemned men and working hard among the convicts. Marriages between convicts were officially encouraged but, according to Collins, many convicts got married because they wrongly thought they would receive 'various comforts and privileges.' When these expectations were not realised, they 'repented' and restored 'their former situations'.[30]

While the building work continued painfully slowly the settlement was having even less success growing food. Until the colony could produce its own food, everyone was issued with a weekly ration from the supplies brought from England. On Phillip's orders, everyone was on the same ration—except that the convicts were not entitled to the grog ration given to the military and civilians. To begin with, the food ration included salted beef, salted pork, rice, peas and flour. Within two months of their arrival the shrinking food stocks required the first of what would be a series of cuts to the food ration; over the next two years the weekly issue would be progressively reduced to starvation levels as successive harvests failed and no new ships arrived from England with more supplies. The situation was made worse by the depletion of local seafood stocks and wildlife by the Europeans and the fact that they learnt little from the Aboriginal population about the nutrition available from local vegetable matter and other bush food.

Almost all the crimes committed in the early days of the colony involved the theft of food. On 27 February, only a month after the fleet's arrival, the court was convened to hear evidence of a plan by some convicts to rob food from the public stores. Thomas Barrett was the first convict to be hanged, but his two accomplices were given a last-minute pardon. The officials were finding that a brutal flogging was not a sufficient deterrent even when it involved more than 100 lashes and left a man's back shredded and bleeding, and his 'shoes full of blood'.[31] Within six months, Judge Advocate Collins was complaining that the floggings and banishments to one of the islands in Port Jackson were insufficient punishment and that executions were 'growing daily more necessary'.[32]

In his first dispatch to London sent in May 1788, four months after the arrival of the fleet, Phillip gave a warning of the slow progress being made in cultivating the land, including the difficulty of cutting and clearing large trees and the 'rocky' nature of much of the soil.[33] In July, Chief Surgeon John White recorded in his journal that the rate of sickness in the colony was increasing because of the shortage of vital food and that 150 marines and convicts were too ill to work:

> The distress among the troops, their wives and children, as well as among the convicts, who have been ill for the want of necessities

> [including] sugar, sago, barley, rice, oatmeal, currants, spices, vinegar, portable soup and tamarins . . . constantly living on salt provisions without possibility of change make them more necessary.[34]

It was also in July that Phillip sent the first clear message to England that the colony was heading for trouble. In a letter to Lord Sydney, he wrote that the original plan of bringing two years' supplies before becoming self-sufficient was unachievable and that further supplies from England would 'be absolutely necessary' for at least another four to five years.[35]

Two months later, on 28 September 1788, Phillip wrote again to say that the first harvest had been a total failure, yielding only enough grain to support the colony for 'a few days'. He said that none of the grain would be fed to the settlers but instead saved as seed for sowing the following year:

> It was now found that very little of the English wheat had vegetated and a very considerable quantity of barley and many seeds had rotted in the ground, having been heated in the passage and so much eaten by weevils. All the barley and wheat likewise, which has been put aboard the *Supply* at the Cape were destroyed by the weevil.[36]

Phillip reported in a similar vein about the loss of farm animals. He said the 'greatest part of the stock' of sheep and cows brought from Cape Town had been lost, either having died or wandered off into the bush, never to be seen again. The settlers' clothing was also wearing out, particularly shoes, which, according to Phillip, soon 'most of the people will be without'.[37]

Despite the colony's dire predicament, Phillip tried to be optimistic about its long-term prospects, saying that eventually it would 'prove the most valuable acquisition Great Britain ever made'.[38]

The head of the marines in Sydney, Major Robert Ross, strongly disagreed with this assessment. He wrote a letter at around the same time as Phillip:

> With respect to the utility of settlement upon this coast . . . it never can be made to answer the intended purpose or wish of Government, for the country seems totally destitute of everything that can be an object of a commercial nation, a very fine harbour excepted, and I much fear that the nature of the soil is such as will not be brought to yield more than a sufficient sustenance for the needy emigrants whose desperate fortunes induce them to try the experiment.[39]

By the end of September and concerned at the growing food crisis Governor Phillip decided to send Captain Hunter on the *Sirius* to Cape Town to fetch grain, seed and flour.

The *Sirius* was the only suitable ship available. All nine of the chartered merchant ships that made up the First Fleet had either been released to resume private shipping or were about to leave Sydney. This left only the two Royal Navy vessels, and the tiny *Supply* was only capable of carrying a small cargo.

In his 28 September dispatch to England Phillip said he was afraid they would not have enough 'grain to put into the ground next year':[40]

> All the seed wheat and most of the other seeds brought from England [have] been spoiled, as well as what wheat was put on board the *Supply* at the Cape. Several acres sown with this wheat have been sown a second time with the seed I procured for next year, in case of any accident happening to what we have in the ground, and which has left us without a bushel of seed in the settlement. Having only a year's flour in store, Captain Hunter has orders to purchase as much as the ship can stow.[41]

Phillip had earlier considered sending the *Sirius* to Cape Town to bring back livestock to replace those lost in the bush. However, the failure of the crops in Sydney left the colony in a more immediate need for grain—and a cargo of livestock would not last as long anyway. Phillip had told Lord Sydney that 'what [livestock] the *Sirius* might procure . . . could not be expected to exceed ten or fourteen days' provisions for the settlement'.[42]

Before it could leave Sydney, the *Sirius* had to be made shipshape as its maintenance had 'been much neglected since its voyage from England'. For the next month Hunter 'employed an old man, the carpenter's yeoman, and a convict caulker' to help prepare the vessel for its voyage.[43]

Hunter sailed from Sydney on the *Sirius* in October 1788. A month later in the Sydney settlement the food ration for everyone was cut by one-third. To reach the Cape of Good Hope and return quickly Hunter decided he would circumnavigate the globe by sailing east under New Zealand and then under Cape Horn at the bottom of South America, and across the Atlantic to southern Africa. 'At that season of the year the route to the eastward by Cape Horn promised fairest and expeditious passage,' he later wrote. 'I therefore steered for the South Cape of New Zealand which I passed on 12th [November] and made the coast of Tierra del Fuego on the 26th November.'[44]

The voyage proved difficult from the start. Within a day of leaving Sydney Cove a major leak was discovered below the waterline, which Hunter said required the water pumps to be manned all the way to Cape Town: 'admitted two feet four inches water in four hours', he said . . . 'we discovered it to be about two feet or three feet below the wale, starboard side'.[45]

Even though it was now approaching the height of the northern hemisphere summer the prevailing winds took the *Sirius* towards the Antarctic and to 'intolerably cold weather' that 'froze the fresh water casks on the deck'.[46] Aboard the *Sirius*, American seaman Jacob Nagle described going around Cape Horn at Christmas and passing dangerously close to more than 30 giant icebergs and large pieces of floating ice. Nagle said giant whales were 'so thick that we could not count them and their spouting soaked all the crew on deck with spray'.[47]

A month after leaving New South Wales a number of the crew fell victim to scurvy, which was not surprising since most had eaten very little fresh food since they were last in Cape Town on their way to New South Wales a year before. Hunter said that by the end of the journey hardly any of the crew was capable of working aloft and three men died before they finally reached the Cape:

> The ship's company, who had been on salt provisions since we left the Cape of Good Hope outward bound, and without any kind of vegetable, fell down very fast with the scurvy. I arrived [at the Cape] . . . having buried three seamen on the passage.[48]

The *Sirius* reached Robbin Island, about 8 kilometres from the mouth of Table Bay, on New Year's Day 1789. Fresh fruit was brought on board and the next day the ship entered Table Bay. Nagle described how he and the others who were stricken with scurvy tried to eat some fruit but when biting an apple, pear or peach, 'the blood would run out of our mouths from our gums'.[49]

Hunter was seven weeks in Cape Town repairing the *Sirius* and loading cargo. The going was very slow as he had been forced to leave his ship's longboats in Sydney Cove and so had only two six-oared cutters to ferry the bags of seed, wheat and flour from the shore to the ship.

Before leaving Cape Town five of the crew—including Jacob Nagle—deserted, no doubt daunted by the prospect of going back to the inevitable hardship of life at Sydney Cove. Nagle claimed they went because a young midshipman on the *Sirius* was sadistic in the beatings he doled out to sailors. When Hunter agreed to admonish the midshipman and banish him to his cabin for three weeks, Nagle was persuaded to return, but the other four crewmen 'never did' and disappeared 'in one of the biggest and busiest ports in the southern hemisphere'.[50]

The three months' voyage back across the Southern Ocean to Sydney was even more hazardous than the trip to Cape Town. Lieutenant Newton Fowell, who was the second-most senior officer on the *Sirius*, later described the journey. After leaving the Cape of Good Hope on 20 February, he wrote that the ship spent two weeks battling into the face of a 'gale of wind' and was unable to make any progress towards the east. When they finally connected with winds from the west and reached 'the south cape of New Holland' (that is, the southern tip of Van Diemen's Land), 'it blew too hard' and tore all the major sails—the ship was being pushed 'directly to the shore'.

Closely avoiding land they were then pushed by huge seas and winds perilously close to the small Bass Strait islands of Swilly and Mewstone. 'We were at this time in a very dangerous situation . . . So heavy a press of sail was on the ship that the sea made a fair breach over her, which obliged every person to be very careful in holding fast for fear of being washed overboard. Indeed the forecastle was constantly under water.'[51]

When they finally reached Sydney Cove the extra rations they had brought gave only a couple of months of respite. The colony was still headed for a full-blown crisis.

5

Epic and Disastrous Voyages

'Upon being brought up in the open air some fainted, some died upon the deck and others in the boat before they reached the shore. When they came to the shore many were not able to walk, to stand, or to sit themselves in the least, hence some were led by others. Some crept on their hands and knees and some were carried on the backs of others.'

Reverend Richard Johnson

When news of the dire situation in Sydney reached London on the *Borrowdale*, one of the First Fleet ships that arrived back in England in March 1789, the government reacted quickly. Within weeks, Lord Sydney wrote to the Admiralty to inform them that King George had authorised the urgent dispatch of a supply ship to relieve the colony:

> The letters which have been received from Captain Phillip Governor of New South Wales representing that a great part of the provisions sent out with him to the settlement . . . have been expended and that there is an immediate occasion for further supply, together with certain articles of clothing, tools, implements for agriculture, medicines etc . . . His Majesty has given orders that one of his ships of war

> of two decks, with only her upper tier with guns, shall forthwith be got ready to carry out the said provisions and stores.[1]

Five months later, in September 1789, HMS *Guardian* commanded by 27-year-old Captain Edward Riou left Portsmouth with a total of 300 passengers, most of whom were convicts, and almost 1000 tons of supplies, including grain and flour, almost 100 pots containing vegetable and fruit plants, as well as cattle, sheep, horses, goats, rabbits and poultry. The government had also responded to Phillip's complaint that too few of the First Fleet convicts knew anything about farming, so 25 'of those confined to the hulks who are most likely to be the most useful' for farming were also sent aboard.

The *Guardian* made good time to Cape Town, arriving on 24 November, where it stayed three weeks to restock food and take on board 150 fruit trees and some additional farm animals. It left the Cape on 11 December and sailed to the south-east across the Southern Ocean, catching the strong westerly winds. Captain Riou was well aware of the hazards of sailing in these waters, which he recorded in his diary:

> We found the great emission of fog from this mountain of ice darken the hemisphere to leeward of it . . . the horizon became clouded all around and in less than a quarter of an hour we were again shut up in a thick, close general mist, and scarce able to see the ship's length before us . . . there were many more such islands of ice floating in the seas, which appeared very dangerous.[2]

At 7.45 p.m. on Christmas Eve, and as the watch was changing, the *Guardian* smashed into a giant iceberg. According to the ship's master, Clements, it happened as he was handing over the watch to Mr Harvey, the master's mate, and he had just remarked 'how much more dreadful it would be [to be] ship wrecked before an island of ice than among rocks, when the noise reached the cabin and gave the fatal signal of failure'.[3]

As the ship shook from end to end Riou ran up the deck to see that the front of the *Guardian* had wedged under a giant iceberg that appeared to be twice as tall as the mainmast of the ship. Within half an hour there was more than two feet of water in the hold and the water level was rising fast. All hands were put to the pumps but they were unable to stem the rise. To lighten the ship Riou ordered the immediate jettisoning of cargo; all heavy items, including live cattle, gun carriages and spare anchors, were thrown over the side.[4]

By 9 p.m. the pumps were all working, but the water level in the hold was over three feet and continuing to rise. At 10 p.m. the water reached five feet and the men were tiring at the pumps so they were split into two shifts, each working for half an hour. Riou also ordered the issue of grog, biscuits and cheese for each man but with the available rum 'nearly expended, the captain thought it extremely dangerous to open the hold to get more'.[5]

At midnight the water level reached six feet, and 'it was blowing a strong gale and an immense sea was running'.[6] All night long the crew continued to pump and by sun-up next morning—Christmas Day—at last the water below decks began to fall. But by the afternoon on Christmas Day, according to Riou, the crew was totally spent: 'About this time the crew became almost unable to perform any duty, from their limbs being benumbed by the frequent transition from the heat of labour and having rested in wet clothes.'[7]

By 5 p.m. the water level began to rise again and by 4 a.m. on Boxing Day it was reaching seven feet for the first time. To make matters worse, during the night the topsails, which had been left unattended, were torn to pieces 'by the violence of the wind and the ship was left to the mercy of a most tremendous sea'.[8]

At six o'clock the next morning the ship's carpenter came up and reported that the water was as high as the orlop, or next deck, and rising by about a foot each hour. It was at this time the crew fully appreciated the seriousness of their predicament. According to Master Clements a number of men, already exhausted, resigned themselves to the sinking of the ship and certain death, and left the pumping to break into the rum store:

> A few of the more profligate escaped with utmost vigilance and secreted themselves below, where they got intoxicated with liquor and became insensible to the danger.[9]

Amazingly, while all this was going on, Lieutenant Riou went to his cabin and wrote a letter to the Admiralty in which he declared that 'there seems to be no possibility of my remaining many more hours in this world'. He praised the crew for their honourable conduct; there was no mention of those who were comatose with alcohol:

> If any part of the officers or crew of the *Guardian* should ever survive to get home, I have only to say their conduct after the fatal stroke against an island of ice was admirable and wonderful in everything that related to their duties, considered either as private men or in His Majesty's Service.[10]

By evening, when the water was up to the lower gun deck and it appeared the ship was about to sink, everyone was given the option of abandoning ship and going aboard one of the five small boats. Riou decided to go down with his ship: '[A]s for me, I have determined to remain in the ship and shall endeavour to make my presence useful as long as there is any occasion for it.'[11]

The boatswain was ordered to make sure every boat had oars, a mast and a sail, a compass, a cask of water and 'other necessities', but their loading proved extremely difficult and resulted in chaos and panic. As the boats were lowered to the sea, they were buffeted against the side of the ship in 'immensely high' seas, the men on the ship trying at the same time to get aboard.[12]

The largest of the five boats was quickly adrift of the *Guardian*, with only seven men on board, and no food or water. In desperation a number of men jumped into the icy water and tried to reach the boats. Riou said he thought it unlikely that the men would have survived for more than a few minutes.[13]

Clements, on one of the boats, watched another boat sink, and then lost sight of another. Sixty-two of the original 123 men stayed on board the ship, either because they could not safely board one of the lifeboats or because they thought their chances of survival were better aboard the *Guardian*, which remained afloat. Among those who stayed was Thomas Pitt, a nephew of the prime minister; two midshipmen; the ship's carpenter; the surgeon's mate, John Fairclough; 30 seamen and boys; 21 convicts; and three convict supervisors.

Only one of the five small boats was heard of again. Among the fifteen survivors who packed on a six-oared 'jolly boat' was Clements, who would later tell of their nine-day ordeal in an open boat in freezing conditions. He described how they eventually lost sight of the only other boat they still had contact with as they were lashed in high seas to the north and away from the stricken *Guardian*. They had with them little food and an eight-gallon cask of water, which they rationed out in the bottom of a tobacco canister at the rate of about two gills, or a little less than a quarter of a litre, for each person each day. After four days in the open boat they divided 'our last fowl . . . and received a small thimble of rum each'.

By New Year's Eve, and with their drinking water almost exhausted, Clements said that 'many people drank their own urine'. There was still some cheese and ham aboard but it remained uneaten: 'We could not eat the smallest crumb till supplied with [an] additional measure of water to moisten our lips. We dropped our bit of biscuit into the water and afterwards sipped a little of it with each mouthful to force it down.'[14]

On 4 January 1790, and about 400 kilometres east of Natal off the southern coast of Africa, they sighted a ship. According to Clements, they were very close to the end:

> One day more of such misery as we suffered in the last twelve hours would have certainly terminated the lives of some, and the others must soon after have paid their debts to nature. At day break the gunner, who was then at the helm, discovered a ship at a little distance from us . . . our joy at this sight was great beyond expression.[15]

It was a French ship, the *Viscountess of Brittany*, on its way to Cape Town from India. Fifteen days later the survivors landed safely in Table Bay, which they had left nearly two months earlier.

When news of the men's survival reached London, *The Times* reported that every effort had been made to save the ship but that the captain and crew were believed to have perished.[16] However, Riou and the 61 crew who had stayed on the waterlogged ship had somehow managed to keep afloat, even though water was above the lower deck and they were lacking an effective rudder. For several weeks the ship drifted across the Indian Ocean, to the south of Madagascar's Cape St Marie and then back towards Africa. On 21 February, and two months after it had been torn open by the iceberg, the *Guardian* was seen by a passing Dutch packet that was carrying mail from the Spice Islands (the present-day Moluccas) and Batavia (Jakarta) back to Europe. The Dutch ship was 'providentially steering a high southerly latitude' and assisted the half-sunken *Guardian* back to Cape Town by which time the ship was totally beyond repair. Riou reported to the Admiralty that much of the *Guardian*'s structure was torn away and repair would be pointless as 'the cost . . . would exceed the value of a new ship'.[17]

On 12 April the ship was torn from its moorings in a fierce gale and beached. The cargo that could be saved was salvaged and put ashore. Over the next three months, first the *Lady Juliana* and then three other convict transports from the Second Fleet—the *Neptune*, the *Surprize* and the *Scarborough*—arrived in Cape Town, and were ordered to take aboard some of the *Guardian*'s salvaged supplies and carry them to Sydney Cove.

Salvaged items from the *Guardian* that finally reached New South Wales included clothing, leather, linen and 200 casks of flour. However, much that was also desperately needed at Sydney Cove—including salt, rice, oatmeal, sugar and medicines—was 'perfectly spoiled and useless'.

In his report to the Admiralty, Riou praised the surviving twenty convicts who had stayed on the stricken *Guardian* and who had now been sent on to New South Wales aboard ships of the Second Fleet. As a result the British government authorised Governor Phillip to grant them pardons, provided they did not return to England until the time of their sentences for transportation was completed.[18]

Meanwhile, at Sydney Cove, unaware that the British had sent the *Guardian* and still less that it had been wrecked, the settlers became increasingly despondent. In April 1790, at the time the *Guardian* was washed ashore in Cape Town, Phillip wrote to England informing the government that all at the settlement were now on severely reduced rations, which was affecting the convicts' ability to work.

'The settlement had been at two thirds of the established rations from the 1st of November,' he wrote, 'and it is now reduced to something less than half a ration; consequently little labour could be expected from the convicts; and they are only employed for the public in the mornings, leaving the afternoons to attend to their gardens.'[19]

Phillip also advised that there would only be enough food for a few more months if he further reduced the settlers' rations:

> It is now necessary to reduce the ration to two pounds and a half of flour, two pounds of pork and two pounds of rice, for seven people for the day. At this ration, which is served to everyone without distinction, the flour will last till the middle of November, the pork till the end of July, and the rice till the first week in September.[20]

In the same month, Chief Surgeon John White wrote to a friend in London and described the desperation enveloping the colony: 'Hope is no more, and a new scene of distress and misery opens our view . . . For all the grain of every kind which we have been able to raise in two years and three months would not support us for three weeks.'[21]

As marine Captain Watkin Tench noted, all attention was on where the next meal would come from:

> Famine . . . was approaching with gigantic strides, and the gloom and dejection overspread every countenance. Men abandoned themselves to the most desponding reflections, and adopted the most extravagant conjectures. Still we were on the tip toe of expectations . . . every morning from daylight until the sun sank did we sweep the horizon, in the hope of seeing a sail. At every fleeting speck which arose from the bosom of the sea. The heart bounded and the telescope was lifted to the eye . . . all our labours and attention were turned to one object . . . the procuring of food.[22]

Finally, two and a half years after the arrival of the First Fleet, when all hope seemed lost, the signal flag was broken out on Port Jackson's South Head. At half past three in the afternoon on 3 June 1790 a ship's sail was sighted. It was the *Lady Juliana*, the first ship of the Second Fleet bringing convicts and, more importantly, food. Tench captured the excitement:

> I was sitting in my hut, musing our fate, when a confused clamour in the street drew my attention. I opened my door and saw several women with children in their arms running to and fro with distracted looks, congratulating each other and kissing their infants . . . [I] instantly started out and ran to a hill where, by the assistance of a pocket glass, my hopes were realised. My next door neighbour, a brother officer was with me but we did not speak. We wrung each other by the hand, with our eyes and hearts overflowing.[23]

Four more ships arrived over the next few weeks carrying enough food to end the immediate prospect of starvation that had threatened the early convict settlement.

Although it saved the colony, the Second Fleet also represents an infamous episode in the early history of Australia and one of the worst chapters in maritime history. Of the 1038 convicts who in England boarded the three largest transports—the *Surprize*, the *Neptune* and the *Scarborough*—nearly a quarter died on the voyage. Of the remaining 756 who arrived alive, 486 were immediately hospitalised in hastily erected tents. One hundred and twenty-four would die during their first days in the colony.

The first ship of the Second Fleet was the *Lady Juliana*, which carried 222 convicts—all of them women—which did not impress those already in Sydney. Judge Advocate David Collins said it was 'mortifying' to receive 'a cargo so unnecessary and so unprofitable as two hundred and twenty-two females' when they would have preferred a cargo entirely of food.[24]

The next ship to reach Sydney was a storeship, the *Justinian*, on 20 June, followed by the *Surprize* three days later, which had left

England with 218 male convicts. When the *Surprize* anchored at Sydney Cove the locals were in for a rude shock. Forty-two convicts had already died during the voyage and half the survivors were ill or dying. The Reverend Richard Johnson, who was the first to go down into the holds of the *Surprize* amid the stench of the dead and the dying, described what he saw in a private letter to a friend in England. Such honesty and anger would never appear in any official report:

> [I] was first on board the *Surprize*. Went down among the convicts, where I beheld a sight so truly shocking to the feelings of humanity, a great number of them laying, some half and others nearly quite naked, without either bed or bedding, unable to turn or help themselves. Spoke to them as I passed along but the smell was so offensive that I could scarcely bear it.[25]

On 28 June the *Neptune* and the *Scarborough* arrived and in both ships the convicts were also in a terrible condition. Johnson proposed to go down among the convicts on the *Scarborough* but was 'persuaded from it by the captain'. He added that the *Neptune* was 'still more intolerable' and he 'therefore never attempted it'. He described the terrible scenes as the dreadful human cargo was unloaded:

> The landing of these people was truly affecting and shocking; great numbers were not able to walk, nor move hand and foot, such were slung over the ship's side in the same manner as they would sling a cask, a box or something of that nature. Upon being brought up in the open air some fainted, some died upon the deck and others in the boat before they reached the shore. When they came to the shore many were not able to walk, to stand, or to sit themselves in the least, hence some were led by others. Some crept on their hands and knees and some were carried on the backs of others.[26]

According to Reverend Johnson, the dead continued to be thrown overboard into the harbour until he complained to Arthur Phillip, after which they were taken to the north side of the harbour and buried. Other officials in Sydney recorded something of the event. David Collins wrote that 'both the living and the dead exhibited more horrid spectacles than had ever been witnessed',[27] while Watkin Tench expressed anger at the shipping contractors who he believed were paid enough to deliver the convicts in reasonable condition but 'violated every principle of justice and rioted on the spoils of misery'.[28]

In Sydney it was learned that during the voyage the convicts had been chained together and kept below decks where the ceilings were too low for them to stand upright. For the limited time they were allowed on deck they remained chained and even when the ship was leaking they were sitting below water often manacled to the dead and the dying. Sometimes a death would be concealed by the other convicts so they could draw on the extra food ration—until the stench of the corpse revealed its presence to the ship's surgeon.

Some of the detail of what happened on the *Surprize* was recorded in a letter penned by Captain Hill, a marine officer, who had travelled on the ship:

> If it blew but the most trifling gale . . . the unhappy wretches, the convicts were considerably above their waists in water . . . but when the gales abated no means were used to purify the air by fumigations, no vinegar was applied to rectify the nauseous streams issuing from their miserable dungeon. Humanity shudders to think that of nine hundred male convicts embarked on this fleet, three hundred and seventy are already dead and four hundred and fifty are landed sick and so emaciated and helpless that very few of them can be saved.[29]

The small hospital on the western side of Sydney Cove could cater for only about one-tenth of the nearly 500 convicts who required medical help. As Reverend Johnson pointed out, there were insufficient beds and bedding and it was the beginning of winter:

> At first they had nothing to lay upon but the damp ground, many scarcely a rag to cover them. Grass was got to lay upon, and a blanket amongst four of them . . . the misery I saw among them was inexpressible, many were not able to turn, or even stir themselves, and in this situation were covered over almost with their own nastiness, their heads, bodies, clothes, blanket, all full of filth and lice.[30]

The death rates of the convicts arriving on the Second Fleet would have been even higher but for the help given to them by the people of the First Fleet when they arrived in Sydney. It is worth speculating on what would have happened if the First Fleet had arrived in the same condition—would enough able-bodied men and women have survived to save the rest?

As *The Times* later pointed out, the Second Fleet was privately contracted, unlike the first, which had been run by the Royal Navy. The shipowners were paid for each convict loaded, not landed, and the greater the number who died, the lower the cost of feeding and clothing the remainder. 'The less of his cargo the Captain brings into port, the more profit he makes,' the newspaper concluded.[31]

Governor Phillip wrote to London complaining that 'it would be a want of duty not to say that it was occasioned by the contractors having crowded too many on board those ships, and from their being too much confined during the passage'.[32]

On their return to England and amid the furore that followed, the *Neptune*'s captain, Donald Trail, and his chief mate, William Ellington (sometimes spelled Ellerington), were charged with murder; but, according to *The Times*, both were acquitted: 'Yesterday the Admiralty sessions finished at the Old Bailey . . . Captain Donald Trail late commander of the *Neptune* and William Ellington the chief mate were indicted for wilful murder of one of the convicts on their passage over; when after a trial that lasted three hours they were both honourably acquitted.'[33]

The arrival of the Second Fleet allowed the restoration of rations from near-starvation levels, but in April 1791, less than a year later, renewed shortages of flour, rice and salted meat meant that cuts had to be reintroduced.[34] The nine ships of the Third Fleet began to arrive between August and October 1791. After this, the arrival of regular fleets bringing convicts and also supplies averted the threat of outright starvation.

However, it did not end the chronic shortage and hardship in the colony, which would continue for many more years. In December 1791 another 'reduction in the ration was directed'.[35] After being restored, the salted meat allocation was again reduced in April 1792,[36] and flour and rice rations were cut back in October 1793.[37] In early 1794, the colony had only two weeks' supply of salted meat when more arrived from England by ship.[38] In November 1797, rations were cut again following a disappointing harvest and a shortage of grain in the government stores.[39]

The amount of land under cultivation progressively increased, but the farmers had to contend with a range of natural disasters, including the regular flooding of the Hawkesbury and Nepean Rivers, west of Sydney, as Collins recorded:

> At the Hawkesbury . . . the river suddenly, and in the course of a very few hours, swelled to the height of fifty feet above its common level, and with such rapidity and power as to carry everything before it. The government store-house, which had been erected at the first settling of this part of the country, was not out of the reach of this inundation, and was swept away, with all the provisions that it contained.[40]

In addition to flooding, the settlers had to adjust to a range of other weather extremes more volatile than anything they had experienced in England, including extreme drought and raging bushfires.

> The wheat proved little better than straw or chaff; and the maize was burnt up in the ground for want of rain. From the establishment of the settlement so much continued drought and suffocating heat had not been experienced. The country was now in flames; the wind northerly and parching; and some showers of rain . . . were of no advantage, being immediately taken up again by the excessive heat of the sun.[41]

It was not only food; the colony was short of all supplies. From very early in the life of the settlement, successive governors pleaded with London for replacement bedding, clothing and footwear. At the end of 1798, and more than ten years after the original settlement, Governor John Hunter wrote to the British government about the people's want of clothing:

> Suffer me here, my dear sir, to beseech you to recollect that the whole colony is actually naked; that no clothing worth mentioning has been received here for more than two years . . . the most studied economy has been practiced to endeavour to cover the nakedness of the people, and at this moment the anxiety which experience from the daily and hourly petitions is excessive. Not a blanket to wrap themselves up in during the night and I fear the consequences to the general health of the settlement.[42]

Less than a year later, Hunter complained that, despite his repeated requests, neither of the two supply ships that had arrived during the year—the *Burwell* and the *Buffalo*—had brought any new clothing. The situation was so dire, he said, that at one point 'four or five hundred' convicts 'naked as they were born . . . had gone in to the fields to work':[43]

> The labouring men have been working in the field and other places literally naked as the natives of the country, and the present inclement season has for want and blankets reduced the people to great distress and placed too many in hospital.[44]

For many years after the arrival of the First Fleet, a majority of the settlers lived in the crudest accommodation, without chairs, tables or proper beds. Permanent dwellings for the convicts remained a lower priority than secure storehouses, which used up the bulk of the iron door hinges and locks brought from England. Governor Phillip and his senior officials had been the first to have better housing built for them. After that, the marines' barracks were constructed, using bricks made at a pit established near today's Haymarket.

Most of the settlers, including the convicts, lived in crude huts built from tree trunks, branches and bark. These tiny shacks offered little protection from heavy rain, the cold of winter or the incessant heat of summer. In a letter to England an unnamed convict woman described a house she was eventually put into after arriving on the First Fleet:

> The inconveniences since suffered for want of shelter, bedding etc., are not to be imagined by any stranger . . . we . . . have . . . four rows of the most miserable huts you can possibly conceive of deserve that name. Windows they have none, as from the Governor's house . . . now nearly finished, no glass could be spared; so that lattices or twigs are made by our people to supply their places.[45]

Constructing durable houses was very difficult; many wooden buildings were attacked by termites and decayed rapidly, as Governor Phillip acknowledged:[46]

> The first huts that were erected here were composed of very perishable materials, the soft wood of the cabbage palm being only designed to afford immediate shelter. The necessity of using the wood green made it also the less likely to prove durable. The huts of the convicts were still more slight, being composed only of upright posts, wattled with slight twigs, and plastered with clay.[47]

Most houses were devoid of basic amenities, and there was very little of the finer things in life, such as chinaware, cutlery or fine furniture. The ships bringing supplies from England were too full of the essential food and equipment for survival, so there was no space for niceties.

By the end of the eighteenth century, and with the settlement well into its second decade, an increasing number of speculator merchant ships called in at Sydney Cove offering 'many articles for sale most of which were very much wanted'. However, few of the settlers could enjoy the goods on offer. As David Collins noted, the prices were beyond the reach even of the officials and would drain the colony of 'every shilling that could be got together'.[48]

6

'A Hostile Menace'

> 'From the wanton manner in which a large body of natives . . . have attacked and killed some Government sheep, and their violent threat of murdering all white men they meet, which they put in to execution by murdering Daniel Conroy, stock-keeper, in the most savage and inhumane manner, and severely wounding Smith, settler; and as it is impossible to foresee to what extent their present hostile menaces may be carried . . . the Governor has directed that this as well as all bodies of natives in the above district to be driven back from the settlers' habitations by firing at them.'
>
> Governor Philip Gidley King

White settlement in Australia was to have dire consequences for the Indigenous population, just as it had in other places where European colonists had dispossessed local peoples of their ancient lands, driven them from their traditional sources of food and exposed them to devastating diseases to which they had no immunity.

As the British settlement expanded west of Sydney, increasingly hungry Aboriginal people turned in desperation to raiding farms for food. In the violent clashes that followed, the killings on both sides escalated into 'open war', striking terror into the farmers' families and the Indigenous communities alike.[1]

The first-known English encounter with Indigenous Australian people was by the pirate William Dampier, eight decades before Captain Cook visited the east coast of the continent. After sailing and marauding for three years around the Caribbean, the Americas and Asia, Dampier landed on the north-west coast of New Holland, in what today is the Kimberley region of Western Australia, in 1688. He returned as the head of a Royal Navy exploration ten years later in 1698. On his first visit he recorded an unflattering assessment of the Indigenous people he encountered:

> The inhabitants of this country are the miserablest people in the world . . . [They] have no houses and skin garments, sheep, poultry, and fruits of the earth, ostrich eggs etc.; as the Hodmadods have; and setting aside their human shape, they differ but little from brutes. They are tall, straight bodied, and thin, with small long limbs . . . their eye lids are always half closed, to keep the flies out of their eyes; they being so troublesome here; that no fanning will keep them from coming to one's face . . .[2]

It was 82 years later that Captain Cook became the first European to encounter Aboriginal people on the east coast of mainland Australia, at Botany Bay in April 1770. In his journal Cook recorded that several men, women and children came to the southern shore of the bay near where the *Endeavour* was anchored:

> I went in the boats in hope of speaking to them . . . as we approached the shore they all made off, except two men, who seemed to oppose our landing . . . they again came to oppose us, upon which I fired a musket between, which had no other effect than to make them retire back.[3]

Over the next few days, Cook and his colleagues recorded other encounters with locals, but there were no violent incidents. 'I do not look upon them to be a warlike people,' he wrote, 'on the contrary I think they are a timorous and inoffensive race, no ways inclinable to cruelty.'[4]

Sir Joseph Banks recorded that after five days at Botany Bay he was able to collect botanic samples 'quite void of fear as our neighbours have turned out such rank cowards'.[5] Banks repeated this nine years later when he gave evidence to a House of Commons inquiry in 1779: '[Banks] apprehended there would be little possibility of opposition from the natives . . . those he saw were naked, treacherous, and armed with lance, but extremely cowardly.'[6]

When the First Fleet arrived in Botany Bay eighteen years later, Commander Phillip carried written instructions from King George III ordering the settlers to develop friendly relations with the Aboriginal people:

> You are to endeavour by every possible means to open an intercourse with the natives, and to conciliate their affections, enjoining all our subjects to live in amity and kindness among them. And if any of our subjects shall wantonly destroy them or give them any unnecessary interruption . . . it is our will and pleasure that you do cause such offenders to be brought to be punished according to the degree of the offence.[7]

Phillip himself had written of the importance of good relations with the Aboriginal people before leaving England: 'I think it is a great point gained if I can proceed in this business without having any dispute with the natives, a few of which I shall endeavour to persuade to settle near us and who I mean to furnish with everything that can tend to civilise them, and to give them a high opinion of the new guests.'[8]

Phillip's colleagues saw little to justify the respect he wanted to show to the locals. Most of them were to record negative views about the local people, and when their journals were published back in England, they would help shape a negative European view of the Aboriginal people that would last for two centuries. This negative view was expressed in a rare written account by one of the early convicts, Thomas Watling, who wrote: 'Irascibility, ferocity, cunning, treachery, revenge, filth, and immodesty, are strikingly their dark characteristics—their virtues are so far from conspicuous, that I have not, as yet, been able to discern them.'[9]

Not all assessments were so condescending and dismissive. Captain Watkin Tench of the marines acknowledged that the Aboriginal people's lack of 'advancement and acquisition' might support the view that they 'were the least enlightened and ignorant on earth' but he argued that on a 'more detailed inspection' they 'possess acumen, or sharpness of intellect which bespeaks genius', and that some of their working tools 'display ingenuity'.[10]

Tench was one of a number of officers on the First Fleet who described how they lived in crude huts that 'consist only of pieces of bark laid together in the form of an oven, open at one end and very low, although long enough for a man to lie a full length.' The canoes they used for fishing were also crude, 'being nothing more than a large piece of bark tied up at both ends by vines', yet they were experts at paddling for miles out in the open sea.[11]

Tench noted that they made fire by 'attrition' from rubbing wood together and nearly always carried a fire on a small pile of sand in the base of their canoes for the immediate cooking of the fish they caught. They cultivated no food and were entirely hunters and gatherers. They used no cooking utensils, cooking their meat and wild vegetables on an open fire. Their diet was based largely on the fish they caught and other shellfish they collected from the shoreline and on the wild berries and fern roots they dug from the ground. Tench observed that to alleviate hunger the locals tied a vine ('ligature') tightly around their stomachs. Tench said that he had seen English soldiers do something similar when short of food some years earlier, during the Peninsular War.

When given bread by the Europeans, they chewed it before spitting it out. They preferred the salted pork and beef they were given but most would not drink alcohol a second time. According to Tench, many kept domesticated dingoes. He said the women were distant and reserved and were missing the top two joints of the little finger of their left hand; the men typically had had one of their incisor teeth ceremonially removed. 'The tooth to be taken out is loosened by the gum being scarified on both sides with a sharp shell. The end of a stick is then applied to the tooth, which is struck gently several times with a stone until it becomes easily moveable, when the "coup de grace" is given by a smart stroke.'[12]

The initial contact between the Europeans and the Aboriginal people had been friendly enough but after a few months the number of attacks on the settlers began to increase. According to John White these were mainly in retaliation for the stealing of food and assaults on the Aboriginal people by the newcomers. Three months after the colony was established the bodies of two convicts were brought to the small hospital. Both men had been out cutting rushes and had been speared to death. 'What was the motive or cause of this melancholy catastrophe we have not been able to discover,' White wrote, 'but . . . I am strongly inclined to think that [the attackers] must have been provoked and injured by the convicts.'[13]

By July 1788 Captain Tench recorded that the Aboriginal people wanted to avoid the white man. 'They seemed studiously to avoid us,' he said, 'either from jealousy or hatred.'[14] By November, Commander Phillip wrote that 'the natives now avoid us more than they did when we first landed', which he believed was due to the 'robberies committed on them by the convicts'.[15]

Phillip had earlier thought that closer relations could be fostered if he could 'persuade a family to live with us' but he soon abandoned the idea as unfeasible.[16] Then on New Year's Eve of the first year of settlement and, in Tench's words, 'tired of this state of petty warfare and endless uncertainty', Phillip decided that some of the Aboriginal people should be abducted and brought into the white settlement. He believed that this would help bridge the cultural gap and provide the British with someone who could help them communicate with the natives.

On 31 December the governor instructed Lieutenant Henry Ball and Lieutenant George Johnston to take two small boats to Manly Cove and to bring back some Aboriginal men:

> Where several Indians were seen standing on the beach, who were enticed by courteous behaviour . . . A proper opportunity being presented, our people rushed in among them, and seized two men: the rest fled; but the cries of the captives soon brought them back, with many others, to their rescue: and so desperate were their struggles, that, in spite of every effort on our side, only one of them was secured; the other effected his escape.[17]

The soldiers hurriedly put off in their boats under a barrage of 'spears, stones, firebrands, and whatever else presented itself'.[18] When they reached Sydney the captive caused 'a lot of excitement' when he was brought out of the boat tied up.[19] After many 'unsuccessful attempts were made to learn his name', he was called Manly by the Europeans, after the name of the beach where he was abducted. Tench, who helped bathe, dress and feed Manly, recorded the episode in considerable detail:

> He appeared to be about thirty years old, not tall but robustly made . . . his hair was closely cut, his head combed and his beard

> shaved. To prevent his escape, a handcuff with a rope attached to it was fastened around his left wrist, which at first highly delighted him; he called it *ben-gad-ee* (or ornament), but his delight turned to rage and hatred when he discovered its use.[20]

The next morning, New Year's Day, Manly was taken by boat back down the harbour to show his people that he was well and not injured. When they reached Manly Cove a number of his colleagues came and asked him why he didn't jump from the boat, but 'he only sighed, and pointed to the fetter on his leg, by which he was bound'.[21]

To help him make his incarceration more bearable, Manly was given more to eat than the standard food ration. He dined at the governor's table and 'heartily' ate fish and duck, which he always allowed to cool down after cooking. Bread and salted meat he smelled but would not taste. When offered, he declined alcohol and drank only water.

Over the next few months Manly managed to communicate his real name, which was Arabanoo, but his detention failed to improve relationships between the settlers and the locals. Two months after his abduction sixteen convicts left their work at the brick kiln and marched to Botany Bay to steal fishing tackle and spears from the locals. They were attacked, and one of the convicts was killed and another seven injured. Phillip ordered that the survivors be flogged in front of the Aboriginal people to demonstrate that such behaviour by the convicts was unacceptable.

This gesture backfired, however, as the locals were appalled at the sight of the Europeans flogging their own people. As Tench observed, Arabanoo was present at the punishment 'and was made to comprehend the cause and necessity of it; but he displayed . . . symptoms of disgust and terror only'.[22]

In April 1789, more than a year after the arrival of the First Fleet, an outbreak of smallpox would kill a high proportion of the Indigenous population. Governor Phillip estimated that 'one half of those who inhabit this part of the country died', while the only European fatality was a sailor from the *Supply*.[23] Lieutenant Newton Fowell described the scene on the shoreline of Sydney in a letter to his father:

> The smallpox raged amongst them with great fury and carried off vast numbers of them. Every boat that went down the harbour found them lying dead on the beaches and in the caverns of the rocks, forsaken by the rest as soon as the disease is discovered in them. They were generally found with the remains of a small fire on each side of them and some water left within their reach.[24]

Smallpox was a greatly feared contagious disease that could spread quickly and kill many, and in the eighteenth century it was a regular occurrence in Europe and in North America. It is a painful disease. Death is slow and often comes as a relief for many of those afflicted. The first symptoms included a fever, headaches, joint and muscle pain, and a feeling of exhaustion, followed by frequent vomiting. After several days of shivering a rash appeared and developed into skin blisters. If the individual survived, the pustules left scars or 'pocks', which by the eighteenth century resulted in the disease being known as the 'speckled monster'.

The eradication of smallpox among Europeans came with the realisation that survivors could not catch the disease a second time. This led to the process of 'variolation' (or inoculation), whereby a healthy person would be deliberately infected with a tiny piece of material from someone with the disease, in the hope of inducing a mild infection and thereby bringing about an immunity. The practice resulted in the death of 2 to 3 per cent of those who were inoculated but saw a dramatic reduction in the number of epidemics.

The Aboriginal people of the Sydney area had no resistance to the disease, which devastated their population. Phillip noted that some who were infected left their camp, saying they 'must have been spread to a considerable distance as well as inland and along the coast'.[25]

The British provided some medical help and Arabanoo went to the aid of as many people as he could, but he was himself struck down and died six days later. By this stage Arabanoo had become popular among the settlers. He was buried in the governor's garden, and Phillip and all the officers attended the funeral.

The white settlers could not account for the outbreak of the smallpox, though it was almost certainly brought into the area by the First Fleet. However, if it had been carried by one of the new settlers it is strange that it had not appeared before now, almost fifteen months after their arrival. In a letter to Lord Sydney, Phillip was unable to explain how the disease had appeared in Sydney.

> Whether the smallpox . . . proved fatal to great numbers of natives . . . before any Europeans visited this country, or whether it was brought by the French ships, we have not yet attained sufficient knowledge of the language to determine. It never appeared on board any of the ships in our passage, nor in the settlement, until some time after numbers of the natives had been dead with the disorder.[26]

Another possibility is that the disease was released from one of the vials that the surgeons had brought as a source of variolation but neither Chief Surgeon John White nor any of the other surgeons admitted to being responsible for the outbreak.

After the death of Arabanoo, the settlers conscripted two other men, Bennelong (also known as Baneelon) and Colebee, into their service. These two men joined two Aboriginal children, Abaroo and Nanbaree, who had been taken into the settlement following the deaths of their parents from smallpox.

Bennelong, who was believed to be about 25 years old, adapted to the ways of the white men with enthusiasm. For most of the time he seemed happy to live among the English; he enjoyed wearing their clothes and proved effective at liaising between his people and Governor Phillip. And, as Tench noted, he enjoyed a drink:

> He became at once fond of our viands [food] and would drink the strongest liquors, not simply without reluctance, but with eager marked of delight. He was the only native we knew who immediately showed a fondness for spirits.[27]

Bennelong went to live in a small house built for him in Sydney Cove. The area later became known as Bennelong Point, and nearly 200 years later the Sydney Opera House was built there. Tench said Bennelong was increasingly appreciated by the English:

> His powers of mind were certainly above mediocrity. He acquired knowledge, both of our manners and language, faster than his predecessors had done. He willingly communicated information, sang, danced and capered, told us all the customs of his country, and all the details of his family's economy. Love and war seemed his favourite pursuits, in both of which he had suffered severely. His head was disfigured with several scars, a spear had passed through his arm, and another through his leg.[28]

In 1790, and notwithstanding his apparent satisfaction at living with the British, Bennelong fled back to his own people. Some months later Phillip was told that Bennelong had been seen at Manly Cove, where he and others were feasting on a beached whale. The governor ordered a boat and an escort of marines to recapture him. With the rowers sitting in the boat Phillip went ashore with his officers carrying gifts for the locals. As a gesture of friendship Phillip withdrew a knife from his belt and threw it on the ground but this alarmed one of Bennelong's colleagues who quickly threw his spear at the governor. The 4-metre-long lance hit Phillip in the shoulder blade and the barb came out of his back. With the help of his colleagues Phillip stumbled down the beach towards the boat. Lieutenant Henry Waterhouse tried to pull the spear out but realised it would cause more damage, so he broke off the shaft instead. As they pulled Phillip aboard, the marines fired a round from their muskets to aid their escape.

It took two hours to row back up the harbour with Phillip lying on the floor of the boat. He was bleeding but conscious and his colleagues expected him to die. When they reached Sydney Cove the surgeon William Balmain at first thought the wound would be fatal, but Phillip pulled through.

Bennelong, who had not been involved in the violence, began calling at Sydney Cove asking after the Phillip's welfare. Eventually contact was re-established and Bennelong moved back to live with the British.

When Phillip left the colony towards the end of 1792 and returned to England on the *Atlantic*, he took with him Bennelong and another young Aboriginal man, Yemmerrawanne, along with two freed convicts, four kangaroos and several dingoes.

The two Aboriginal men were a novelty in England but were by no means unique as the practice of bringing people back from the 'New World' for exhibition in Europe was quite common. One of the few newspaper reports of their arrival in England gave an unflattering account of the Australians:

> Governor Philip [sic] has brought home with him two natives from New Holland, a man and a boy, and brought them to town. The *Atlantic* had on board four kangaroos, lively and healthy, and some other animals peculiar to that country. From the description given [of] the natives of Jackson Bay they appear to be a race totally incapable of civilisation, every attempt at the end having proved ineffectual . . .

> no inducement, and every means have been perseveringly tried, can draw them from the state of nature.[29]

Bennelong and Yemmerrawanne were taken to see St Paul's Cathedral and the Tower of London, to the theatre and the beach and for a boat ride on the Thames. At a tailor's they were fitted out with silk stockings and blue and buff striped waistcoats and then were presented to the colonial secretary Lord Sydney. It is believed they were also presented to King George III but there is no surviving record of the encounter.

Yemmerrawanne was thought to be homesick and towards the end of his first year in England he became ill. He died five months later on 18 May 1794 and was buried at Eltham Anglican church in south-east London. The cause of his death is not known but is thought to have been tuberculosis.

While Bennelong had seemed reasonably happy in London, after the death of Yemmerrawanne he increasingly wanted to go home, and he eventually secured passage on HMS *Reliance*. Even while the ship was still in port and waiting to leave Bennelong's health deteriorated. Captain John Hunter, who was then returning to Sydney, expressed concern at Bennelong's condition: 'Disappointment has much broken his spirit, and the coolness of weather here has so frequently laid him up that I apprehend his lungs are affected—that was the cause of the other's [Yemmerrawanne's] death.'[30]

Bennelong finally reached Sydney again in September 1795. Soon he was drinking heavily and was constantly involved in fights, including with the man who had taken up with his wife during his absence in England. By the early nineteenth century he was living on the north side of Sydney near present-day Ryde, on Wallumedegal land. He died a rather sad figure on 3 January 1813; he was about 50 years of age.

When Governor Arthur Phillip sailed from Sydney on 11 December 1792 aboard the *Atlantic*, the lieutenant governor, Major Francis Grose, commander of the marines, took over. Grose departed in December 1794 and was succeeded by his deputy William Paterson before Captain John Hunter returned to Sydney Cove in September 1795 to become Phillip's official replacement as governor.

Following Phillip's departure there were many more years of violent incidents between the newcomers and the Indigenous people of the area. Much of the conflict arose as the settlement spread and farms opened west of Sydney along the fertile banks of the Nepean and Hawkesbury rivers.

The European settlers had already taken a large proportion of the traditional sources of food around the Sydney basin by fishing and hunting kangaroos, wallabies and birds. As the farms spread westward many more of the traditional owners were forced off their lands and, driven by a need for food, they began to steal crops, which inevitably provoked violent responses from farmers. In most cases the killing was not undertaken by the military but by squatters, and much of it not officially recorded.

In February 1794 Judge Advocate David Collins typified the view that the violence was the fault of the Aboriginal people. Describing the 'natives' as again being 'troublesome', he said several accounts had been sent from Parramatta of farms being attacked and 'great quantities of corn being stolen'.[31] Later the same year he reported that, in defending their farms from robbery, the farmers had killed a number of Aboriginal men:

> A body of natives having attacked the settlers, and carried off their clothes, provisions, and whatever else they could lay their hands on, the sufferers collected whatever arms they could, and following them, seven or eight of the plunderers were killed on the spot.[32]

Collins described how the raids were striking terror into the settlers and their families: having 'attacked, robbed, and beaten some of the settlers' wives' one woman 'was so severely wounded by a party who robbed and stripped her of some of her wearing apparel, that she lay for a long time dangerously ill at the hospital'.[33]

However, Collins conceded that not all the violence was caused by the locals when he acknowledged an attack on a Hawkesbury farm was likely to have been in retaliation for an atrocity committed by the settlers:

> From the Hawkesbury were received accounts which corroborated the opinion that the settlers there merited the attacks which were from time to time made upon them by the natives. It was now said, that some of them had seized a native boy, and, after tying him hand and foot, had dragged him several times through a fire, or over a place covered with hot ashes, until his back was dreadfully scorched, and in that state threw him into the river, where they shot at and killed him . . . it appeared that a boy had actually been shot . . . from a conviction of his having been detached as a spy upon the settlers from a large body of natives, and that he was returning to them with an account of their weaknesses.[34]

By the following year, 1795, 'upwards of four hundred persons' were living on farms on either side of a 50-kilometre stretch of the Hawkesbury and Nepean rivers and a state of 'open war' had 'commenced between the natives and the settlers'.[35] Acting governor William Paterson ordered that as many Aboriginal people as possible be killed and that their bodies be publicly hanged and left to rot as a terrible example to the others:

> To check at once, if possible, these dangerous depredators, Captain Paterson directed a party of the corps to be sent from Parramatta,

> with instructions to destroy as many as they could meet with of the wood tribe [Be-dia-gal]; and, in the hope of striking terror, to erect gibbets in different places, whereon the bodies of all they might kill may be hung.[36]

In a dispatch to London, Paterson justified the military action, carefully omitting some details of the terror.

> It therefore became absolutely necessary to take some measures which might secure to the setters the peaceable possession of their estates, and without which . . . I very much feared they would have abandoned the settlement entirely, and given up the most fertile spot which has yet been discovered in the colony . . . I therefore sent a detachment . . . to drive the natives to a distance, as for the protection of the settlers.[37]

According to Judge Advocate David Collins the savage reprisals did not discourage the locals. 'It might have been supposed,' he said, that the punishments would have taught the natives 'to keep a greater distance', but 'nothing seemed to deter them from prosecuting the revenge they had vowed against the settlers for the injuries they had received at their hands.'[38]

In September 1795 Hunter arrived and formally became governor of New South Wales. In February 1796, and in response to the high level of violence, he issued a general order encouraging the white farmers in the Hawkesbury–Nepean district to form their own militias as there were too few marines to permanently guard more than 100 kilometres of farming settlements. 'The frequent attacks . . . renders [sic] it indispensably necessary . . . that they should on all occasions of alarm mutually afford assistance to each other,' Hunter decreed, 'by assembling without a moment's delay whenever any numerous body of the natives are known to be lurking about the farms.'[39]

According to Collins, the 'kindness that had been shown' the Aboriginal people had brought on 'all the evils', and firmer action was required. He recorded that Governor Hunter expressed the view that any Aboriginal thieves should be hanged in trees as a discouragement to the rest: 'The Governor also signified his determination, if any of the natives could be detected in the act of robbing the settlers, to hang one of them in chains upon a tree near the spot as a deterrent to the others.'[40]

In February 1798, Governor Hunter ordered reprisals following an incident in which three settlers were killed and several others injured when local Aboriginal men raided three farms to steal the harvest:

> It became, from these circumstances, absolutely necessary to send out numerous well-armed parties, and attack them wherever they could be met with; for leniency or forbearance had only been followed by repeated acts of cruelty.[41]

As the eighteenth century drew to a close the killing on both sides continued. In August 1799 John Wimbow and Thomas Hoskisson went on a hunting expedition and their 'naked and mangled bodies' were found a fortnight later.[42] Wimbow had been transported to New South Wales for robbery in 1790. He gained fame and a small fortune by securing the reward for killing the notorious bushranger nicknamed 'Black Caesar' in 1796. His companion, Hoskisson, was fifteen years old when he arrived in New South Wales, having also been transported for robbery in 1790. At the time of his death he was married to Sarah Pigg, with whom he had three children.

In what was widely believed to be a 'clamour for revenge' the following month two Aboriginal boys were barbarously murdered by several whites at the Hawkesbury River.[43] The two boys, named Jemmy and Little George, were shot and then hacked with a cutlass in what was believed to have been 'a frenzied settler retaliation'.[44]

The killing by both sides continued into the second decade of white settlement as farming intensified on traditional Aboriginal land west of Sydney. In 1801 Governor Philip Gidley King, who had replaced Hunter the year before, established a drastic new policy to drive the Indigenous people from the area. Following more raids against farms along the Georges River and other settlements, King issued a general order on 1 May 1801 directing 'that this and all the other bodies of natives in the above district to be driven back from the settlers habitations by firing at them'.[45]

Not everyone agreed that the violence was the fault of the Aboriginal people, including 30-year-old botanist George Caley, who had arrived in the colony in 1795 with the support and patronage of Sir Joseph Banks. Caley, who according to Governor King was 'eccentric', wrote to Banks in August 1801: 'I believe the Governor gave strict orders to shoot them, and the military went in quest of them several times . . . I have every reason to believe that the whites have been the greatest aggressors upon the whole.'[46]

Three months later, in November, King gave orders that the military protect the new harvests from Indigenous people: 'A detachment [of troops] . . . are to fire on any natives they see, and if they can, pursue them with a chance of overtaking them. Every means is to be used to drive them off, either by shooting them or otherwise.'[47]

By now the British government was aware of the extent of the conflict in the colony. In a rare expression of concern at the violence inflicted on the Aboriginal people, colonial secretary Lord Hobart wrote to Governor King asking him to ease the hostilities:

> I cannot help lamenting that the wise and humane instructions of my predecessors, relative to the good will of the natives, do not appear to have been observed in earlier periods of the establishment of the colony. The evils resulting from this neglect seem to be now sensibly experienced, and the difficulty of restoring confidence of the natives,

> alarmed and exasperated by the unjustifiable injuries they have too often experienced will require all the attention which your active vigilance and humanity can bestow . . . and I should hope that you may be able to convince those under your Government that it will only be by observing uniformly a great degree of forbearance and plain, honest dealing with the natives that they can hope to relieve themselves from their present dangerous embarrassment.[48]

There is little evidence that Hobart's letter made any significant difference to the ongoing tensions in the colony. The growing European population and the continued expansion of farming led to the increased dispossession of Aboriginal land, and with the loss of their traditional sources of food the local people were forced to raid the farms. Increasingly, the settlers repelled them with a violence that the local British authorities had limited ability, and even less will, to stop.

One of the most prominent Aboriginal men in the early days of the colony was the outlaw and warrior Pemulwuy, who for more than a decade terrorised and harassed the white settlers.

Pemulwuy first gained notoriety when he speared Governor Phillip's gamekeeper, John McIntyre, in December 1790. McIntyre, who had been transported for seven years for robbery, was out hunting kangaroos and was confronted by a group of Aboriginal men when Pemulwuy suddenly 'threw a spear, hitting McIntyre in the ribs and piercing his left lung'.[49] McIntyre staggered back into the Sydney settlement, where he was treated by John White, but he died five weeks later.[50]

Phillip was enraged by the incident. According to his own account, Watkin Tench was summoned by the governor and ordered to 'strike a decisive blow' in order 'at once to convince them of our superiority, and to infuse an [sic] universal terror, which might operate to prevent farther mischief'.[51]

Tench was ordered by Phillip to take a force of soldiers on 14 December 1790 and capture 'two natives as prisoners' and 'to put to death ten': 'We were to destroy all weapons of war, but nothing else: that no hut was to be burned: that all women and children were to remain uninjured'. Tench was also ordered 'to cut off, and bring in the heads of the slain, for which purpose, hatchets and bags would be furnished'.

Tench took with him a substantial force, including Captain William Hill, Lieutenants William Dawes and John Poulden, as well as three sergeants, three corporals and 40 marine privates. Also in the expedition were surgeon George Worgan and assistant surgeon John Lowes, presumably included to sever the heads of those killed. 'By nine o'clock this terrific procession reached the peninsula, at the head of Botany Bay,' Tench wrote, 'but after having walked in various directions until four o'clock in the afternoon, without seeing a native, we halted for the night.'[52]

Every time they saw the locals 'they darted into the wood and disappeared'. The heavily armed and heavily equipped Europeans moved too slowly and could not keep up with the 'naked unencumbered Indians', as Tench referred to the Indigenous people.

When the men returned to Sydney weary and hungry after several days, with the 'expedition having so totally failed', Phillip sent them on a second attempt. Leaving on 22 December, they surrounded and attacked an Aboriginal village the following night but found it had been abandoned:

> [W]e found not a single native at the huts; nor was a canoe to be seen on any part of the bay. I was at first inclined to attribute this to our arriving half an hour too late, from the numberless impediments

> we had encountered. But on closer examination, there appeared room to believe, that many days had elapsed since an Indian had been on the spot, as no mark of fresh fires, or fishbone, was to be found.[53]

On Christmas Eve, 'disappointed and fatigued', they again abandoned the quest without killing the ten men, taking captives or even setting eyes on Pemulwuy. Phillip had to live with the disappointment of having no heads of dead Aboriginal men, which he had intended sending to Sir Joseph Banks in England.

For several more years Pemulwuy regularly attacked and robbed white settlers and farms. In May 1795 he was believed to have been involved in a daring robbery of a farm at Brickfields close to the heart of the Sydney settlement during which a convict was injured.[54] In December of the same year it was reported that he had been killed but the story turned out to be false.[55]

According to Judge Advocate David Collins, by 1797 Pemulwuy was 'the most active enemy' to the settlers, plundering them of their 'property, and endangering their personal property'.[56] In March 1797 Pemulwuy was shot but survived, which only added to his legendary standing among the Aboriginal people and settlers alike. In March, a 'body of savages' said to number 100 attacked a government farm at Toongabbie. At dawn the next day troops and armed settlers pursued the attackers to the outskirts of Parramatta. During the fighting that ensued, Pemulwuy threw a spear that wounded one of the soldiers. From the soldiers' gunfire five of the Aboriginal men were killed and Pemulwuy had seven buckshot wounds to the head.

Pemulwuy was captured, put in irons and taken to hospital, where he not only recovered but also made a successful escape. He was next seen two months later on the Georges River south of Botany Bay, 'perfectly recovered' from his wounds.[57] His remarkable ability to survive this and other injuries led to a curious and widespread belief that he could not be killed by white men's bullets:

> A strange idea was found to prevail among the natives respecting the savage Pe-mul-wy, which was very likely to prove fatal to him in the end. Both he and them entertained an opinion that, from his having been frequently wounded, he could not be killed by our fire arms. Through this fancied security, he was said to be at the head of every party that attacked the maize grounds; and it certainly became expedient to convince them both that he was not endowed with any extraordinary exemption.[58]

On 1 May 1801 and in response to more killing that was believed to have been led by Pemulwuy, Governor King issued a general order that any Aboriginal man seen in the area should be shot:

> From the wanton manner in which a large body of natives . . . have attacked and killed some Government sheep, and their violent threat of murdering all white men they meet, which they put in to execution by murdering Daniel Conroy, stock-keeper, in the most savage and inhumane manner, and severely wounding Smith, settler; and as it is impossible to foresee to what extent their present hostile menaces may be carried . . . the Governor has directed that this as well as all bodies of natives in the above district to be driven back from the settlers' habitations by firing at them.[59]

In November 1801 King offered a reward for the capture of Pemulwuy 'dead or alive'. The governor described Pemulwuy as having 'great influence' over them, and being 'known to commit violent acts of depredation in conjunction with the natives . . . whom they excite to the most diabolical and outrageous offences on the public'.[60]

The reward offered to settlers was 'the labour of a prisoner for twelve months'; to a prisoner serving life or fourteen years, the reward was 'conditional emancipation'; and to someone already emancipated it was 'a free pardon and a recommendation for a passage to England'.[61]

Pemulwuy was finally killed on 1 June 1802, more than twelve years after he began to terrorise the white settlers. He was shot by Henry Hacking, a seaman and early explorer of part of the New South Wales coast.[62] After the killing Pemulwuy's head was cut off and preserved in spirits and in 1803 sent to Sir Joseph Banks. It is known that the head was kept for a time at the Royal College of Surgeons in London, but it now appears to have been lost.[63] After Pemulwuy's death Governor King wrote to Banks that although Pemulwuy was a 'terrible pest to the colony', he was also 'a brave and independent character'.[64]

In the early decades of settlement of the Australian mainland the dispossession of traditional Indigenous hunting lands was limited to coastal areas, but after the crossing in 1813 of the Blue Mountains, west of Sydney, and the subsequent spread of farming to the hinterland, the savage treatment of the Aboriginal people continued.

For more than a century the spread of British settlers led to cases of abduction and rape of Aboriginal women and indiscriminate killings of local Aboriginal people across the hinterland, and by escaped convicts and sealers along the vast Australian coastline. It would be another 30 years before there was any official recognition of the disaster when a British House of Commons inquiry acknowledged how damaging white colonisation had been. During that inquiry parliament was told by Bishop William Broughton, who had returned after eight years in Australia, that the Aboriginal people were worse off than they had been before British settlement:

> They are, in fact, in a situation much inferior to what I supposed them to have been before they had any communication with Europe . . . it is an awful . . . appalling consideration, that, after an intercourse of

> nearly half a century with a Christian people, these hapless human beings continue to this day in their original benighted and degraded state . . . while, as the contagion of European intercourse has extended itself among them, they gradually lose the better properties of their own character, they appear in exchange to acquire none but the most objectionable and degrading of ours.[65]

The impact of settlement was even more savage in Britain's second colony, Van Diemen's Land. Having endured for thousands of years, practically the entire Aboriginal population was killed or exiled within 30 years of the arrival of the British. At the time of the first British settlement in 1803 it was estimated that between 4000 and 7000 Aboriginal people were living on Van Diemen's Land. In 1830 the British colonial secretary, Sir George Murray, would state that the Aboriginal population on the island was on the brink of extinction:

> The great decrease which has of late years taken place in the amount of the Aboriginal population, renders it not unreasonable to apprehend that the whole race of these people may, at no distant period become extinct.[66]

7

The 'Troublesome' Convict Women

'The continual complaints which are made to the Governor of the refractory and disobedient conduct of the convict women call aloud for the most rigid and determined discipline among those troublesome characters, who, to the disgrace of their sex, are far worse than the men, and are generally found at the bottom of every infamous transaction committed in this colony.'

Governor John Hunter

Life in the colony was tough for settlers, convicts and officials alike. But for the convict women, particularly those with children, it was far more difficult.

Most convict men served out their sentences working either on road and other building works, on government farms or on settlers' farms. After being emancipated or pardoned, they could perform paid work, take up land grants and become farmers or open their own businesses. In time, many became successful, rich and powerful. For women there was little prospect of paid work, and ordinarily they were excluded from owning their own land. Most spent their lives working for board and lodging, and caring for children.

In the early days of the colony, convict women and their relatively few children represented little more than 20 per cent of the population. Over the next twenty years and with the birth of many more children, the number of women and children grew to nearly 46 per cent of the population.[1]

There was little rationale for the inclusion of women in the convict colony other than the obvious need to provide men with sexual gratification.[2] To survive most were forced to become concubines or prostitutes. If a convict woman was not taken as a 'wife', she might be made a 'hut keeper' or 'set to make shirts, frocks, trousers, etc., for the men'. Occasionally women were forced to work with the men harvesting grain.[3] Others were employed as domestic servants to officials and farmers.

With so little opportunity it was not surprising that so many women were forced into prostitution. In a rare surviving account, a female convict on the First Fleet describes how the abuse of women started before they even reached the colony:

> As for the distresses of the women, they are past description, as they are deprived of tea and other things they are indulged in the voyage by the seamen, and as they are all totally unprovided with clothes, those who have young children are quite wretched. Beside this, though a number of marriages have taken place, several women, who have become pregnant on the voyage, and are since left by their partners, who have returned to England, are not likely even here to form any fresh connections.[4]

Many of the female convicts met and married male convicts during the voyage to New South Wales or when they reached Sydney Cove. Some met officers or civil officials and either married them or became their concubines. Some of these relationships lasted a long time, and in others the convict women were abandoned in the colony with small children.

Esther Abrahams was believed to be twenty years old (though she may have been as young as fifteen[5]) in 1786, when she was convicted at the Old Bailey and sentenced to seven years' transportation for stealing about 20 metres of silk lace valued at around £2.10s. While in Newgate prison she gave birth to a baby daughter, Rosanna, who sailed with Esther to New South Wales on the *Lady Penrhyn.* On board she met 23-year-old Lieutenant George Johnston of the marines and after landing in Sydney became his de facto wife. In 1790 she gave birth to a son, George. Over the next decade she had another six children, two more boys and four daughters. In Sydney she lived first on Johnston's farm at Bankstown before moving into the principal family home on the Annandale property.

In addition to the generous land grants given to George Johnston, Esther Julian, as she now called herself, was herself granted a large allotment of land of 520 acres (210 hectares) at Bankstown. Later, when Johnston was forced to return to England between 1811 and 1813 to face trial for his role in the overthrow of Governor William Bligh, Esther capably managed their joint estates. In 1814 and after Johnston returned from England—having been cashiered from the army by the court, but allowed to return—the two of them were finally married, having been together for twenty-six years. When George Johnston died in 1823, he left his large estates to his wife, who died in 1846, aged about sixty.

Even if the convict women were not abused during the voyage they were often subject to sexual selection as soon as they reached Sydney Cove. The controversial cleric and magistrate Samuel Marsden, who arrived in New South Wales in 1794 and spent most of the next 44 years in the colony, claimed that women were picked as soon as they arrived in the colony, and before they disembarked:

> It has been a common custom (a custom that reflects the highest Disgrace upon the British Government in that colony) that shortly after a ship has anchored in the Cove with female convicts, settlers, soldiers, and prisoners, have been permitted to go on Board, and make their respective selection amongst them, and to induce these unfortunate women, some by threats and some by promises, to accompany them to their habitations and to become their mistresses; and to make room for them a former wife or mistress with their children are not unfrequently turned out into the street in the utmost want and distress. These women having never set Foot in New South Wales and being totally ignorant of the circumstances, characters and dispositions of the admirers; are not likely to derive any happiness from their new connections; but almost certain accumulated misery, and wretchedness. These abandoned men will keep them as long as it is agreeable or convenient or until some other female object strikes their fancy when they are immediately turned off with perhaps one or more natural children to struggle with. In this miserable situation, oppressed with hunger, and in want of every necessary; the unfortunate woman is happy to form a second connection, with the meanest wretch, who will receive her into his hut; and give her and her starving children a loaf of bread.[6]

Many of the convict women who met and had children with officials and military officers were abandoned when the men then married someone else or met another convict woman. Thirty-two-year-old Ann Inett was sentenced to seven years' transportation for theft in Worcester in 1786 and sailed on the *Lady Penrhyn*, leaving two children behind her. Shortly after arriving in New South Wales, she was included in a small party led by Lieutenant Philip Gidley King to settle Norfolk Island, more than 1600 kilometres to the north-east in the Pacific Ocean. Assigned to Lieutenant King as a house servant, Inett bore him two sons: Norfolk, born in January 1789, and Sydney, born in July 1790. Four months before Sydney was born King left Inett and returned to England where he married Anna Coombe, a distant cousin, in March 1791.

King and his wife subsequently returned to Norfolk Island where she bore him a son and four daughters. Meanwhile, Ann Inett married a fellow convict, Richard Robinson, who had arrived in New South Wales on the *Scarborough* as part of the Second Fleet. Together they later operated a small farm near Parramatta growing maize and breeding pigs. King may have abandoned Ann Inett but he did not completely abandon their two sons, Norfolk and Sydney, both of whom he had educated in England before arranging their careers as officers in the Royal Navy.

Not all abandoned convict mothers had their illegitimate children educated by the deserting fathers. Nineteen-year-old Anne 'Nancy' Yeats (sometimes Yates) was convicted of burglary and transported on the *Lady Penrhyn* as part of the First Fleet. In Sydney she became the mistress of the colony's first Judge Advocate, 31-year-old David Collins; he was married but his wife, Maria, was still in England. With Collins Anne had two children: Marianne, born in September 1790, and George, born in April 1794.

In September 1796 Collins left Anne and their two children and returned to London, and to his wife. Seven years later, in 1803, he was appointed by the British government to establish a new penal settlement on the southern coast of New South Wales (in what would later become Victoria). Again leaving his wife in London, he sailed with more than 400 convicts, marines and a few free settlers to start a new colony at Port Phillip; when that failed, Collins relocated to the Derwent River, in Van Diemen's Land. As lieutenant governor of what was to become Tasmania, Collins entered into a relationship with Margaret Eddington, the young teenage daughter of convict parents, Thomas Eddington, who arrived on the First Fleet in 1788, and Elizabeth Gregory, who arrived on the Second Fleet in 1790. Collins had two children with young Margaret. The first was John, born in 1806, when Margaret was only fourteen years old, and the second, Elizabeth, came four years later.

Captain William Bligh, who was later in Hobart Town in 1809 seeking refuge after having been overthrown as governor of New South Wales by the marine corps, was highly offended by Collins's relationship:

> [He] was walking with his kept woman (a poor low creature) arm in arm about the town and bringing her almost daily to his office adjoining the house, directly in view of my daughter. As a military offence this was very great; but it was in a moral and civil point of view as great an insult as could be offered.[7]

David Collins died suddenly in office in Hobart on 24 March 1810, aged 54. According to his wife, Maria, in England, he died insolvent leaving her with only £36, the pension of a captain's widow. In 1813 Maria successfully appealed to the Colonial Office and was granted an allowance of £120 a year.[8] There is no record of either of the mothers of his children receiving any financial support.

Only a minority of the convict women managed to make a success of life entirely on their own. Margaret Catchpole boasted that she was one of the few who did. In 1811 and after ten years in the colony, she wrote of her pride in living independently and being, she said, one of the few convict women who led a decent and industrious life: 'I am living all alone as before in a very honest way of life,' she wrote. 'There is not one woman in the colony lives like myself.'[9]

At 33 years old and the domestic-servant daughter of a ploughman Margaret Catchpole was first imprisoned for stealing a horse in 1797. Nearly three years later she made a daring escape from Ipswich gaol using a clothesline to scale a 7-metre wall. She was later recaptured on a Suffolk beach, tried, convicted and transported to New South Wales, where she arrived in December 1801.

Initially she was assigned as a servant to John Palmer, who had arrived in the colony almost fourteen years earlier with the First Fleet. Palmer had been the settlement's first commissary, responsible for managing the government's food stores. After nearly six years in the colony Palmer had returned to England in 1793; after three years back there, he decided to come back to New South Wales as a settler. In 1796 he had sailed for Sydney with his wife and two children, his two sisters and his younger brother, Christopher.

Palmer proved to be an astute businessman and quickly became a successful farmer, operating a number of enterprises, including a windmill and a bakery. On his Woolloomooloo farm and orchard he built a grand family home where the Palmer family 'elegantly entertained the first rank of colonial society'.[10]

When Margaret Catchpole reached Sydney Cove she complained it was 'the wickedest place I ever was in all my life'.[11] At first, she had 'no government work to do; nor they have nothing to do with me—only when there be a general muster, then I must appear to let them know I am here.'[12] Eventually she was assigned work as a 'cook and a dairy servant' in the Palmer family home, where in the normal way she was given food and lodgings but paid no wages. Pleased by her improved circumstances she wrote to an uncle in stumbling and broken English to say she was happy: 'I am well beloved by all that know me and that is a comfort for always go into better company than myself is a mark of free people where they make as much of me as if I were a lady—because I am the commissary's cook.'[13]

In addition to working on and off for the Palmers for many years she also worked for several other established farming families, including that of William Faithful, a marine private who became a free settler. She spent time in the employ of Richard Rouse, one of the earliest free settlers who arrived in 1801, who, Margaret said, respected her 'as one of their own family'.[14] She wrote that she had the opportunity of marrying but preferred to stay single, saying that she had 'a man that keeps me company and would marry me if I like but I am not for marrying'.[15]

Many of the convict women had multiple partners and multiple fathers to their children. Ann Davis was seventeen years old when she was convicted of the theft of a gown, five bonnets and some other clothing and sentenced in the Gloucester court to transportation for seven years. Sailing on the *Lady Juliana* she reached Sydney Cove in 1790.[16] In 1792 she bore a son to 26-year-old First Fleet convict Samuel Richards, who had arrived four years earlier on the *Scarborough* as part of the First Fleet. They named their son Samuel after his father but the baby died less than three years later, in February 1795. The following year Ann gave birth to a daughter she named Elizabeth. The father was convict Thomas Fowles, who had arrived on the *Atlantic* in 1791. By 1798 Ann was in a relationship with another convict, Thomas Williams, and with him had a son, Thomas, in 1799 and a daughter, Mary, in 1802.

But it was with another convict that Ann finally entered a long-term relationship: Simon Moulds, who in 1792 had been convicted in the Essex court for stealing 'a cow, a heifer and some chattels'.[17] Over the next decade the couple had four children: Simon (1805), Susannah (1808), Charlotte (1811) and John (1814), who was born when Ann was 41 years old. The two finally married in 1820 when Ann was 46 and Simon was 44. Together they farmed on land at Toongabbie west of Parramatta and later at Windsor and, after the Blue Mountains were crossed, at Bathurst. Simon died in 1843, aged 67, and Anne in 1854, aged 80.

The convict woman who is believed to have had the most number of children in early New South Wales was Mary Wade, who was only eleven years of age when she was convicted of 'violent theft and highway robbery' at the Old Bailey in January 1789.[18] Mary, who up to then had spent most of her time begging on London's streets, and another girl, fourteen-year-old Jane Whiting, were sentenced to death for having stolen from an eight-year-old girl a cotton frock, a linen shawl and a linen bonnet, which they then sold to a pawnbroker. In March that year their death sentences were commuted to transportation. After 93 days at Newgate Mary Wade was put aboard the *Lady Juliana*, which was part of the Second Fleet and the first ship to carry only women convicts. After an eleven-month voyage she arrived in Sydney in June 1790 and was shipped three months later to Norfolk Island. There she had two children. The first, a daughter Sarah, in 1793, when she was fifteen years old; the father was 22-year-old convict Edward Harrigan; her second child, a son she named William, was fathered by 34-year-old convict Jonathon Brooker.

Mary Wade returned to Sydney with Edward Harrigan and they lived together in a tent on the banks of the Tank Stream, where she had another son, Edward, in 1803. Three years later, in 1806, Harrigan, who had served his sentence, left to go on a whaling expedition and never returned. In 1811 Mary Wade went back to Jonathon Brooker, the father of her second child, William. By now Brooker had also completed his sentence and was farming on a land grant of 60 acres (24 hectares) on the Hawkesbury River. In 1816 they moved to another farm near Campbelltown.

Mary is believed to have had 21 children, almost all of them with Jonathon Brooker; seven of them lived to have their own children. Jonathon Brooker died in 1833, aged 62, while Mary died in 1859, aged 82. When she died she had an estimated 300 living relatives. Today she has thousands of descendants, including former Australian prime minister Kevin Rudd.

From the earliest days in the colony, women faced strong prejudices from male authority. Even before the fleet sailed from England, Captain Arthur Phillip reflected the prevailing official attitude when he wrote that the women convicts 'were worse than the men' and 'possessed neither virtue nor honesty'.[19]

A problem they may have been but the British authorities wanted to supplement the women convict numbers in order to satisfy the larger number of men. In his original instructions Captain Arthur Phillip had been ordered, after settling New South Wales, to send ships to neighbouring islands in the Pacific to bring back more women. However, after only three months of struggling to build the settlement at Sydney Cove, he wrote to Lord Sydney to say that it was not a suitable place for women from the Pacific Islands, and ask that more convicts be sent from Britain instead.

> The very small proportion of females makes the sending out an additional number absolutely necessary, for I am certain your Lordship will think that to send for women from the islands, in our present situation, would answer no other purpose than that of bringing them to pine away in misery.[20]

Nor did Phillip implement his own private plans to establish government-organised brothels using convict women, a system he believed existed at London's Millbank prison.

The prejudice against convict women continued after Phillip left New South Wales to return to England in 1792. His successor Governor John Hunter also complained that the women convicts were worse than the men:

> The continual complaints which are made to the Governor of the refractory and disobedient conduct of the convict women call aloud for the most rigid and determined discipline among those troublesome

> characters, who, to the disgrace of their sex, are far worse than the men, and are generally found at the bottom of every infamous transaction committed in this colony.[21]

Hunter was joined in his condemnation of the convict women by David Collins, who, rather hypocritically, described their 'vices' as being 'too conspicuous and prominent':

> Great complaints were now made of the profligacy of the women, who, probably from having met with more indulgence on account of their sex than in the general conduct entitled to them, were grown so idle and insolent, that they were unwilling to do anything but nurse their children; an excuse from labour which very few were without.[22]

Unlike Phillip, who saw the relative shortage of women as a problem and wanted more to be sent, Governor Hunter, a bachelor, wanted fewer. Hunter complained that women convicts could not be found productive work in the colony and with their children would only be a bigger drain on the colony's inadequate food and other supplies. In 1796 and on hearing another shipment of 300 convicts was destined for Sydney he wrote to Lord Portland saying that he hoped they would not include women:

> I must express my hope that the three hundred are all men, and not part men and part women, for of the latter we have already enough. We have scarcely any way of employing them, and they are generally found to be worse characters than the men; if we had more work for them it would be often difficult to employ them for we find those of a certain age taken up in the indispensable duties of nursing an infant.[23]

The lack of any real opportunities for women and their dependence for survival on men led to large numbers of illegitimate children. Nearly twenty years after the establishment of the settlement, the Reverend Samuel Marsden calculated that 1025 of the colony's 1832 children, or nearly 60 per cent, were illegitimate. According to Marsden, the fathers were 'under no obligation to maintain the mothers and their children', and the women and children were 'constantly likely to be turned out of doors poor, friendless and forsaken'.[24]

Soon after arriving to take over as governor of the colony from John Hunter in 1800, Philip Gidley King identified most of the children in the colony to be abandoned or orphaned:

> Finding the large part of the children in this colony so much abandoned to every kind of wretchedness and vice, I perceived the absolute necessity of something being attempted to withdraw them from the vicious examples of their abandoned parents.[25]

Like his predecessors, King had a low opinion of convict women, complaining of their 'ill behaviour', which 'no kindness or punishment can ever reclaim'.[26]

Despite his misgivings about convict women, King attempted to address the problem of the large numbers of homeless young girls, opening a Female Orphan School in August 1801. The guiding mission of this institution was to train girls in the skills they would need as domestic servants, which would allow them to escape the life of poverty, idleness, immorality and prostitution that would otherwise befall them.[27] Many of the girls at the Female Orphan School did in fact have parents. Initially opened in Sydney, it was moved by Governor Lachlan Macquarie in 1813 to Parramatta, where the girls could be 'more secluded' and brought up in the 'habits of religion and morality'.[28]

The opening of the orphan school made little difference. Initially it could only accommodate 100 children, which was only a fraction of the 'remote, helpless, distressed and young' people who were homeless and wandering the streets. In a letter to the London Church Missionary

Society in 1813 the Reverend William Pascoe Crook claimed that a large proportion of the girls released from the institution into the Sydney environment became prostitutes, and were little better while they were inmates.[29]

It was not until the colony was nearly a quarter of a century old that the British parliament established an inquiry into convict transportation, which included an examination of the plight of convict women and their children in the New South Wales colony. In a report that was tabled in the House of Commons in July 1812 the parliamentary committee found that many women, after being allocated to work as domestic servants, were being regularly sexually abused.

> In the distribution of female convicts, greater abuses have formerly prevailed; they were indiscriminately given to such inhabitants as demanded them, and in general received rather as prostitutes than as servants; and so far as being induced to reform themselves, the disgraceful manner in which they were disposed of, operated as an encouragement to general depravity of manners.[30]

By this time Lachlan Macquarie was governor of New South Wales. Two of his predecessors—William Bligh and John Hunter—were back in England, and both gave evidence to the committee. The two men painted a bleaker picture of the circumstances faced by convict women than they had conveyed in their earlier dispatches from Sydney.

Hunter told the committee there 'was but little work' for the women and 'it was so common to see them with a young child in their arms that they had no time for work'.[31] Many 'were born before wedlock, and a great number after; a considerable number of children were born without knowing who was their father'.[32]

Bligh noted that after twenty years of settlement nearly half of the colony's children were born to prostitutes and that the children of convicts were equally likely to become prostitutes:

> From the number of people in the colony prostitution is too common a great deal; it has been dreadfully bad, I mean extremely common. I do not observe any difference between the women convicts who have come from Europe and the women born in the settlement.[33]

Bligh acknowledged that there was 'no pubic means of providing for' the children born in this way, 'except for a small number that had been taken by the orphan school'. He added that, in some cases, the father cared for the illegitimate child, but 'when it [the pregnancy] happens by accident he would go away and leave her, just as men do in all other countries'.

Bligh was asked about the proportion of women who were married compared with those living in prostitution in his time as governor. 'Nearly about the same proportion,' he said, 'perhaps there might be half and half.'[34]

As for illegitimate children, he said that he believed about two-thirds of children were born out of wedlock, and only about a third were legitimate.

Women were particularly disadvantaged if they wanted to return to England at the end of their prison term. This was possible, but convicts had to pay for their own passage. And that was easier for men, who had many more opportunities to find paid work in the colony, particularly those who had skills or some trade. Generally women had no skilled qualifications that would allow them to earn money enough to pay for a passage home.

Also, many men were able to work their passage as crew, which was not an option for women. Former convict James Duce Harris was sent to New South Wales in 1798. After six years in the colony he had no difficulty obtaining a passage back to England. He said the returning ships charged £50 for the passage home but he was able to work for his fare as a member of the ship's crew. Harris mentioned that no convict women were able to secure a passage home when he did.[35]

Maurice Margarot, one of the convicts known as the 'Scottish martyrs', was in New South Wales between 1794 and 1810. He said there were 'many hundreds' of women 'whose period of transportation was expired' but who were 'obliged to remain in the settlement because they could not procure the means of returning to Europe'.[36]

Former governor John Hunter admitted to the British parliamentary inquiry that convict women could only return home by prostituting themselves:

> Q. You said in your former examination that the women had no means of returning except by making interest with the officers of the ship to give them passage?
>
> A. Very true.
>
> Q. Had they then any means of returning, except by prostitution?
>
> A. I should think they had no other means.[37]

8

The Corrupt Military Take Control

'The conduct of the military . . . is of so flagrant a nature, and so directly tending to endanger the safety of your Government, that I cannot well imagine anything like the justifiable excuse for not bringing the four soldiers who were disposed against to bring a Court-martial, and punish them with the utmost severity.'

The Duke of Portland

With the departure of the first governor, Arthur Phillip, who returned to England, political and economic control of the colony fell into the hands of an increasingly corrupt military. Major Francis Grose, who would run the colony until he was replaced by William Paterson and finally Governor John Hunter, was 34 and had a successful military career behind him when he arrived at Sydney Cove with his wife and two-year-old son in February 1792 to take command of the New South Wales Corps. Grose was born in London in 1758 into a reasonably well-to-do family. His father was a well-known antiquarian and his grandfather a fashionable jeweller whose clients had included King George II.

Arthur Phillip, who was still governor when Grose arrived, found him unassertive and easygoing, in contrast to his 'testy and uncooperative' predecessor, Major Robert Ross.[1] Others felt that Grose was lacking in distinction and leadership talent,[2] including William Bligh, who met Grose in Cape Town when Grose was on his way to take command of the New South Wales Corps and Bligh was on his Second Breadfruit Voyage. At the time Bligh wrote to his friend and mentor Sir Joseph Banks in London to say that he thought Grose was 'not blessed with any moderate share of good knowledge to give much stability to the new settlement'.[3]

The first major commercial venture by the officers of the New South Wales Corps occurred before Governor Phillip left for England. Two months before he sailed Phillip heard rumours that the *Britannia*, which had delivered supplies to Sydney, had been chartered for a private trading venture. Eleven marine officers had together put up the £200 for the *Britannia* to go to the Cape of Good Hope and bring back supplies, which the officers would then be able to sell in the young settlement for a handsome profit.

Phillip summoned and questioned Grose about the 'propriety, as well as the necessity' of the venture. He wanted it stopped, even though as he pointed out in a dispatch to Lord Dundas in England he did 'not have the power to prevent it'.[4]

Grose was unapologetic, claiming that the marines were living in unacceptably bad conditions. In a written response to Phillip he complained that the marines were on the same food rations as the male convicts, their uniforms were threadbare and their boots worn out.

> The situation of the soldiers under my command, who at this time have scarcely shoes on their feet, and who have no other comforts than the reduced and unwholesome rations served out from the stores, has induced me to assemble the captains of my corps for the purpose of consulting what can be done for their relief . . . Amongst us we have

> raised a sufficient sum to take up the *Britannia*, and as all money matters are already settled with the master.[5]

Grose was not only resolute in supporting the marines' trading venture but he audaciously invited Phillip himself to invest in the *Britannia* cargo.[6]

Within a month of Phillip's departure, Grose began to transform the colony to military rule. A week after Phillip left, on 10 December 1792, Grose increased the food rations of the civil and military personnel. As Grose explained to Lord Dundas, he 'considered it expedient . . . to make some little distinction between the convicts and the civil and military people'.[7]

Grose then transferred the powers of the five civil magistrates to the marine officers and gave the marines generous land grants, which were to be worked by convict labour. Grose also actively encouraged his marine officers to become involved in trade, believing it would 'hasten the transition from near starvation to abundance'.[8] At first this involved the officers buying in bulk from any private merchant ships that called in at Sydney Cove with provisions to sell. The officers would then resell the goods in the settlement at highly inflated prices, often at profits of 1000 per cent.[9]

The monopolisation of trade by military officers in the colony was almost complete by the middle of 1798, when they entered a formal agreement stipulating that only 'two officers be chosen and nominated from amongst ourselves' to negotiate with arriving ships' captains to buy 'goods, wares and merchandizes'. The agreement was designed to keep the cost of goods arriving on merchant ships as low as possible since the captains had no one else to sell to.[10]

The single most valuable commodity to come under the control of the military was grog, as people then called any fermented liquor. Heavy drinking of grog was a dominant feature of the early decades of New South Wales; however, while consumption was probably twice the levels of the modern era, it was no different from England, where the drinking of gin reached epidemic proportions in the eighteenth century.[11]

No grog ration was issued to convicts but increasingly the whole community became attracted to it, leading to a number of deaths through excessive drinking.[12] As early as 1793 Judge Advocate David Collins said grog 'had found its way' to the convicts, and that intoxication had become 'common among them':

> The fondness expressed by these people for even the pernicious American spirit was incredible; they hesitated not to go to any lengths to procure it, and preferred receiving liquor for labour, to every other article of provision or clothing that could be offered them.[13]

Later the same year, Collins claimed liquor 'operated like a mania' at all levels in the colony, and that there was 'nothing that they would not risk to obtain it'.[14] The New South Wales Corps, which earned the nickname 'the Rum Corps', dominated the rapidly growing grog trade. Increasingly, the officers monopolised the sale of imported liquor and owned the still that was used to produce spirits locally.

Grose also dramatically increased the amount of land granted to officers for farming. Behind the generous grants was Grose's belief that the colony would benefit more from the exertions of his officer colleagues than from the public farms established by Governor Phillip. In a letter to Lord Dundas only two months after Phillip left, Grose stated that he intended to press on with the favoured treatment of his fellow officers:

> I have allotted to such officers as have asked one hundred acres of land which, with great spirit, they, at their own expense are clearing . . . their exertions are really astonishing; and I absolutely expect, if they

> continue as they begin, that in the space of six months the officers will have a track in cultivation more than equal to a third of that has been cleared in the colony . . . As they are the only . . . settlers on whom reliance can be placed, I shall encourage their pursuit as much as is in my power.[15]

Officers were able to accumulate even more land by getting marine privates to take up their grant entitlement of 25 acres, which would then be bought by the officers.[16] The generosity of the land grants inevitably led to a conflict for the marine officers between their public duty and their private interest.

At the same time as Grose was justifying the big land grants he made, before he could be sent to engage in any serious fighting, he appointed 26-year-old marine Lieutenant John Macarthur as Inspector of Public Works, which gave the young officer immense influence over the allocation of convict labour.[17] Macarthur's pursuit of wealth and power would put him at odds with many officials for the next two decades and in time he would become the most powerful and most disruptive figure in the early days of the Australian colony.

Born into modest circumstances in Plymouth in 1767, John Macarthur was the son of a mercer and draper. His family was sufficiently connected to secure for him an ensign's commission in the army when he was fifteen. He was initially trained for the American War of Independence but that war ended and his corps was disbanded in 1783 before he could be sent to fight. After being retired on half-pay and working a farm in Devon for five years he returned to full pay in 1788, when he was stationed at Gibraltar. In 1789 he 'enhanced his rank and opportunity' by signing up as a lieutenant in the New South Wales Corps, which was then being enlisted for duty in Sydney on a lieutenant's salary of £79 a year.[18]

Twenty-three-year-old Macarthur sailed on the *Neptune* in January 1790 with his wife, Elizabeth, whom he had married the year before, and their infant son, Edward. Elizabeth, who was one day younger than her husband, came from a farming family in Cornwall. They were not rich but she was well educated and was the 'first woman of education and sensitivity' to reach the colony.[19] For many years she was the centre of what passed for Sydney society, even though in later years her husband's political position was too controversial for any governor to socialise with the Macarthur family.

The voyage on the *Neptune*, which left England with 424 male and 78 female convicts, got off to a bad start. Even before the ship had left English waters Macarthur complained to the ship's master Captain Gilbert that his wife was exposed to the stench of the convict women's sanitary buckets, as well as their foul language and behaviour.[20] Elizabeth complained of the 'hourly effusions', the 'noisome stenches' and the threat of 'infection' from the convict women who were immediately below.[21] Gilbert made light of the matter and in an ensuing argument the two men agreed to a duel on the shore near Plymouth harbour. The duel, which was illegal, was fought around four in the afternoon in the seclusion of an old wharf. When the two men fired, Macarthur's ball struck Gilbert's coat but not his body, while Gilbert's shot missed Macarthur altogether.[22] The seconds reloaded the pistols and the two men shot again but both balls safely missed their target.[23]

As was the convention of the times, Macarthur's wife was not officially told of the duel but she described how shaken she was when she found out about it afterwards:

> On the afternoon of the day we arrived at Plymouth, Mr Harris, our surgeon, and Mr Macarthur went ashore; at their return, which was early evening, I gathered from some distant hints that a duel had taken place between Mr Gilbert and Mr Macarthur. To describe my feelings on the occasion would now be a difficult task, though, they were by no means so acute as reflection has since rendered

> them . . . I therefore did not so seriously consider what I now think of with trembling—the unhappy consequences that might have arisen from so presumptuous a meeting; nor can I be sufficiently thankful to the Almighty.

Conditions on board the *Neptune* did not improve. Elizabeth Macarthur wrote of the sickness of her infant son Edward, the 'narrow limits of a wretched cabin' and the 'totally dark passageway' to the deck, which 'was always filled with convicts, and their constant attendants—filth and vermin'.[24] On 9 February, and before reaching Cape Town, Macarthur asked that he, his wife and son be transferred to the *Scarborough* for the remainder of the voyage. The request was gladly approved by Captain Gilbert, who was happy to get rid of a man he thought was a troublemaker.

At Cape Town, John Macarthur was struck by a serious illness that 'continued to rage until every sense was lost, and every faculty but life destroyed'.[25] Although he made an unexpected recovery the sickness left Macarthur with recurring symptoms for the rest of his life. After leaving the Cape young Edward also became sick and Elizabeth, who was pregnant, gave premature birth to a baby girl, who died after only one hour and was buried at sea.[26]

Macarthur and his wife reached Sydney on 28 June 1790. In his first year the ambitious young lieutenant trod a 'path strewn with minor hostilities', which led to him clashing with Governor Phillip in October 1792.[27] Macarthur had approached Phillip to complain about a trivial matter involving the registration of a keg of imported grog rations. According to Macarthur's later account of the incident Phillip flew into a rage and threatened to have the persistent Macarthur arrested. Macarthur insists that he defied Phillip's threat: 'Sir, you may please yourself. You are the first officer that ever threatened me with arrest. And I give you my word of honour if I am put under arrest, I shall require a full and sufficient explanation of cause before

I consent to sit quietly down under such a disgrace.'[28] Macarthur also said in his recollection of the incident that for the next months until Phillip left Sydney to return to England in December 1792 he refused all invitations to dine at the governor's house.

When Lieutenant Governor Francis Grose promoted the 26-year-old Macarthur over more senior officers to the position of Inspector of Public Works at Parramatta he justified the appointment to London by saying that with Macarthur, 'we get a great deal more done than we used to' and that 'the work in general is much better done'.[29] The position gave Macarthur considerable economic power, including the allocation of almost half the colony's convict labour. Macarthur's power extended to his being spokesman for the army officers.

As result of the grant of land and livestock from Lieutenant Governor Grose, Macarthur and his wife established Elizabeth Farm in 1793 on 100 acres (40 hectares) of some of the best farming land discovered near Parramatta. On the farm the Macarthurs built a fine house, which was 68 feet (20.7 metres) long and 18 feet (5.5 metres) deep, consisting of four rooms, a large hall, closets and cellar, and kitchen and adjoining accommodation for servants. The house was sufficiently close to the Parramatta barracks for Macarthur to continue his military duties without much difficulty. The house, much of which survives today, was surrounded by 3 acres (1.2 hectares) of vines, orchards and vegetable gardens.

In a letter to a friend in England, Elizabeth recorded her gratitude to Francis Grose:

> The Major had given us a grant . . . of land on the banks of the river close to the town of Parramatta. It is some of the best land that has been discovered, and ten men are allowed us for the purpose of clearing and cultivating it. I have one more gift to speak of—it is a very fine cow in calf, of which I am very proud, and for this too

> we are indebted to Major Grose, and to a family in this country in its present situation it is a gift beyond any value that can be placed on it.[30]

With the help of unpaid convict labour Macarthur quickly cleared and cultivated 50 acres (20 hectares), which earned him another 100-acre (40-hectare) grant. By 1794 Macarthur had horses, cows, 130 goats, 100 pigs and 'poultry of all kinds', as well as 1800 bushels of corn in his granaries. Within two years he was selling large amounts of grain to the government stores and reinvesting in more farming.[31]

Macarthur also began breeding and cross-breeding sheep. The foundations of the Australian wool industry are thought to lie in his cross-breeding of Bengal ewes with Irish rams. In 1796 he acquired a few merinos that had been brought to Sydney from Cape Town. A few years later he bought some of the best merinos from the royal farms at Kew, England. Within a decade Macarthur was by far the biggest and the richest sheep farmer in the colony.

After two years in charge of the colony, Francis Grose, now aged 36 and 'debilitated' by injuries he sustained fifteen years before in the American War of Independence, quit Sydney in December 1794 and returned home. Over the next decade he served in a number of military roles in England and Europe, and twice unsuccessfully applied to become governor of New South Wales. Dogged by ill health and with the rank of lieutenant general he lived in Croydon, Surrey. His first wife died in January 1813 and in April 1814 he married again, this time to William Paterson's widow, Elizabeth Driver—but he died little more than a month later in May 1814, aged 56.

In December 1794 Grose's deputy, 39-year-old William Paterson, an avid botanist and a marine veteran of India, took over as lieutenant governor. Paterson had arrived in Sydney with his wife, Elizabeth, in 1791 and spent his first two years on Norfolk Island. In the nine months Paterson was in charge of New South Wales he made land grants of another 5000 acres (2000 hectares) of land, much of it to his military colleagues. He made no attempt to control the trading and farming activities of the officers, or to monitor the propensity of the troops under his command to take the law into their own hands when they felt aggrieved. In 1796 he returned to England on sick leave.

The new governor of New South Wales, Captain John Hunter, took control of the colony in September 1795. Officially, he was replacing Arthur Phillip, who had left the colony almost three years before at the end of 1792.

Hunter's career in the Navy prior to his appointment to the First Fleet had been 'somewhat uneventful'.[32] It was not until 1786, by which time he was 49, that Hunter was promoted to post-captain and second captain to Arthur Phillip on the First Fleet's flagship, the *Sirius*.

When Arthur Phillip returned to England it was thought that he would resume as governor of New South Wales when his health recovered. But when it became clear that Phillip was not going back to Sydney, Hunter applied for the job.[33] At the time Hunter was serving on Lord Howe's flagship, the *Queen Charlotte*, and he wrote to colonial minister Lord Dundas claiming he had the entire requisite experience and 'the most unremitting zeal and attention to the various duties of the office'. He was supported by a written reference from Lord Howe, who testified to Hunter's 'conduct and qualifications' and recommended the appointment.[34] It was another four months before Hunter was officially appointed, in January 1794, and another year before he sailed on the *Reliance* in February 1795.

Aged nearly 60, and looking forward to 'a life of dignity and ease', Hunter was much older than most among the small band of 30 officials in the colony. Reaching Sydney on 7 September 1795, Hunter's difficulties started almost as soon as he took office. In a letter to the Minister for Colonies, the Duke of Portland, a week after arriving he complained that there was 'scarcely a pound of salt provision in store' to feed the nearly 60 per cent of the settlement's population of more than 3000 people who were still dependent on public stores for their food.[35]

Hunter also began complaining to the Duke of Portland about the under-resourced colony. He claimed the military was understaffed and the settlement had no 'granary, barn, or storehouse', it was 'destitute of every kind of tool used in agriculture', and was so short of convicts that he could not carry out vital public works.[36]

In a personal letter he later wrote to his friend, Sir Samuel Bentham, Hunter said that given his experience and knowledge he had hoped and expected an easy time of it but that the reality was harder and the problems of office deeply entrenched:

> My former knowledge and acquaintance with this country encouraged me in a hope . . . that I should with ease to myself . . . have been able to manage all the duties of my office; but I had not been long entered upon it before I was awakened from that dream of comfort and satisfaction the prospect of which I had so vainly indulged; the seeds of these vexations, which had so disappointed me, had been sown for a very considerable time.[37]

Hunter may have been unable to do much about shortages of supplies from England, but he did little to address the other problems in the colony—particularly the threat posed by the increasingly powerful and out-of-control military.

From the moment of his arrival Hunter was aware of the impropriety of much of the military—yet did nothing to stop it. Throughout his term as governor he sent dispatches to the Duke of Portland and

Under-Secretary John King alerting them to the military involvement in the trafficking in spirits, the erection of stills and the bartering of grain for spirits—but at no stage did he give a clear and specific order for the military to stop their involvement in illegal activities. This was despite a specific instruction Hunter received when he was appointed to the position:

> And whereas . . . great evils have arisen from the unrestrained importation of spirituous liquors . . . whereby both the settlers and the convicts have been induced to barter and exchange . . . for the said spirits to their particular loss and detriment. We do therefore strictly enjoin you, on pain of our utmost displeasure, to order and direct that no spirits shall be landed . . . without your consent.[38]

Five months after assuming the governorship, Hunter failed in his first big run-in with the 'violent and mutinous' military.[39] In February 1796 four off-duty members of the New South Wales Corps raided the house of a carpenter who had caused one of their comrades to be arrested. After beating up the carpenter they burned his house to the ground and destroyed all his furniture. An outraged Hunter demanded that the perpetrators be brought to justice and told the corps commander Paterson that the crime was 'the most violent and outrageous that was ever heard of by any British regiment whatever'.[40] Hunter added that in the prosecution of justice the offenders would have to 'answer for it, most probably with their lives'.[41]

Before warrants for the arrest of the offenders were executed, Hunter was approached by John Macarthur, who had by now become a very powerful man. Macarthur proposed to Hunter that rather than face punishment, the offenders would express their contrition and pay the sufferer for the damage done to him and his property. In an act that seriously undermined his authority Hunter accepted this proposal and the arrest warrants were withdrawn.

London was underwhelmed by Hunter's weakness. The Duke of Portland, when he heard that the offending marines had escaped punishment, was highly critical. But, being so far away, it took eighteen months for his response to reach Sydney:

> The conduct of the military . . . is of so flagrant a nature, and so directly tending to endanger the safety of your Government, that I cannot well imagine anything like the justifiable excuse for not bringing the four soldiers who were disposed against to bring a Court-martial, and punish them with the utmost severity.[42]

Hunter continued to complain about the lack of discipline and corruption in the colony, comparing it unfavourably with the administration of earlier days. In a letter to London after his first year as governor, in November 1796, he described the out-of-control grog trade and the damage it was doing to the settlement:

> The original discipline of the original colony is sadly relaxed or sadly lost, but, it is to be hoped, only for a time; all is confusion, disorder and licentiousness, and a total inattention to, nay, I might also say, a direct disobedience to—Public Orders. All of this my Lord, has, in my opinion, proceeded from those who . . . have been but too much engaged in the most destructive traffic with spirituous liquors . . . It has been as eagerly imported by those who had the means of purchasing, and sold again to the settlers at an immense profit . . . Very considerable sums have been realised in a very short time by this ruinous trade—ruinous to many who might have lived now independently on their farms; to the destruction of all order; to the almost total extinction of every spark of religion; to the encouragement of gambling; the occasion of frequent robberies. And, concerned am I to add, several recent and shocking murders . . . This spirit for trade, and, I may say . . . has been carried

> so far, that although it originated with those whose situations gave the respectability and influence, it has descended to all the inferior appointments so that the duties of their respective offices have become a secondary attention.[43]

Hunter added his concern that the involvement of military officers in the grog business was 'highly disgraceful to men who hold in their hand a Commission held by his Majesty'.[44]

But an impatient Duke of Portland reminded Hunter that as governor he had both the power and the responsibility to stop the military officers trading in grog:

> With respect to the sale of spirits, it is certainly within your power, as well as it is your duty, to prohibit, by the most positive orders, all officers of the Government, civil or military, from selling any spirituous liquors to the convicts or the settlers.[45]

Relations between Hunter and the powerful John Macarthur appear to have begun well but within months Hunter was wary of Macarthur's excessive influence and power. Those who complained to him about Macarthur included the colony's Chief Surgeon, William Balmain, who accused the marine commander of causing 'turbulence', being 'contentious' and undermining 'civil authority'.[46] On another occasion Balmain branded Macarthur 'a base rascal and an atrocious liar and villain'.[47]

The growing general disillusionment with Macarthur must have had an effect because in February 1796 he resigned as Inspector of Public Works, complaining that Hunter had 'increasing difficulties' with him.[48] Seven months later on 14 September 1796 Macarthur took the step, unprecedented for a relatively junior officer, of setting down his complaints in a letter sent directly to the Duke of Portland in London. He wrote that Hunter had started by promising to reduce government spending but that 'this resolution has never yet been put into practice'.[49] Claiming that Hunter was mismanaging the colony's resources and the governor was unable to control the settlement, Macarthur called for his dismissal:

> It is a melancholy truth, my Lord, that vice of every description is openly encouraged, and it cannot therefore excite much surprise that the lower order of people continue their former practices when those whose situations require the most particular circumspection of conduct are the most openly dissipated and abandoned.[50]

Surprisingly, when the Duke of Portland received this letter he did not regard it as serious insubordination and did not rebuke Macarthur. He acknowledged to Hunter that Macarthur had not used the 'proper channel', and he then ordered Hunter to respond to each of his allegations:

> I now return to you Captain Macarthur's letter, and I will transmit you the answer I shall judge proper to return to him, when I have heard from you upon the subject. I have at the same time so high an opinion of your penetration and judgment as to leave no doubt upon my mind of your availing yourself of every suggestion contained in Captain Macarthur's letter, which appears to you to tend to the advantage of the colony, and to diminish the public expense.[51]

One area of success for Hunter was his support for further exploration of the New South Wales coast, which resulted in a vast increase in newly charted territory. During Phillip's almost five years as governor the new settlers explored barely 100 kilometres of the coastline around Sydney. During Hunter's almost five-year tenure, thousands of kilometres were explored to the north and south, including what became the coasts of Victoria, Tasmania and northern New South Wales.

Hunter was lucky in that when he arrived back in the colony aboard the *Reliance* in September 1795, the ship also brought two young navy officers who were to conduct hugely important voyages of discovery. They were 24-year-old navy surgeon George Bass and 21-year-old ensign Matthew Flinders who would become good friends as well as accomplished explorers.

Bass was already an accomplished navigator; he spoke fluent Spanish and carried with him more than 90 books covering a wide range of subjects. Despite being younger than Bass, Flinders was even more experienced, having been a midshipman for two years from 1792 on the *Providence* under the command of Captain William Bligh on his Second Breadfruit Voyage, which was after the mutiny on the *Bounty*.

Hunter had requested a bigger official commitment from England to further exploration of the Australian coastline, and had sought the support of his mentor, Sir Joseph Banks. However, Banks warned Hunter that the war with Napoleonic France had intensified, and this made exploration in the remote south-east Pacific a very low priority:

> The situation in Europe is at present so critical, and His Majesty's Ministers so fully employed in business of the deepest importance, that it is scarce possible to gain a moment's audience on any subject but those which stand foremost in their minds, and colonies of all kinds, you may be assured, are now more put into the background.[52]

Only a month after arriving in Sydney and with the blessing of Governor Hunter, Bass and Flinders went to explore the bays and rivers south of Sydney, on what was probably the smallest expedition in British exploration history. There was a shortage of spare boats in Sydney—shipbuilding had been restricted in New South Wales, for fear that vessels would be stolen and used by convicts to escape—so the only vessel available was a 3-metre-long dinghy from the *Reliance*. Naming their little boat the *Tom Thumb*, Bass, Flinders and Bass's servant boy, William Martin, sailed from Port Jackson in 1795. After rounding Cape Banks and crossing Botany Bay, they came to the mouth of the Georges River, which opens into the south-west of the bay. Pushing 30 kilometres up the river, beyond which they could sail the *Tom Thumb* no further, they found good fertile soil, suitable for farming. Encouraged by their discovery Governor Hunter later established a settlement there and named it Bankstown after Sir Joseph Banks.

On his return to Sydney, Flinders was reassigned to the *Reliance* and in January 1796 sailed on it with supplies to Norfolk Island. Here he met Philip Gidley King, who was on his second tour of duty of the tiny island settlement. When Flinders and King met, neither could have known that seven years later they would both be back in Australia and their collaboration would be critical in Flinders' greatest achievement: the charting of what would become the complete British map of Australia.

Later in 1796, back in Sydney from Norfolk Island, Flinders once more teamed up with his friend George Bass and, again with Hunter's blessing, set off on 25 March on a second expedition south of Sydney. This time they took a slightly bigger dinghy, which they again called *Tom Thumb*, to explore a river that was not on Cook's earlier maps.[53] Over the next five days, battling high seas, in which the *Tom Thumb* was nearly sunk and their provisions nearly lost, Flinders first charted Port Hacking River and what would later become known as Lake Illawarra, south of current-day Wollongong.

Back in Sydney, Bass made an attempt to become the first European to cross the Blue Mountains west of Sydney. For many years there had been speculation as to what might be on the other side. Some believed there would be a great inland sea, or a strait that separated the Dutch-charted New Holland in the west from New South Wales in the east.

But now there was a more pressing need to cross. The Sydney basin, which extended about 100 kilometres to the north and to the south, and only about 60 kilometres to the west, had a limited amount of fertile soil; it was hoped more could be found on the other side, to grow food in sufficient quantities to support the colony's growing population.

For his attempt to cross the mountain range Bass took two reliable seamen and used boathooks to climb the steep rock faces and ropes to descend into the ravines. But after fifteen exhausting days he returned to Sydney and declared the range to be impassable.[54]

Bass's failure, and the failure of a number of other attempts, led to the widespread belief that the Blue Mountains simply could not be crossed. As late as 1812 and after returning to England, Matthew Flinders told a House of Commons committee that the mountains 'cannot be penetrated' from Port Jackson.[55]

Any hope of further exploration by Flinders or Bass in 1796 was dashed when Hunter ordered the *Reliance*, under the command of Henry Waterhouse, to sail to Cape Town to buy horses, cows, goats and sheep, because the settlement was again sorely lacking in livestock. The *Reliance* left Sydney in September and, sailing via Cape Horn, reached Cape Town in just under four months on 16 January 1797. They spent ten weeks in Table Bay, where they refitted and repaired their ship and loaded about 250 cows, bulls, sheep, horses and goats.

The officers also bought animals for themselves; as most of the deck space was needed for the colony's purchases, many of the privately bought animals had to be accommodated in the officers' own cabins. The *Reliance* left the Cape on 11 April 1797 and, with almost all the livestock in good health, reached Sydney on 16 May. They had been away for almost eight months.

In December 1797 George Bass took a longboat with six sailors and went exploring again south of Sydney. Four hundred kilometres south he discovered Twofold Bay, which later became a prominent port for whaling ships and the site of the town of Eden. Sailing further south he passed Point Hicks—from which, nearly 30 years before, Captain Cook had begun his exploration northward along the New South Wales coast.

Bass then sailed around the southern tip of the mainland, where no European had sailed before, charting Wilsons Promontory, which he reached on Christmas Day, and then Western Port, which he reached on 4 January 1798. It was here that he encountered strong currents and what was known as the 'Venturi effect'—the speeding up of the flow of fluid when its movement is restricted. Bass knew that this was characteristic of a tidal current pushed between two bodies of land[56] and, while not conclusive, strengthened his belief that he was sailing in water that separated Van Diemen's Land from the rest of New South Wales.

Bass was now running short of supplies, and returned to Sydney on 25 February 1798, having been away for 84 days. An appreciative Governor Hunter granted Bass 100 acres (40 hectares) of land near Bankstown on the Georges River, the area Bass and Flinders had explored just over two years earlier.

By now Governor Hunter, too, was convinced that Van Diemen's Land was separate from the mainland and to prove it he decided to send Matthew Flinders and George Bass on their most important expedition yet: to circumnavigate Van Diemen's Land.

Since the First Fleet had sailed to Australia more than a decade before, the standard route to New South Wales from Europe had been to sail south under Van Diemen's Land, and then north to Botany Bay and Sydney. For some years navigators had speculated that a sea might separate Van Diemen's Land from the mainland. Governor Hunter himself had suspected it in 1789 when he was on his way back to Sydney on the *Sirius* after his emergency voyage to Cape Town and he experienced a strong easterly current and high seas, which led him to conjecture that 'either a very deep gulf, or a straight [sic] . . . may separate Van Diemen's Land from New Holland'.[57] Hunter was well aware that a strait could significantly reduce the distance—and the danger—of sailing between England and Sydney.

Hunter wrote to the Admiralty in England, telling them of his intention to order the expedition and adding that he already had charts from Flinders and Bass which indicated that Van Diemen's Land might be separate from the mainland:

> From this little sketch it will appear . . . the high land in latitude 39 degrees south . . . is the southern extremity of this country, and the land called Van Diemen's Land is a group of islands to the southwards . . . and probably leaving a safe and navigable passage between; to ascertain this is of some importance, I am endeavouring to fit out a decked boat of about fifteen tons . . . in which to send two officers [Flinders and Bass].[58]

The boat chosen for the expedition was a small, 10-metre-long sloop, the *Norfolk*, which had been built from pine timber on Norfolk Island earlier in 1798. Flinders and Bass left Sydney on 7 October accompanied by a visiting merchant ship, the *Nautilus*, which was heading south to hunt seals. After battling severe weather for six days, they sheltered in Twofold Bay, before reaching the Furneaux Islands. At Cape Barren Island, where in early November George Bass became the first European to record seeing a wombat, they left Captain Charles Bishop of the *Nautilus* to begin his seal hunting.[59]

Flinders and Bass then sailed westward, into strong headwinds along what they later confirmed was the north coast of Van Diemen's Land, naming Cape Portland (after the Duke of Portland) and Waterhouse Point (after a colleague, the captain of the *Reliance*). Pressing further west, they found the mouth of a river, which would later be named the Tamar, and where Launceston would be founded six years later.

Pressing on further west they were repeatedly forced backwards in the face of gales and heavy seas.

Then at the end of December, they noticed as they reached the north-west coast of Van Diemen's Land, the tide began coming from the west. They also saw that the shoreline tended to the south, away from New South Wales. Flinders was now satisfied that they had at last confirmed a strait separated the island from the mainland, and he named it Bass Strait after his friend. He described how he and Bass 'hailed the discovery with joy':

> This we considered to be strong proof, not only of the real existence of a passage betwixt this land and New South Wales, but also that the entrance into the Southern Indian Ocean not be far distant.[60]

After sailing around the island's mountainous north-west corner—named Cape Grim by Flinders—they sailed for the next four days southward along the rugged west coast, which Flinders said was 'amongst the most stupendous works of nature I have ever beheld' and 'the most dismal and barren [coast] that can be imagined'.[61]

By now the *Norfolk* had been away for more than nine weeks. In the last days of the year they reached the south-west of Van Diemen's Land and camped in the same bays that had sheltered Abel Tasman more than 150 years before, as well as the later British and French explorers who had sailed along the south coast, including Cook, Hayes, Furneaux, Bligh and Bruni d'Entrecasteaux. On Christmas Day they explored the Derwent River, which later became the site of the city of Hobart.

Early in the New Year, with its provisions almost exhausted, the *Norfolk* headed out of Adventure Bay and 1000 kilometres up the east coast of Van Diemen's Land, across the recently charted strait, to reach Sydney on 11 January 1799.

Shortly after celebrating their momentous discovery, Bass was granted sick leave and abruptly left the colony. He arrived back in England in July 1800, and on 8 October married Elizabeth Waterhouse, sister of his and Flinders' old shipmate and friend Henry Waterhouse, the captain of the *Reliance*. Within months of his marriage, Bass became a business partner of a merchant trader, and in January 1801 he sailed with goods to sell in Sydney. Next he sailed to Tahiti, returning with a shipment of pork that he sold for a handsome profit.

In early 1803 Bass arranged to sail to the coast of Chile to buy further provisions, which he planned to bring back and sell in Sydney. He left Port Jackson on 5 February 1803 and was never seen again. To this day his fate remains a mystery.

Matthew Flinders also returned to England, in March 1800, after the historic voyage of discovery with George Bass. There he married his girlfriend, Ann Chappell, in Lincolnshire in April 1801 at the age of 28.

However, only three months later, Flinders was commissioned by the Admiralty to return to New South Wales to explore the thousands of kilometres of uncharted southern coastline, to find out if the west coast of New Holland and the east coast of New South Wales were part of the same land mass, or separated by a sea or a strait. From 1606, various European explorers had progressively charted most of the coast of the Great Southern Land; by the end of the eighteenth century only several thousand kilometres remained uncharted—this was referred to the 'unknown' south coast.

Flinders sailed from England on the 30-metre-long HMS *Investigator* on 18 July 1801 with a crew of 75, which included a number of scientists—a botanist, a naturalist, an astronomer—as well as two artists and two gardeners. Shortly before embarkation, Flinders tried to smuggle his new bride aboard but she was discovered in the captain's cabin by Admiralty inspectors 'without her bonnet' and barred from going.[62] It would be another nine years before Flinders saw his wife again.

Flinders left England seven months after Frenchman Nicolas Baudin, who sailed from France with two ships, *Naturaliste* and *Géographe*, on exactly the same quest as Flinders. Baudin's expedition had been authorised by Napoleon. It was the British fear of France's colonial ambitions that had prompted the hasty preparation of Flinders' voyage.

Because Baudin decided to first chart the east coast of Van Diemen's Land, Flinders was the first to chart the southern coast of the mainland, naming the Gulf of St Vincent—later the site of the city of Adelaide—and the Spencer Gulf. In doing so he confirmed that Australia was not divided by a sea or a strait.

After sailing on to Sydney, Flinders then sailed completely around Australia in 1803, recharting some of the north coast before heading to England, where, with his new charts, he could draw a complete map of Australia. However, on his way back to Europe, and against the advice of his friend and supporter the governor of New South Wales, Philip Gidley King, Flinders called in at the French-controlled island of Mauritius for fresh supplies. Because Britain and France were now at war, Flinders was arrested, charged with being a British spy and detained for six and a half years.

Meanwhile, Baudin's French expedition had completed its exploration of the Australian coast and following the death of Baudin returned to France, where in 1811 the French produced the first complete map of 'Terra Australis'.

Flinders was finally released from Mauritius in 1810. He returned to London, where he produced his own map on which he was the first to use the name 'Australia'. Flinders died on 18 July 1814, the day after his map and journal were published. He was only 40 years old.

Back in Sydney in the last year of the eighteenth century Governor Hunter was still struggling administratively. By early 1799

Lord Portland was taking more and more notice of the complaints he was receiving from the colony and in February 1799 he wrote to Hunter with a list of allegations. Portland acknowledged that many of the claims against Hunter were from anonymous sources and assured the governor that if he knew who the author of the complaints was, 'you should not be left unacquainted with them'.[63]

The long list included claims 'that the price of necessary articles is of late doubled' and that 'spirits continued to be bought by the officers and retailed at the most exorbitant prices to the lowest order of settlers and to the convicts'. It was also claimed that the rum trade was not limited to the officers but also 'carried on in Government House', and 'that officers and favoured individuals' were being allowed to sell their grain to the government stores at higher prices, while others were forced to sell to 'hucksters' at a lower price. Portland demanded Hunter answer the allegations: 'I cannot too strongly impress upon you the duty and necessity of satisfying me of the falsehood or futility of the charges which have been made against you.'[64]

At this same time, Secretary to the Army Robert Brownrigg was ordering Major William Paterson back to New South Wales to help Hunter clean up the illegal grog trading by the military.

> The Duke of Portland having stated . . . that the most serious representations have been made to his grace of the abuses which are practiced and countenanced by the officers of the New South Wales Corps, who, among other instances of impropriety, are stated to be in the habit of purchasing spirits and other articles . . . and retailing them at the most exorbitant prices to the lower orders of the settlers and the convicts, and that the profit received on such articles is often at the rate of one hundred shillings to one I am directed to make known to you the above circumstances . . . with a view to ascertain who are the officers that have transgressed, and to bring them to punishment . . . you will embrace the earliest opportunity of

> proceeding to join your regiment, where, it is hoped, your presence will materially contribute in some measure to restore the credit which has hitherto attached to the character of a British officer, but in this instance been sullied.[65]

Hunter was put into an unfair position. Portland wrote to Hunter on 26 February 1799 but the governor did not receive this letter until 3 November. Two days later on 5 November 1799, and before Hunter could defend himself, Portland wrote another letter sacking Hunter and demanding his early recall:

> I cannot but be apprehensive [that the officers' arrangement] . . . has been considered as a sanction to officers engaged in traffic, and as an apology for the proceedings which I have but too much reason to fear may be found to have disgraced his Majesty's service in the persons of several officers of the New South Wales Corps . . . Having now made all the observations which appear to me . . . I felt myself called upon . . . to express my disapprobation in the manner in which the government of the settlement has been administered by you in so many respects—that I am commanded to signify to you the King's pleasure to return to this kingdom by the first conveyance which offers itself after the arrival of Lieutenant Governor King.[66]

Hunter was replaced by Philip Gidley King who, to take up the governorship, was making his third trip to New South Wales. He had been a 29-year-old second lieutenant when he sailed with Phillip and Hunter on the First Fleet in 1787. After setting up the new settlement on the tiny Norfolk Island in 1788, King was sent to England by Governor Phillip in 1790 to report on the problems of the early colony and he'd returned in 1792 with his new bride, Anna Coombe. Newly promoted to lieutenant governor of the colony, King spent most of the next four years back on Norfolk Island before returning to England again in 1796. At that time he was in poor health and suffering from gout so severely that 'much doubt was entertained of his recovery'.[67]

In England, with his health sufficiently recovered and with the help of Arthur Phillip and the support of Sir Joseph Banks, King was given a dormant commission in January 1798 to succeed John Hunter in the event of Hunter's death or absence from the colony. At the time of his appointment there was no question of Hunter being recalled.

King had originally been recommended by Phillip just over five years earlier, when Phillip quit the colony in 1792. The exiting governor had written to the government saying that King was the 'most likely' person to meet its requirements. King's performance as head of the Norfolk Island colony, Phillip said, had been 'highly satisfactory'; 'no other officer' possessed the 'knowledge' and 'perseverance' so 'requisite in an infant colony'.[68]

After receiving his January 1798 commission King did not reach Sydney for another two years. He was scheduled to sail from England on a newly built ship but the ship was not ready in time. When they set sail in August 1799, the vessel was found to be unseaworthy and forced to return to Portsmouth. When King finally sailed on the *Speedy* on 5 December 1799 he carried the Duke of Portland's dispatch recalling Hunter.

When he reached Sydney on 15 April 1800, 42-year-old Philip Gidley King was still in poor health, 'ravaged' in appearance and possessing a violent temper that put him at odds with many in the colony.[69] In his nearly six years as governor, he would attract widespread criticism.

Impatient to take up office, King was soon arguing with his former colleague and friend Hunter who had been ordered to return to England at the earliest opportunity but did not leave the colony until the end of September. Five months before Hunter left on the *Buffalo* the men were no longer on speaking terms and exchanges between them degenerated into increasingly terse letters. At one point in their letter-writing war Hunter accused King of making an 'attack' on Hunter's character.[70] King replied by saying Hunter's letter contained a 'marked insult'.[71]

King had a poor opinion of what the colony had become. In a letter to his mentor Sir Joseph Banks only two weeks after arriving, he said that he had been well received but predicted the mood of the locals would soon change when he began to clean up the colony:

> My arrival and remaining here gives general satisfaction, but I believe many will change their tone when their nefarious proceedings are arrested. Vice, dissipation, and a strange relaxation seems to pervade all descriptions . . . cellars from the better sort of people to the blackest characters among the convicts are full of that fiery poison. The rising generation are abandoned to misery, prostitution, and every vice of their parents, and in short, nothing less than a total change in the system of administration must take place.[72]

In a similar letter sent on the same day to his namesake, Navy under-secretary John King, he accurately predicted that he would meet strong opposition and that complaints would flow to London: 'I will persevere, and trust you will consider when calculating on my success the sets of villains I have to contend with . . . I must count on having for decided enemies those from whom I ought to have support.'[73]

In September 1800 and on the day Hunter finally left Sydney, King sent a letter on the same ship to the Duke of Portland: 'My observation confirms me in the opinion that the only inducement many people have in this colony of being employed by the Crown, is that it gives them opportunity . . . to impose on the public and . . . sharing the immense profits that have been made of the shameful monopolies that have long existed here.'[74]

As governor, King had mixed success but was probably more effective than his predecessor. He was initially able to limit the importation of liquor and reduce the colony's grog consumption but he found it increasingly difficult to suppress the growth in illicit local distillation. Nor was he successful in breaking the economic power of the military officers.[75]

As had been the case with his predecessors, relations between Governor King and John Macarthur became bitter when in November 1801 King was given the opportunity of ridding the colony of the troublesome Macarthur.

Macarthur had organised a social boycott of King, whereby none of the marine officers would accept invitations to Government House. However, the colony's most senior military officer, William Paterson, disagreed with the idea and continued his normal relationship with the governor. The 46-year-old Paterson had been in the colony for ten years, including a stint as acting governor before Hunter arrived.

Macarthur was enraged with his superior officer and threatened to 'divulge all their private and public conversations, correspondence and transactions', which he claimed would embarrass Paterson. Deeply offended and believing Macarthur had disclosed the contents of a private letter sent by his wife, Elizabeth, to Elizabeth Macarthur, Paterson challenged Macarthur to a duel.[76]

The duel took place near Parramatta on 14 September 1801. A coin was tossed, which Macarthur won giving him the right to shoot first. Paterson stood sideways so as to minimise the target and Macarthur fired, shattering his opponent's right shoulder. Paterson was seriously wounded and was unable to take his shot at Macarthur. At first it was thought Paterson would die but after a week in the infirmary he slowly recovered. The wound would bother Paterson for the rest of his life.

Duelling was illegal. Governor King censured Paterson for 'calling an inferior officer out', which he said was 'highly detrimental to His Majesty's service'. He sent Macarthur back to England for trial for having shot his superior officer. King admitted that he could have tried Macarthur in Sydney, but was not confident that a local court couldn't be corrupted: 'Experience has convinced every man in this colony that there are no resources which art, cunning, impudence and a pair of basilisk eyes can afford that [Macarthur] does not put in practice to obtain any point he undertakes.'[77] In a separate letter to the British government, Governor King gave vent to his feelings about Macarthur:

> He came here in 1790 more than £500 in debt and is now worth more than £20,000 . . . [which] enables him to boast of his indifference of whatever change happens to him. His employment during the eleven years he has been here has been making a large fortune, helping his brother officers make small ones (mostly at public expense), and sowing discord and strife . . . if the records of this colony, now in your office, are examined you will find his name very conspicuous. Many and many instances of his diabolical spirit had shown itself before Governor Phillip left this colony, and since, altho' in many instances he has been the master worker of the puppets he has set in motion.[78]

Macarthur left Sydney on the *Hunter* in November 1801 on a voyage that took almost a year. As it turned out the forced exile was a great piece of luck for John Macarthur: being the owner of more than 4000 sheep he was able to take to England high-quality wool fleeces, which he hoped to sell on the British wool market. At that time the price of wool was very high because it was difficult to import it from Spain due to the French blockade during the Napoleonic Wars. Macarthur not only managed to convince the British wool industry of the quality of his fleeces but he also obtained British government backing for his private plan to massively expand his wool operations when he returned to Sydney. Lord Camden authorised Macarthur to receive an unprecedented land grant of 5000 acres (2000 hectares) of the colony's best farmland and free convict labour to develop it into a massive sheep farm:

> I am commanded by His Majesty to desire that you will have a proper grant of land. Fit for the pasture of sheep, conveyed to the said John Macarthur, Esq., in perpetuity . . . containing not less than five thousand acres. Mr Macarthur has represented that the lands he wishes to be conveyed to him for this purpose are situated near Mt Taurus, as being particularly adapted for sheep; and I therefore am to express my wishes that he may be accommodated in this situation . . . it will be impossible for Mr Macarthur to pursue this unless he be indulged with a reasonable number of convicts (which he states to be not less than thirty) . . . and I doubt not you will provide him with such as shall appear most suitable to his objects.[79]

The charge of duelling, which Macarthur had come to England to face, was conveniently brushed aside with 'official censure liberally scattered over him'.[80] There was no penalty for the serious charge of shooting his superior officer. The Army's adjutant General Harry Calvert said Governor King had 'judged ill' in sending Macarthur away from where the alleged offence took place because there were no witnesses in Britain except Macarthur himself.[81]

Offered the chance to become an extremely rich farmer in the colony Macarthur quit the Army after a 24-year career, although most of it had been combined with his extensive private businesses. He arrived back in Sydney on 5 June 1805 on the *Argo* having been away for nearly four years. No doubt humiliated, Governor King had no alternative but to accept Macarthur's elevated status with all the grace he could muster and made his peace with his former nemesis:

> He [Macarthur] soon after waited on me, and gave me a polite and highly satisfactory letter from [Lord Camden], pointing out that as

> Macarthur was no longer a military man, that everything might be settled . . . Such a communication was not to be disregarded by me, and, whether right or wrong . . . I offered Macarthur my hand, who very gratefully received it . . . so much for our meeting after four years of suspense and vicissitude.[82]

Macarthur had not been King's only critic and while Macarthur was in England a number of others in the colony had been trying to undermine the governor. One of his most irritating and persistent critics was the convict Sir Henry Browne Hayes. In 1797 the Irish-born 37-year-old widower with four children had been convicted of kidnapping 21-year-old heiress Mary Pike and forcing her into a 'spurious' marriage. She was later rescued and Hayes was convicted and sentenced to death but his sentence was commuted to life transportation to New South Wales.

In contrast to the common criminals the wealthy Hayes lived a life of comparative comfort for a convict. He built the original Vaucluse House, which much later became the family home of the Wentworth dynasty. In Sydney Hayes mixed with other malcontents and intransigents and was a constant critic of Governor King. On a number of occasions he protested to King about various issues, including King's opposition to Hayes establishing a Freemasons' lodge in the settlement. In May 1803 he wrote to the colonial secretary in London, questioning King's character:

> I entreat you to lay my complaint [before His Majesty] against a man who, unable to guide his own passions . . . a man who mistaking arrogance for authority and dignity, and caprice for wisdom, and power for authority, conscious only of his own hereditary meanness, knows no other way of aggrandising himself than by the coarsest language and most brutish behaviour, degrading men down to his own level . . .[83]

King was well aware that his reforms had offended many in the colony—and that his critics were writing to the British government to complain about him. In a letter to Sir Joseph Banks in October 1802, King said:

> Believe me, dear sir, that my situation here is not a very pleasant one; the obnoxious character of a reformer is not calculated to appear often on the theatre of this world. I have had the most flagrant and dishonourable abuses to do away, and I have succeeded, but at the expense of being hated by those whose interests have been hurt.[84]

When John Macarthur returned to the colony in June 1805 King was in poor health. He continued to drink excessively and his foul temper had become more obvious to everyone in the colony. Two years earlier in May 1803, and tired of the opposition he was still experiencing from the military, he had asked the British government to conduct an inquiry into the colony. He also wrote to say that he had been 'seized with a dangerous attack of illness' that was life-threatening: 'I humbly solicit [you] . . . to appoint . . . a commission . . . to enquire into what the real state of this colony is, and my conduct has been, from the time of my taking command.'[85]

If the inquiry did not take place, King added, he would like to return to England: 'But in case any consideration should render this request [for an inquiry] I humbly implore your lordship procuring me His Majesty's leave of absence to enable me to submit my conduct to your lordship's consideration.'[86]

Lord Hobart received King's letter in November 1803. Surmising that King had had enough and was offering to resign, the colonial minister recalled the governor. He began his letter by congratulating King on the improvements the colony had seen under his leadership but qualified this praise by referring to 'the unfortunate differences which have so long subsisted between you and the military officers of the colony'.[87]

> These considerations have led me to recommend to His Majesty to comply with your application for permission to return to Europe as soon as the important trust with which you are charged can be placed in the hands of some person competent to exercise the duties thereof.[88]

It would take more than two years to replace King, who finally handed over to his successor on 13 August 1806; however, he was in such poor health that he could not sail from Sydney until February 1807. He finally reached England in November 1807, and died the following year on 3 September. He was buried in the churchyard of St Nicholas in Tooting.

King had done a reasonably good job as governor. He had presided over the successful expansion of government farms, quadrupling the publicly owned flocks and herds. He also took the settlement close to being self-sufficient in the production of grain other than in years of floods, drought or bushfire. He began the mining of coal, which he hoped would become a major export from the colony, and the experimental growing of grape vines, tobacco, cotton, hemp and indigo.[89] Like his predecessor, King promoted expeditions to discover more of the south and north coasts of Australia.

King was the first governor to try to address some of the appalling social conditions, including the establishment of an orphanage to accommodate the growing army of abandoned children, many of whom were already prostitutes.

Initially, King had some success in reducing the settlement's grog consumption by restricting the importation of liquor into the colony. However, he had increasing difficulty controlling the growing number of illicit local stills and was only partially successful in his attempt to curb the officers' grip over the colony's grog trade and other commerce.[90]

The man sent to replace King was Captain William Bligh of the Royal Navy. It was intended that Bligh was to bring some much-needed stability to the young colony but in a little more than a year he would be at the centre of the settlement's most turbulent episode of all.

9

The Fear of the French and the Threat of the Spanish

> 'The entirely helpless state in which I observed that settlement [at Port Jackson] in 1793, and the general discontent of its inhabitants, would so facilitate its conquest that I believe it would be achieved with the surprise that the convincing presence of our fleet would cause. But even if some resistance were offered, it could never triumph over the gunfire from our ships or prevent the total destruction of houses, warehouses and goods located in the principal settlement.'
>
> Spanish naval commander José de Bustamante y Guerra

In the fifteen years following the arrival of the First Fleet in New South Wales the British established a number of other colonial settlements in Australia, including at Norfolk Island, Port Phillip (later Victoria) and in both the south and north of Van Diemen's Land (later Tasmania). In all cases the decision to build the settlement was driven largely by British fears of the territorial ambitions of its arch rival France—even though there is no firm evidence that the French ever planned to establish a colony in Australia.

But in the minds of the British in Sydney there was good reason to fear the French. For almost 30 years from late in the eighteenth century France and Britain were almost constantly at war. And as the world's two most powerful colonists for more than a century the nations had regularly fought each other over competing territorial claims in India, North America and the West Indies. To the British it seemed entirely possible that the French would seek to contest the British possession of the newly discovered southern continent.

Nearly all of the senior officers in Sydney had personal experience fighting the French enemy, which no doubt contributed to their heightened suspicions. Arthur Phillip, John Hunter and Philip Gidley King had all served in the Royal Navy during the wars against France. All the leading early chiefs of the Marine Corps had fought the French in North America. Major Robert Ross, who sailed on the First Fleet, was part of the British siege of the French at Louisburg, and the later capture of Quebec. On his way back to England on the HMS *Ardent* in 1789, he was captured by the French before later being released in an exchange of prisoners. Ross's successor, Major Francis Grose, also fought against the French-backed Americans in the War of Independence, where he was twice wounded before being sent back to England. Major George Johnston, who became head of the New South Wales Corps in 1803, fought the French in North America and later in the East Indies, where he was severely injured in 1781.

It is in many ways remarkable that in the late eighteenth and early nineteenth centuries France managed to maintain a commitment to global scientific exploration, discovery and the expansion of human knowledge during what was the most tumultuous time in the country's history. The Bastille had been stormed in 1789, which was followed by the guillotining of King Louis XVI in 1793 and the period known as the Reign of Terror. Then, during the fifteen years of the Napoleonic era, France was almost permanently at war with most of its European neighbours. In 1814 the monarchy was restored first under Louis XVIII and then from 1824 under his brother Charles X but the new governments were often in conflict with many of the still prevailing principles of the revolution. Popular uprisings in Paris and the July revolution in 1830 saw Charles X abdicate and Louis-Philippe take his place.

Yet throughout all this chaos and upheaval France continued to send well-equipped and expensive scientific expeditions to explore the world, including Asia and the Pacific. The period between 1715 and 1789 later became known as the Age of Enlightenment, which was characterised by great intellectual developments in all fields, including science, art, philosophy, literature, architecture and music. This new cultural force, which swept across Europe and America, was prominent in France and the salons of the *ancien régime*, and the force of its ideas continued during the Revolution and the Napoleonic era.

Until the Revolution most of the commanders of the French exploration ships tended to come from the aristocracy, whereas many of their British counterparts came from more modest backgrounds. The first Frenchman believed to have seen Australia was Abraham de Bellebat de Duquesne-Guitton who, on his way to establish a French presence at the kingdom of Siam (Thailand) in 1687, had sailed along the coast of New Holland near what became known as the Swan River and later the site of the city of Perth.

A little more than 80 years later in 1768, Louis Antoine de Bougainville was sent by Louis XV to investigate the lands of the southern oceans. After sailing via Cape Horn and Tahiti and encountering the Solomon Islands he reached but did not penetrate the Great Barrier Reef off the north-east coast of Australia. When Bougainville returned to France in 1769 as the first Frenchman to have circumnavigated the world, Captain James Cook was already on his way to chart the east coast of Australia.

Three years later, Marc-Joseph Marion du Fresne was sent to explore Terra Australis and became the first European to set foot on Van Diemen's Land since Abel Tasman 130 years before. Du Fresne claimed the country for France but the French did not establish any settlement there to protect their territorial claim. Also in 1772, while Du Fresne was sailing from Van Diemen's Land towards New Zealand, another Frenchman was 4000 kilometres to the west exploring the coast of New Holland. Thirty-four-year-old aristocrat Louis François Marie Aleno de Saint Aloüarn sailed over 1000 kilometres from Cape Leeuwin to Shark Bay, claiming the territory for Louis XV.

All these explorations raised British suspicions that its rival, France, harboured territorial ambitions over land claimed by Cook on behalf of King George III when he reached Possession Island at the northern tip of the Australian continent in August 1770.

The first site to be settled by the English after Sydney—largely to discourage the French—was the tiny Norfolk Island, which was less than 36 square kilometres in size, making it smaller than the Isle of Wight. It had been charted by Cook on his second voyage and named after the Duchess of Norfolk. Cook had gone ashore on 11 October 1774 and reported that the island grew tall and straight trees that would make good masts for the Royal Navy's ships. He also noted that the island grew the flax plant, which was used for making rope.

When Captain Arthur Phillip was sent to create the convict settlement in New South Wales his written orders included an instruction to thwart the French by establishing a British presence on the uninhabited Norfolk Island as soon as possible after reaching Botany Bay:

> Norfolk Island . . . being represented as a spot which may hereafter become useful, you are as soon as circumstances will admit of it, to send a small establishment thither to secure the same to us, and prevent it being occupied by the subjects of any other European power.[1]

These instructions to Phillip issued before he left England came as news reached London that French explorer Admiral Jean-François de Galaup La Pérouse was heading towards New South Wales, and followed London press reports of a 'strong presumption that a squadron from [France] are now, or soon will be, in possession of the very spot we meant to occupy in New Holland'.[2]

Only days after arriving in New South Wales in January 1788, the British saw La Pérouse and his two ships arriving in Botany Bay. When Captain Phillip sent Lieutenant Philip Gidley King to pay a courtesy call on La Pérouse he learned that the Frenchman had already visited Norfolk Island on his way to Botany Bay. But when La Pérouse reached Norfolk Island on 13 January 1788, five days before the English ships began to anchor in Botany Bay, he had decided that the high seas and lack of a good landing spot made an attempted landing too dangerous. 'It is obvious,' he recorded, 'that I would have to wait maybe for a very long time for a moment suitable for a landing and a visit to this island was not worth the sacrifice.'[3]

Having heard from King that La Pérouse had already been to Norfolk and had only decided against landing because of bad weather, Phillip immediately ordered his young protégé to take a small party to settle the island. At 7 a.m. on 14 February King sailed for his new post on the tiny *Supply* with perhaps the smallest-ever party to establish a colony for the British Empire. The group of 23 included a surgeon, a carpenter, a weaver, two marines, eight male convicts and six female convicts. In his instructions from Phillip, King was ordered to take the 'necessary measures to securing' the island, and to start growing food and 'proceed to the cultivation of the flax plant'.[4]

When King arrived on 8 March, he quickly found that the flax plant was difficult to cultivate and the giant pine trees less than ideal for ships' masts. He did, however, discover the soil to be more fertile than that of Sydney and Norfolk Island soon became a productive farm that was able to provide the Sydney settlement with vegetables and grain in the early days when starvation threatened. As Sydney struggled, more convicts were sent to Norfolk Island, which in turn produced more food to relieve the shortages in Sydney.

After the departure—and disappearance—of La Pérouse and his two ships, the *Astrolabe* and *Boussole*, there was no further French presence off the New South Wales coast to unnerve the British for more than a decade. A French expedition was sent in 1792–3 to try to discover what happened to La Pérouse but it did not call in at Sydney or bother the English elsewhere. Under the command of 55-year-old Antoine Raymond Joseph de Bruni d'Entrecasteaux the *Recherche* and *Espérance* landed in Van Diemen's Land before their search for La Pérouse took them around Australia and Papua New Guinea. Subsequently, the French became the first to circle Australia ten years before Matthew Flinders performed the same feat in 1803.

If the presence of Bruni d'Entrecasteaux in the South Pacific didn't frighten the English, Nicolas Baudin's French expedition of 1800–3 was a different matter. Baudin was sent by the French to complete the charting of the coastline of Australia, the same task the English set for Flinders seven months later. In May 1802 Baudin arrived in Sydney, where he enjoyed a good relationship with the French-speaking Governor King.

Shortly after Baudin left Sydney to resume his expedition, King was alarmed to hear a rumour from his deputy Captain William Paterson that the French intended to establish their own colony on Van Diemen's Land.[5] Concerned that his friend Baudin had made no mention of such a plan King hastily dispatched Navy captain

Charles Robbins on the *Cumberland* to deliver letters to Baudin, who was anchored in Bass Strait off King Island to the north-west of Van Diemen's Land:[6]

> You will be surprised to see a vessel so soon after you . . . but this has been hastened by a report communicated to me soon after your departure, 'that the French intended to settle in Storm Bay [Van Diemen's Land] . . . and that it was recommended to you by the Republic' . . . as a proof of which a chart, pointing out the situation . . . was, as Colonel Paterson informs me, given him a short time before he sailed by a gentleman of your ship. You will easily imagine that if any information of that kind had reached me before your departure, I should have requested an explanation . . .[7]

Baudin replied immediately, saying he had no knowledge of French plans to establish a settlement. However, his response left room for anxiety, as Baudin reminded King that the French had explored southern Van Diemen's Land before the British:

> I have no knowledge of the claims the French Government may have upon Van Diemen's Land, nor of its designs of the future . . . However, if it were sufficient (according to the principle you have adopted) to have explored the country in order to vest it in those who made it known first, you would have no claims. To convince one's self well that it was not the English, it is but necessary to cast eyes on the ideal maps prepared by your geographer, Arrowsmith, and compare them with those of Charles-François Beautemps-Beaupré,[8] which will leave nothing to be desired.[9]

King was sufficiently concerned about the ambitions of the French that he advised the British government of his plan to send a party to occupy the Derwent River. He reported that he had made the decision because he had heard that a 'principal objective' of the French was 'to form a settlement'.[10]

The man he chose to lead the expedition to start a new British colony was 23-year-old naval lieutenant John Bowen. Bowen left Sydney in August 1803 with 48 people, including 21 male and three female convicts, an escort of fifteen marines and several free settlers and their families.[11] He took with him six months' supplies (and the promise that more would be sent later) and was ordered to 'proceed to the clearing of ground on the public account for the cultivation of wheat and other plants'.[12]

In separate confidential instructions, King also ordered Bowen to prevent any French attempt to establish a settlement on Van Diemen's Land—notwithstanding that he had only fifteen soldiers with which to do it:

> In case any French ships, or ships of any other nation, should attempt to form an establishment anywhere in the neighbourhood of where you are settled, you will inform the Commanding Officer of His Majesty's right to the whole of Van Diemen's Land . . . if they persevere after this, you will endeavour to prevent them carrying their intention into effect, but without any act of hostility if it can be avoided.[13]

As he prepared to send Bowen to the Derwent River, King was unaware that the British government, alerted to Baudin's expedition was planning to establish a major colonial settlement on the northern side of Bass Strait as a further deterrent to the French. In early 1803, the government commissioned 47-year-old David Collins as lieutenant governor, instructing him to establish a sizeable settlement at Port Phillip, on the south coast of New South Wales, in what is now the state of Victoria, about 60 kilometres south of what became modern-day Melbourne.

Collins was a veteran of the First Fleet, having sailed with Arthur Phillip on the flagship *Sirius* in 1787. Although his wife, Maria, remained in England, Collins had served as the colony's first judge for almost a decade before returning home in 1796—the longest term of any senior officer who was part of the First Fleet. When Collins got back to England, having sailed on the *Britannia*, he found Maria in poor health. Over the next two years with her help, he wrote his two-volume *Account of the English Colony of New South Wales.* Although promoted to the rank of lieutenant colonel in 1798 Collins was unable to secure a senior role until he accepted the position of lieutenant governor of the new expedition to Port Phillip.

Although not on as grand a scale as the First Fleet the Collins expedition was similar in design. He was to take a total of 500 people, including around 300 convicts, on two large ships to settle at 'Port Phillip on the southern coast of New South Wales to the northward of the Bass Straights'.[14] The instructions given to Collins were similar to those Phillip had received fifteen years before. He was to take the HMS *Calcutta* and the *Ocean*, 'properly victualled' and with 'such tools, implements and utensils' for their 'subsistence' as well as building their own 'habitations'.[15]

The *Calcutta*, a navy man o' war, would carry most of the convicts and a marine escort of 50 men as well as eighteen free settlers and their families. The *Ocean* was a commercial merchant ship that was hired to convey most of the supplies, equipment and about 100 people, including some civil officers and free settlers, before heading for China to load a cargo of tea.

Port Phillip and the north coast of Bass Strait had been first explored by 27-year-old Lieutenant John Murray early in 1802, three years after Bass and Flinders had discovered that Van Diemen's Land was separate from the mainland. Murray had originally named it Port King but, when he returned to Sydney, King changed it to Port Phillip in honour of the founding commander of the Sydney settlement.

In addition to taking enough food and seeds for growing food in Port Phillip, Collins was instructed to load 'corn and other seed grain' and plants at Rio de Janeiro, and to buy farm animals, including cattle, sheep, goats and pigs.[16]

There were a number of differences about this expedition, compared to the First Fleet, including that some the convicts were allowed to take their wives with them because of their good behaviour.[17] Twenty-seven-year-old Lieutenant James Tuckey on the *Calcutta* expressed admiration for the sacrifice made by the convict's wives, who had agreed to travel with their husbands:

> They had married in sunshine and prosperity when the world smiled deceitfully and their path in life appeared strewed with unfaded flowers; in the season of adversity they would not be separated but reposed their heads on the same thorny pillow; and as they had shared with them the cup of joy, they refused not the one of sorrow. Those alone who know the miserable and degrading situation of the transported felon can appreciate the degree of connubial love that could induce these women to accompany their guilty husbands in exile.[18]

Before leaving England, Collins was warned by British secretary of state Lord Hobart of the 'destructive consequences' New South Wales had seen from the trafficking of grog by 'officers of the military establishment', and ordered to take all steps to 'prevent any attempts' by the marine officers to do it at Port Phillip.[19] Another difference was that the British government recognised the problem of developing an agricultural colony with the labour of convicts who had little or no farming experience and so a number of free settlers and their wives and children were included in the expedition. Each settler was to be given a grant of land for farming, free convict labour and a food ration until they could grow their own food. Collins was also authorised to give them farm animals if the government's supply reproduced enough.

Collins was also given more skilled convicts. Arthur Phillip had protested, when he led the First Fleet, that barely any of the convicts possessed skills of any value. In the Collins expedition there were four carpenters, nine timber workers, four skilled in brickmaking and bricklaying, fifteen bakers and butchers, cooks, fishermen, mariners and caulkers. Other occupations included clerks, brewers, gardeners, shoemakers and clothes makers, as well as 45 people experienced in working with boats.[20]

The two ships sailed from Portsmouth on 24 April 1803 and reached Tenerife, where four convicts were reported as having died, two of whom had already been sick with advanced tuberculosis.[21] While in the port of Santa Cruz, Collins purchased a 'large quantity of vegetables and lemons' when 'an indication of scurvy' was observed among the convicts.[22] After a stay of only four days, primarily to load more drinking water, the ships sailed across the Atlantic and the equator, reaching Rio de Janeiro on 29 June.

In a dispatch sent to Lord Hobart, Collins noted there had been no further deaths since Tenerife and everyone from both ships was in 'perfect health'.[23] While in Rio harbour the convicts were fed a small ration of fresh meat and some fresh oranges. Collins had bought corn seed and a few goats and pigs but had not found any cattle, which he said they would buy when they reached Cape Town.

They left Rio on 19 July. The *Calcutta* reached the Cape of Good Hope on 12 August, but it had lost contact with the slower-sailing *Ocean*, which did not stop at Cape Town. The two ships did not see each other again until they reached Port Phillip. Collins said the *Calcutta* was well received by the Dutch authorities and he was able to buy the cattle they needed. He also reported a fatality: a sixteen-year-old convict who was caught stealing from one of the officers had jumped overboard into the Atlantic and swum off to his death. After leaving Cape Town on 23 August, the *Calcutta* reached Port Phillip nearly seven weeks later, on 9 October, and was surprised to find that the *Ocean* had already anchored in the bay two days before.

Despite the glowing promises that they had been given before leaving England the new settlers found Port Phillip to be as unsuitable for settlement as Arthur Phillip had found Botany Bay fifteen years before. Lieutenant James Tuckey said that, within a week of arriving on the *Calcutta*, they had reached the conclusion that the site could not support a settlement:

> The week following our arrival at Port Phillip was occupied in searching for an eligible place to fix settlement . . . Here to our great mortification, we observed a total want of fresh water, and found the soil so extremely light and sandy to deny all hope of successful cultivation.[24]

A few days after landing, the unloading of convicts, settlers and stores began at the best spot they could find. Collins named Sullivan Bay after the British secretary of state for war and the colonies, John Sullivan. Over the next month, a settlement of tents was erected and 12 acres (5 hectares) allotted for the planting of vegetables and corn.

The settlers' initial encounters with the local Aboriginal people were, as at Botany Bay and Sydney, entirely peaceful. According to Lieutenant Tuckey, on the day of the *Calcutta*'s arrival 'the natives came to the boats entirely unarmed, and without the smallest symptom of apprehension'.[25] However, within weeks relations became hostile when the newcomers shot several Aboriginal men who threatened to steal supplies.[26]

Three weeks later on 5 November 1803, Collins wrote a long letter to Governor King in Sydney—who was his commanding officer given that he had landed in what was part of New South Wales. Collins complained that a comprehensive search of Port Phillip had failed to find adequate water or good soil: '[Officers] had been searching some

William Hogarth depicts the squalor of eighteenth-century England. The Industrial Revolution had started and while the rich got richer, the overwhelming majority living in overcrowded towns and cities continued to live and die poor. Crime rates spiralled despite an increase in the number of offences that attracted the death penalty. By the end of the century, one in eight people in London lived on the proceeds of crime. The prisons and hulks were so full and disease-ridden, it was feared that a plague would break out in wider society. William Hogarth, *Gin Lane*, c. 1750.

Because of the overcrowded prisons, many of the convicts spent years on prison hulks before being transported to New South Wales. The hulks were decommissioned navy ships stripped of their masts, rudders and rigging, and were anchored on the Thames and at other English ports. Originally intended as a temporary measure, the 'floating prisons'—which had neither sanitation nor sewerage—housed thousands of prisoners over more than 80 years. George Cooke, *Prison Ship at Deptford*, 1826.

Aristocrat botanist Joseph Banks was a major influence in sending the convicts to Botany Bay, which proved totally unsuitable for settlement and had to be abandoned within a few days. For many years Banks had the ear of the government, the Admiralty and the king on all matters relating to the penal colony and was regularly consulted on a wide range of subjects, including botany, earthquakes, sheep breeding, exploration and who should be appointed as the colony's governors. Thomas Phillips, *Sir Joseph Banks*, c. 1801.

There was nothing particularly outstanding in Arthur Phillip's career when he was plucked from semiretirement at nearly 50 years of age to lead the expedition to New South Wales, but he proved to be a good choice. Despite enlightened and compassionate views, Phillip believed that sodomites and murderers should be fed to cannibals and that the most 'abandoned' of the colony's female convicts should be forced to work in government-run brothels. Francis Wheatley, *Arthur Phillip*, 1786.

The First Fleet called in to Rio de Janeiro harbour in August 1787. The eleven tiny wooden ships carried nearly 1500 people, including around 800 convicts, of whom 25 per cent were women. The fleet carried enough food for two years; tools and equipment to build a new colony in the Australian bush; plants and seeds to grow grain, vegetables and fruit; and over 500 farm animals—some from England and others bought at ports on the way. At Rio they bought 65,000 litres of rum.
William Bradley, *City of St. Sebastians, Rio Janeiro: Sirius & Convoy at Anchor, 1787.*

A view of Sydney more than six months after landing shows that the building of the new colony was very slow. Having abandoned Botany Bay as unsuitable, the colonists found the clearing of the bush around Sydney difficult. After the successive failure of the first harvests, the colony was on the brink of starvation and only survived because the Second Fleet arrived two and a half years later with provisions.
William Bradley, *Sydney Cove, Port Jackson, 1788.*

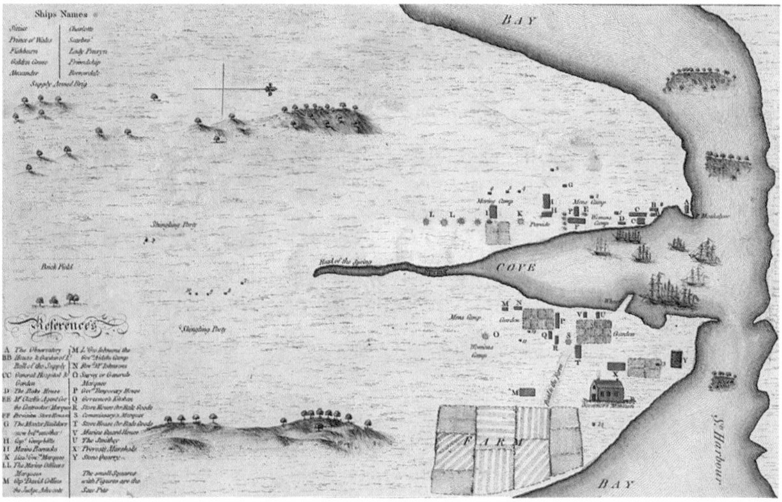

Drawn less than three months after the arrival of the First Fleet, this map shows prospective sites for the first gardens and farm, bakehouse, storehouses, blacksmiths and tent hospital. Only a few senior officers were to have their own houses. The marines and the convicts lived in tents, in some cases for many years. The map shows ten of the eleven ships of the First Fleet still in the harbour, unloading supplies. The eleventh, the *Supply,* was at the time taking a small detachment to settle Norfolk Island. Map of Sydney Cove, probably by Francis Fowles, 1788.

This hand-coloured aquatint shows the *Guardian* being shipwrecked on its way to Sydney on Christmas Eve 1789 after hitting an iceberg in the Southern Ocean. The ship was carrying over 1000 tons of urgently needed supplies for the starving colony. Thomas Begg, *Distressing Situation of the Guardian Sloop, Capt. Riou, after striking on a floating Island of Ice*, 1809.

Governor Arthur Phillip narrowly escaped death when he was speared through the shoulder at Sydney's Manly Cove. He was rescued and taken by boat to safety by colleagues. Port Jackson Painter, *The Governor making the best of his way to the Boat after being wounded*, c. 1790.

More than a decade after the establishment of the colony, Governor John Hunter complained about continuing serious shortages of food and supplies. For many years the overwhelming majority of those in the colony lived in crude shacks that had leaking roofs; there was no bed to sleep in, no chair to sit on and no table to eat at. In 1799 Hunter reported to London that hundreds of convicts were harvesting crops 'naked as they were born' because they had no clothes. William Bennett, *Vice-Admiral John Hunter*, c. 1813.

England's Matthew Flinders unexpectedly encountered France's Nicolas Baudin in 1802 when the rival navigators were sent at the same time by their respective governments to chart the remaining 'unknown' southern coast of Australia. The British held strong fears that the French also proposed to set up colonies in Australia in competition with the British as they had done in India, the West Indies and North America, which had led to years of warfare between the two countries. John Ford, *The Encounter 1802*, 2002.

Twenty-year-old Esther was convicted of stealing 20 metres of silk lace and sentenced to seven years' transportation. Sailing on the First Fleet's *Lady Penrhyn,* she met 23-year-old marine Lieutenant George Johnston, with whom she had seven children before he married her 26 years later in Sydney. In 1808 she effectively became the colony's First Lady when her husband led the military overthrow of William Bligh and installed himself as acting governor. Richard Read Senior, *Esther Johnston*, c. 1820.

As the British settlement expanded, Aboriginal people were driven from their land and their traditional food sources. Increasingly hungry, they turned in desperation to raiding the settlers' farms. In the violent clashes that followed, the killing on both sides escalated into 'open war' that struck terror into the hearts of farmers' families and Aboriginal communities alike. Thomas Watling, *View of Sydney Cove,* 1794–1796 (?).

This engraving is the only known depiction of warrior and resistance leader Pemulwuy, who terrorised white settlers for more than a decade. That he was shot and wounded a number of times but did not die led to the widespread local belief that he could not be killed by the white man's bullets. Governor Philip Gidley King offered a reward for his capture 'dead or alive' and he was shot dead six months later in June 1802. Samuel John Neele, *Pimbloy,* 1804.

Fernando Brambila was part of a friendly visit to New South Wales by Spanish explorer Alessandro Malaspina in 1793. The British were unaware that, after the visit, Spain drew up plans for the invasion and destruction of Sydney because they saw the British presence in the South Pacific as a threat to Spanish interests in the region. Fernando Brambila, *View of Sydney*, 1793.

Philip Gidley King returned with his family to Sydney in 1800 to take up the post of governor following the recall of his predecessor, John Hunter. But King already had a family in the colony. When he had arrived on the First Fleet more than a decade earlier and was sent to establish the settlement on Norfolk Island, he fathered two children with convict woman Ann Inett. King served as governor for six years before returning to England in November 1807. Robert Dighton, *Philip Gidley and Anna Josepha King with Their Children*, 1799.

Lieutenant John Macarthur arrived in Sydney with his wife, Elizabeth, and infant son in June 1790. Over the years he became an unofficial leader of the colony's corrupt military and the colony's richest and most powerful man, having amassed a fortune from trading, selling grog and pioneering the Australian wool industry. Haughty and argumentative, he was involved in two illegal duels and in one of them he seriously wounded his superior officer. Macarthur clashed with all of the colony's governors and in 1808 was the primary instigator of the overthrow of Governor William Bligh. Artist unknown, *John Macarthur*, c. 1850s (?).

John Macarthur's wife, Elizabeth, was the settlement's first educated woman. For two decades she held court among the officers of the New South Wales Corps, hosting musical recitals on the colony's only piano, which was given to her by naval surgeon George Worgan. Eventually none of the early governors would accept invitations to the Macarthur home because of her increasingly controversial husband. Artist unknown, *Elizabeth Macarthur*, date unknown.

Political reformer Thomas Muir, a member of the 'Scottish Martyrs' and transported for sedition, was one of hundreds of convicts who successfully escaped from the colony. After leaving Sydney in January 1796 aboard an American sealing ship, he reached Vancouver Island before sailing to California, Mexico, Cuba and Spain. Off the coast of Cadiz he lost an eye during a battle with the British navy but finally reached France in November 1797, where he was given sanctuary by the revolutionary government. He died near Paris a year later aged 33. François Bonneville, *Thomas Muir*, 1800.

Many convict women were forced into prostitution to survive and others became the concubines of military officers and civil officials, even when the men were already married. David Collins left his wife, Maria, in England when he sailed with the First Fleet to become the colony's first Judge Advocate. In Sydney he took up with convict girl Anne Yeats and fathered two children before returning to England, leaving the family behind. Later he became lieutenant governor of Tasmania, where he took up with a fourteen-year-old daughter of convicts, Margaret Eddington, and fathered two more children. John T. Barber, *David Collins*, c. 1797–c. 1803.

Farmers who crossed Bass Strait from Tasmania in 1835 to take up farming in Victoria were surprised to find a white man among the local Aboriginal people. He was convict William Buckley, who had escaped from the convict settlement that had been established and then abandoned at Port Phillip more than 30 years earlier. Buckley had been away from white people for so long that he had forgotten how to speak English. Frederick Woodhouse, *The First Settlers Discover Buckley*, 1861.

An artist's impression of the escape from Sydney of convict Mary Bryant, her husband, her two small children and seven other convicts in March 1791. In a stolen boat it took them 69 days to reach the Dutch port of Kupang in Timor, 5000 kilometres away. Masquerading as shipwreck victims, they were imprisoned and handed over to the next English ship to arrive in port. Over the next two months, Mary's husband and son died, along with three of the other convicts. Her daughter later died off the coast of Africa. Mary and the four surviving convicts eventually reached England, where they were freed after they had served their original sentences. Bill Lacey, *They Rowed to Freedom*, 1966.

In another plan to thwart French settlement in Australia, the British sent a large expedition to settle Port Phillip in October 1803 on what would become the south coast of Victoria. Under the command of David Collins, it comprised nearly 500 people, including 300 convicts, a marine escort and eighteen free settlers and their families. After less than three months, the settlement was abandoned. George Gordon McCrae, *Sullivan Bay, Port Phillip*, 1803.

Water casks found at Sorrento were left there by the Collins expedition to Port Phillip when the settlement was abandoned in early 1804 and moved across Bass Strait to Hobart. It would be another 30 years before the British formally settled what would become Victoria.

After years of struggle, the settlement faced its biggest threat to survival in March 1804, when hundreds of Irish political prisoners in Sydney attempted to overthrow British rule and return to Ireland, where they could continue to fight for the creation of an Irish republic. Artist unknown, *Convict Uprising at Castle Hill*, 1804.

Fearing that the French were threatening to establish rival colonies in Australia, the British established their own settlement first in Van Diemen's Land (Tasmania). The initial expedition of 48 people sent in August 1803 were under instruction to prevent a French landing, with force if necessary. Like Sydney, the Hobart colony struggled in the early years to survive. *Hobart Town*, probably by George Prideaux Harris, 1805.

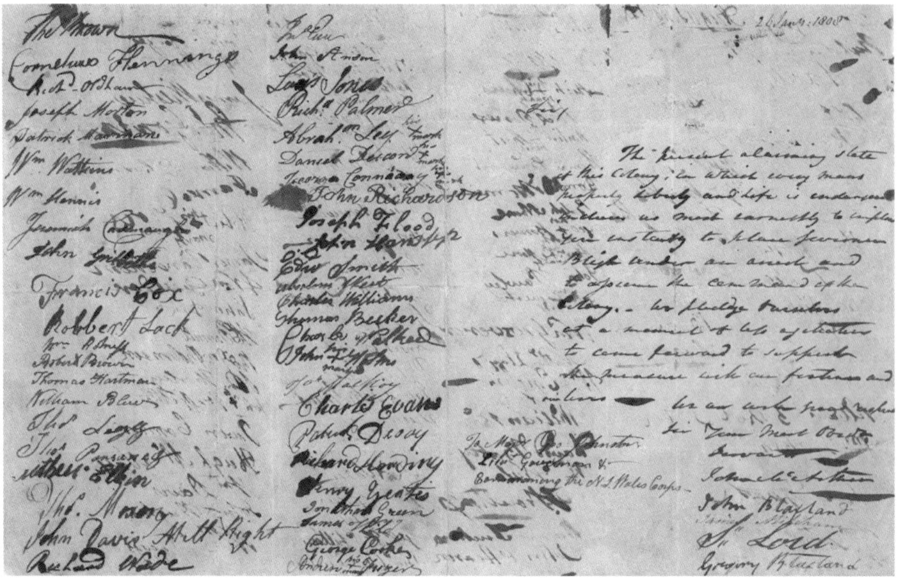

26 Jany 1808

The present alarming state of this Colony, in which every man's property, liberty and life is endangered, induces us most earnestly to implore you instantly to place Governor Bligh under an arrest and to assume the command of the Colony. We pledge ourselves at a moment of less agitation to come forward to support the measure with our fortunes and our lives. We are with great respect, Sir, Your most obedient servants

The petition calling on marine commander George Johnston to arrest Governor William Bligh and take over the role of governor was signed by 151 leading citizens. Bligh had survived the mutiny on the *Bounty* when he was appointed governor to clean up the corrupt colony in 1806. A year later the unpopular leader was arrested and deposed by the colony's powerful military.

Governor Lachlan Macquarie and his wife, Elizabeth, who accompanied her husband on his extensive travels throughout the colony, including Van Diemen's Land (Tasmania). The most progressive of all the early colonial governors, Macquarie was responsible for ending the colony's struggle for survival and for transforming Australia from a prison camp to the beginnings of a country. Artist unknown, *Lachlan Macquarie*, c. 1819 (left); artist unknown, *Elizabeth Macquarie*, c. 1819 (right).

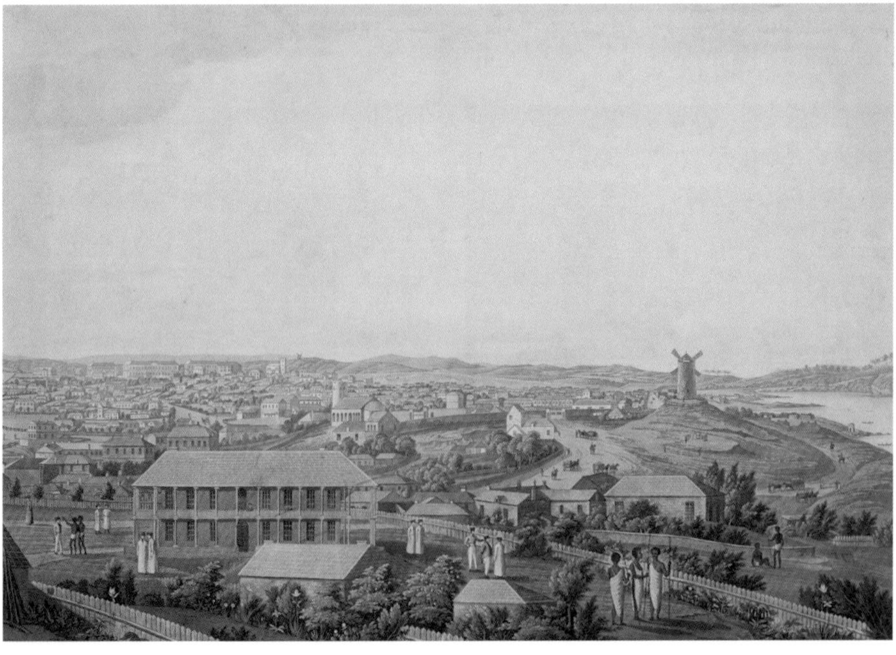

After struggling against the odds in the early decades of the nineteenth century, the colony's future now looked more secure. In a little over a decade of the Macquarie era, the European population increased almost fourfold to nearly 40,000 people. Over the next quarter of a century it would grow to 400,000 people. Major James Taylor, *Panoramic views of Port Jackson*, c. 1821.

part of the bay. I received the first unfavourable impression of it, which I am truly concerned to observe a more minute survey thereof has only intended to strengthen.'[27]

Collins asked King for permission to abandon the settlement. As there was no established way of delivering mail between Port Phillip and Sydney, which was more than 1000 kilometres' sailing to the north, Collins fitted out a six-oared cutter with a single sheet sail under the command of his cousin William Collins, one of the settlers, who volunteered to deliver the dispatches.[28] By this time the *Ocean* had completed its commitment to deliver supplies to Port Phillip and was being readied to sail to China to pick up its commercial cargo.[29] For the voyage to Sydney the little cutter took six convict volunteers, all of whom were later granted conditional pardons.[30] The cutter was nine days at sea when it was picked up by the *Ocean*, which had left Port Phillip six days later. The *Ocean* towed the little boat the last hundred kilometres to Sydney before heading on to Canton.

On receiving the dispatches from Collins on 24 November 1803 King quickly wrote back giving Collins permission to abandon the Port Phillip settlement. By this time King had received a corroborating report about Port Phillip from the colony's surveyor Charles Grimes, who had examined the port the year before:

> It appears . . . that Port Phillip is totally unfit in every point of view . . . from this circumstance I shall presume it will appear to you that removing from thence will be the most advisable for the interests of His Majesty's Service.[31]

King gave Collins the option of moving the entire settlement to Port Dalrymple on the Tamar River in the north of Van Diemen's Land, or to Risdon Cove on the Derwent River in the south of the island, where John Bowen had gone a year earlier. King re-chartered the *Ocean* on behalf of the British government and, cancelling its planned voyage to China, sent it back to Port Phillip to help with the evacuation of the settlers to Van Diemen's Land.[32]

Collins chose the Derwent: 'The advantages which I must derive from establishing myself in a place already settled,' he said, 'had certainly great weight with me.' He added that he thought the Derwent was preferable because its fledgling sea port was increasingly used by visiting whaling ships, and thus 'better adapted to commercial purposes'.[33] He also noted that he'd had discipline problems with some of his marines at Port Phillip, which resulted in one private being given 700 lashes and another 500. Collins told King he thought the example set by the marines at Risdon Cove would encourage 'a spirit of emulation' within his own disaffected troops.[34]

Collins left Port Phillip on 30 January 1804 on the *Calcutta*, with nearly 300 of the people who had landed there the previous October. The remaining 193 had to wait another three months for the *Ocean* to come back from Sydney and pick them up.[35]

Before quitting Port Phillip, Collins recorded that a number of convicts had escaped the Sullivan Bay settlement. A total of twelve were recaptured or returned and were punished by flogging. The remainder who had disappeared into the bush were believed to have died—except one.

After the departure of the Collins expedition in early 1804, the southern coast of New South Wales was not officially settled again for three decades, until farmers crossed from Van Diemen's Land with their sheep to begin farming in what became the colony of Victoria. On 6 July 1835 three farmers near Indented Head on the western arm of Port Phillip saw a white man approach them wearing kangaroo skins and carrying Aboriginal weapons. His name was William Buckley and he was one of the earlier convict escapees, who had been in the bush for more than 30 years and had difficulty speaking English. He began to understand the farmers when they offered him some bread. He later recalled that, when they called it by its name, 'a cloud appeared to pass from over my brain'.[36]

Buckley had escaped from Collins's settlement with four other convicts but they became separated in the bush and he was eventually taken in by the local Wathaurung people. The Van Diemen's Land farmers organised for Buckley to sail to Hobart in December 1837, where he saw an established town for the first time since he had left England in 1803. In Hobart he married, was given a pardon by Lieutenant Governor George Arthur and was found jobs as an assistant storekeeper and gatekeeper. He died in 1856 aged seventy-six.

After abandoning Port Phillip on 30 January 1804 and making an uncomfortable fifteen-day crossing of Bass Strait, Collins reached the Derwent, where he met up with John Bowen and his party. Collins and his colleagues were disappointed with Risdon Cove, which they said lacked sufficient water and was 'unsuitable for a town'.[37] The following day they explored what they thought was a better site to the south-west on the other side of the Derwent, and Collins, who was senior in rank to Bowen, ordered the settlement to be moved across the river to the new location. Collins named the new settlement Hobart Town after the man who had ordered his mission, Lord Hobart, the secretary of state for war and the colonies at the time.

Lieutenant Bowen did not stay long in Hobart after the arrival of Collins, returning to Sydney six months later, in August 1804, and then to England in early 1805, leaving behind Martha Hayes, a convict's daughter, who had already had one child with him and was pregnant with another. Bowen had met Hayes when she was believed to have been around fourteen years old, on HMS *Glatton*, which had brought her convict mother and Bowen to Sydney in 1803.

When Bowen was ordered to establish the Derwent River colony in August 1803, he took the pregnant Martha with him. Their first child, Martha, was the first European born in Van Diemen's Land, in March 1804. Martha was pregnant to Bowen again six months later, and gave birth to a second daughter, Henrietta. In England, Bowen later married Elizabeth Clowes, the niece of the Countess of Newburgh.[38] He left the abandoned Martha Hayes with a land grant and living in a timber shack. In 1811 Martha married ex-convict William Whitehead, with whom she had two more children. When Whitehead died, she married police clerk Bernard Williams, who was almost twenty years her junior. She died aged 85 in 1871.

Collins's struggle to establish Hobart was similar in many ways to the earlier experience of the First Fleet in Sydney. Most of the convicts were unqualified to work in the wilderness and the English tools they had were not strong enough to cut through the tough Australian trees that needed to be cleared. A year later Hobart Town was still dominated by tents and wooden shacks; the lieutenant governor's own small house was 'no more than a cottage'.[39]

Although the land was more fertile than in New South Wales the new settlement struggled with food shortages. The provisions they had brought with them were intended to last for a year, but were much damaged by many loadings and exposure and had to be supplemented by kangaroo and other game. Supplies came from Sydney but only irregularly and often much was ruined and rotten. Many of the sheep and cattle sent from Sydney died in transit.

By carefully husbanding their stores and buying what they could from occasional whalers and trading ships the settlement struggled along, often on reduced rations and never far from starvation.[40] Collins's deputy, Lieutenant Edward Lord, said the situation was made worse because of the lack of necessities: 'The whole settlement was called upon to endure hardship of no ordinary kind. The Governor himself, the officers, the whole settlement for eighteen months, were without bread, vegetables, tea, sugar, wine, spirits, or beer, or any substitute, except a precarious supply of the wild game of the country.'[41]

Only months after Collins had arrived in Hobart Town, Governor King in Sydney received orders to establish yet another British settlement on Van Diemen's Land. Although the letter arrived in early 1804 it had been penned by Lord Hobart in June 1803, before the government in London knew that King had organised for Lieutenant Bowen to begin a settlement at Risdon Cove.

Governor King was ordered to establish the new settlement at Port Dalrymple on the Tamar River in the north of the island. King was specifically instructed to send his deputy, Lieutenant Colonel William Paterson, the officer who had first heard the rumours in Sydney that the French planned to establish their own colony on Van Diemen's Land. In a veiled reference to the French threat, Lord Hobart said his decision 'renders it in a political view peculiarly necessary that a settlement should be formed' to protect Bass Strait from others. King was also ordered to include in Paterson's expedition people still living on Norfolk Island, which was now less valuable as a supplier of food to Sydney and no longer thought to be coveted by the French.

Paterson left Sydney in May 1804 taking with him his wife, Elizabeth, a captain, two subalterns, four sergeants, two drummers, 58 privates and 74 convicts. He settled on the Tamar River on the other side of what would later become Launceston. Within a year Paterson—a weak man and a heavy drinker, who was severely afflicted with gout—was complaining that the new settlement was struggling. The convicts, he said, were averse to work, the marines insubordinate, their shoes falling to bits and their tools not strong enough.

For the next eight years the British maintained two settlements under separate command in the north and south of Van Diemen's Land. In early 1809 Paterson finally left Port Dalrymple after more than four years there and returned to Sydney, where he was required to serve as governor following the overthrow of William Bligh.

Overwhelmed by the pressures of office and drinking heavily, Paterson stayed until the new governor, Lachlan Macquarie, took office in January 1810. Paterson then left Sydney on HMS *Dromedary* on 12 May 1810 bound for England but he died at sea on 21 June as the ship rounded Cape Horn.

Although fearful of the French, the English were unaware that the Spanish had also posed an even direr threat to their young colony in New South Wales. The Spanish—along with the Portuguese—had been in the Pacific centuries before the British and had established a Pacific empire that included large tracts of the North and South American coast as well as the Spanish East Indies, which included the present-day Philippines.

In 1788 the Spanish government decided to conduct its own vast exploration of the Pacific, including the coast of New South Wales. This five-year expedition was similar in scope to that undertaken by Cook on behalf of the British and that by La Pérouse on behalf of the French. For what was to be largely an expedition to carry out studies in 'natural history, cartography, ethnography, astronomy, hydrography and medicine',[42] the Spanish commanders were Alessandro Malaspina and José de Bustamante y Guerra. Thirty-four-year-old Malaspina, like Christopher Columbus more than 300 years before, was born in Italy but spent his adult life as an officer in the Spanish Navy. Twenty-nine-year-old Bustamante was born in Cantabria, in northern Spain.

Malaspina, so as to honour James Cook's ships, named the two ships that had been especially built for his expedition *Descubierta* (after the *Discovery*) and *Atrevida* (meaning 'bold', after the *Resolution*). His five-year expedition left Cadiz on 30 July 1789, crossing the Atlantic and rounding Cape Horn before navigating the entire west coast of

South and North America up to Alaska. They then sailed back to Mexico, before crossing the Pacific to Manila, and then headed south-east to New Zealand and New South Wales before heading back to Cadiz, arriving on 21 September 1794.

The expedition was a scientific success. It resulted in a more precise charting of the entire western cost of America, and a more accurate measurement of glaciers and mountains in Alaska, and suggested the feasibility of building the Panama Canal.

Although the Malaspina expedition was chiefly understood to be a scientific expedition, it also had clear political objectives, especially in connection to New South Wales. In a letter dated 24 April 1789 Malaspina wrote to the Spanish maritime minister, Antonio Valdés:

> [I]t is important to decide on . . . whether New Holland and New Zealand are to be looked at with political rather than naturalist's eyes, that is to say whether from the study of various parts of those vast regions solidly-based conclusions with relation to particular products can be developed beyond the few recently established in those areas.[43]

At the time, Britain and Spain had recently become allies of convenience against revolutionary France. Judge Advocate David Collins recorded in his journal that the settlement at Sydney was told to expect the arrival of the two Spanish ships, which anchored in the lower part of Sydney Harbour on 12 March 1793 and stayed for a month.[44] In a dispatch to London, Lieutenant Governor Francis Grose assured the British government that the first foreign visitors to New South Wales were made welcome:

> His Majesty's instructions regarding their reception. I have executed to the utmost in my power, paying them every compliment and attention due to their rank and situation; and I have the pleasure to report

> that on their leaving us, as well as on many occasions before their departure, they did not omit to give every testimony on their part of the satisfaction and gratitude they felt at the hospitality they had been treated with.[45]

One of the Spanish expedition's botanists on the expedition, Thaddäus Haenke, expressed a similar view in a letter to Sir Joseph Banks when he wrote 'the public testimony of a grateful soul for the very extraordinary humanity and kindness with which the English in their new Colony welcomed us'.[46]

While in Sydney the Spanish conducted a raft of scientific measurements, storing their instruments in the 'small brick hut' that had been built for Bennelong, who had returned to England with Governor Phillip three months before.[47] The Spanish also made a number of paintings and drawings; twelve of these survive, providing an important record of the progress of the five-year-old settlement.

The English and the Spanish got along well. Collins wrote that the visitors gave a 'pleasant diversity to the dull routine' and that despite being 'severed from the mother country and residing in the woods and among savages' the British had not forgotten the 'hospitalities due to a stranger'.[48]

Before they left, the Spanish reciprocated when Malaspina hosted a lavish dinner aboard the *Descubierta.* They ate a small cow 'sacrificed for the occasion' and cooked by the Spanish 'after their own custom'.[49] Shortly before leaving Sydney Malaspina left a 'packet with dispatches' that Lieutenant Governor Francis Grose agreed would be taken on the next British ship bound for England to be given to the Spanish ambassador in London.[50]

Behind all the pleasantries, however, the Spanish were forming the view that their English hosts constituted an emerging threat to Spanish interests in the Pacific. This was Spain's first look at the five-year-old British settlement and one of Malaspina's officers, Francisco

Muñoz y San Clemente, reported that he thought the English settlement could be used to disrupt Spanish trade in peacetime and provide a base for an invasion in the event of war:

> The colonists will be able to fit out lucrative privateers so as to cut all communication between the Philippines and both Americas . . . These possessions will have a navy of their own, obtaining from the Southern region whatever is necessary to establish it, and when they have it ready formed, they will be able to invade our nearby possessions.[51]

Commander Malaspina also saw the settlement at Sydney as a serious issue, writing that if left unchecked the English could pose a terrible threat to Spanish interests:

> [W]ith the greatest ease a crossing of two or three months through healthy climates, and a secure navigation, could bring to our defenceless coasts two or three thousand castaway bandits to serve interpolated with an excellent body of regular troops. It would not be surprising that in this case—the women also sharing the risks as well as the sensual pleasures of the men—the history of the invasions of the Huns and Alans in the most fertile provinces of Europe would be revived in our surprised colonies . . . The pen trembles to record the image, however distant, of such disorders.[52]

Soon after his stay Malaspina compiled a report in which he denounced Britain's colonial greed and the settlers' abuse of power in New South Wales:

> [T]he transportation of the convicts constituted the means and not the object of the enterprise. The extension of dominion, mercantile speculations, and the discovery of mines were the real object; and to these, albeit vain, hopes, were sacrificed the restraints of legislation,

> the principles of sane policy, and above all the compassionate cries of oppressed humanity.[53]

In September 1794 the explorers were welcomed back to Spain after their long and successful expedition. Malaspina was presented to King Charles IV and promoted to fleet brigadier in March 1795. However, he soon fell from grace when he involved himself in local politics and opposed the prime minister, Manuel de Godoy. The following year he was gaoled and banished to a remote fortress prison in Galicia, where he spent almost six years. He was released in 1802 and exiled to live in Pentromoni, in his native Italy.

Meanwhile, Bustamante remained free of his boss's political troubles. His career continued to flourish and in 1796 he was appointed governor of Spanish-controlled Paraguay. It was in the 1790s after returning from the visit to New South Wales that Bustamante is believed to have composed a detailed plan for the Spanish to invade Sydney as the prospect of Spain and Britain going to war became more likely. It is claimed that Bustamante's detailed plan was approved by the Spanish cabinet shortly before Spain declared war against Britain in August 1796.[54]

Bustamante's plan proposed that the Spanish send a fleet of gunboats disguised to look like British supply vessels to raid and destroy the settlement at Sydney. The ships were to be equipped with 'hotshot' cannon balls heated in a furnace so that when they landed they would ignite fires in the colony's buildings.

According to Bustamante, the entire population of Sydney and Norfolk Island—around 7000 people—would be captured and transported. 'I believe that the destruction of the English colony in Botany Bay, today transferred to Port Jackson, is one of the points most of interest to the Crown [and] easy to execute in the space of six or seven months by the Royal Squadron in Peru,' Bustamante wrote in his proposal, dated 29 July 1796.

> The entirely helpless state in which I observed that settlement in 1793, and the general discontent of its inhabitants, would so facilitate its conquest that I believe it would be achieved with the surprise that the convincing presence of our fleet would cause. But even if some resistance were offered, it could never triumph over the gunfire from our ships or prevent the total destruction of houses, warehouses and goods located in the principal settlement . . . If the orders of His Majesty foresee the total destruction of this colony by taking all its English inhabitants prisoner to transport them to our possessions, embarking all the effects that may be useful, it will then proceed to ruin its warehouses and buildings so that, if England should attempt the reconstruction of the settlement in peacetime, she may renounce her desires, and also because of the exorbitant expenses which she must make to restore it to the footing on which it is today.[55]

Spain went to war with England a few months later and Bustamante's ambitious plan was quickly overtaken by events. Early in the war in February 1797 the Spanish Navy was heavily defeated in the Battle of Cape St Vincent off the Portuguese coast, despite having more ships than the British. Having incurred serious losses to its navy Spain was forced to concentrate on the European theatre and all hope of invading Sydney was abandoned.

Spain's war with England continued on and off for more than a decade until 1808 by which time Spain, already an empire in decline, was in no position to threaten the British territories in the south-west Pacific.

10

The Unstoppable Loss of Escaped Convicts

> 'It is becoming necessary to restrain the practice of several vessels carrying the American flag, who having received assistance and relief according to their wants, have with very few exceptions, taken persons from hence who are under sentence of the law . . . who have been secreted on board those ships . . . The master of every ship or vessel, whether English or foreign, before they are allowed any communication with the settlement, shall give security [of] £500 . . . not to carry off any person whatsoever without the Governor's certificate.'
>
> Governor Philip Gidley King

In the first two decades of the settlement at Sydney, there were about 40 officially recorded escape attempts, involving about 250 convicts.[1] However, reports were only lodged when there was some evidence of an escape attempt—nothing was noted when convicts simply disappeared, never to be heard of again. As a result, there is no reliable record of how many men and women successfully escaped in the first decades of the convict settlements in Australia but it could have been thousands.[2] And since the escapees tended typically to be the more enterprising and most qualified of the convicts, the high number of absconders seriously reduced the skilled labour needed for the building of the colony.

One of the reasons the British had decided on New South Wales as the location of the convict colony was that it was surrounded by inhospitable bush and vast oceans. It was so remote that even without walls and iron bars 'it is hardly possible for persons to return' to England 'without permission'.[3]

However, the innate urge for freedom prompted an array of ingenious attempts to escape. The first recorded plot came when the First Fleet was barely out of the English Channel when two convicts on the *Scarborough*, Phillip Farrell and Thomas Griffiths, planned to free other convicts so they could take control of the ship and silently 'quit the fleet in the night'.[4]

Both Farrell and Griffiths were experienced sailors. Prior to being sentenced at the Old Bailey for stealing a handkerchief worth one shilling, 24-year-old Farrell had been a boatswain's mate in the Royal Navy. Twenty-eight-year-old Griffiths had been the master of a French privateer during the American War of Independence before being sentenced—also at the Old Bailey—to seven years' transportation for stealing cloth valued at £2 in 1784.

The plot was uncovered when another convict heard of the plan and warned the ship's officers. Once their plan was exposed the two men were shackled and rowed over to the *Sirius*, where they were flogged, put in irons and then sent for the rest of the voyage to another ship, the *Prince of Wales*. Despite the high drama Captain Phillip sent a letter from Tenerife three weeks later to say that, at the time, the officers on the *Scarborough* 'did not think they had reason to be seriously alarmed'.[5]

The first recorded escape was by convict John Powers, when the fleet called in at the Tenerife port of Santa Cruz to load fresh water and provisions. The night before the ships' departure, Powers managed to get up on the deck of the *Alexander*, lower himself into a small boat and make his escape. He first rowed over to a Dutch East Indiaman anchored in the harbour, but his offer to sign on as a member of their crew was rejected. He then rowed to a nearby beach, where he intended to hide until the fleet left Tenerife. Early the next morning, when he was reported missing, Captain John Hunter said 'orders were immediately given' for a party of marines to set out in search of him. They found him asleep on the west side of the town, 'concealing himself in the cleft of a rock not having been able to get up the precipice'.[6] John Hunter said that the marine's officer pointed a gun at Powers and threatened to shoot him if he didn't get into the boat: 'The fellow complied rather than run the hazard of being shot and was taken on board, punished and put in irons until we got to sea, when he was liberated in same manner as the rest.'[7]

Others were luckier. In October 1791 four convicts managed to escape from the *Pitt* when it stopped at Rio de Janeiro on its way to Sydney. The ship's commander, Captain Edward Manning, reported that the convicts had escaped and may have been given sanctuary in a monastery by local Catholic priests:

> I am sorry to tell you that we have lost four of the convicts. I was under the necessity of permitting them to go on shore with the boats, from whence they did, or at least attempted to make their escape. I rather think they were drowned in making their attempt, or if not, they must have been secreted in a convent of the Friars. I applied to the Viceroy and every step was taken that was possible for their recovery without effect.[8]

Another convict made his escape when the *Pitt* reached Cape Town. After getting away, 29-year-old forger Thomas Watling went into hiding until the ship left for Sydney. Excited about his freedom, he wrote enthusiastically to his aunt in England from his hiding place:

> Your loved Watling is at liberty! True, I am in a remote clime, where slavery wields her iron sceptre, and where slaves are at this moment attending me—yet blessed be Divine Mercy, I enjoy freedom! . . . That but yesterday I had the ignominious epithet convict adhibited [affixed] to my name, am again myself! To-day all nature seems renovated. The sun that has been clouded for three years has regained his splendour . . . 'Tis the jubilee of creation.[9]

Watling thought it unwise to say in the letter how he escaped, but wrote that he was waiting for the convict ship *Pitt* to leave:

> I hold it imprudent to commit to paper how I have obtained emancipation. I will only say, that the ship *Pitt* lies opposite my window, and means to sail by Sunday next; after when, should any other vessel here tend to Europe, if possible, I will procure a passage—and be happy.[10]

He was at large for around three months trying to arrange a passage back to England when he was recaptured—having been, he said, 'betrayed by the mercenary Dutch' authorities.[11] He was held in a local prison for seven months and handed over to the next British convict transport the *Royal Admiral*, which arrived in Sydney in September 1792.

In New South Wales, Watling became a prolific painter in the young colony. He had been born in Dumfries in Scotland in 1762 and received a 'better than average' education despite being made an orphan at a young age.[12] He was 29 years old when convicted of forging banknotes and sentenced to fourteen years' transportation. After arriving in Sydney, he was first assigned to work with Chief

Surgeon John White, who was also an enthusiastic naturalist. Watling flourished as a painter and produced a large number of drawings and paintings of the early days of the Sydney colony, including landscapes, natural history and the local Aboriginal people. More than 100 of his works survive.[13]

In 1797 Watling received a pardon from Governor Hunter, himself something of an artist, who greatly admired Watling's work. As a free man Watling managed to arrange a passage to Calcutta, where between 1801 and 1803 he earned a 'precarious living' as a painter of miniatures before returning to Scotland after a fifteen-year absence. In 1806 he was again charged with forgery but the case was dismissed. He lived his final years in 'indigent circumstances' in London and was known to have cancer. It is thought that he died around 1815 aged 53 years old.

Probably the earliest escape from the colony by sea occurred in the first weeks of the Sydney settlement. French-born convict Peter Parris, who had arrived on the First Fleet, walked from Sydney to Botany Bay where the French ships *Boussole* and *Astrolabe* were anchored. According to John White, Parris 'might have been concealed through pity by his countrymen and carried off without the knowledge of the commanding officer'.[14] Parris's freedom would have been short-lived, however, because sometime after leaving Botany Bay the French ships were lost with all crew believed to have perished.

There is evidence that other convicts of the First Fleet also tried to get away with the French. According to White a number of prisoners made the same overland trek as Parris had done, where they were 'met with the most hospitable, polite and friendly reception and treatment'. However, when they offered themselves to the French 'not one of them' was taken aboard and they were forced to return to

Sydney. 'When they came back they were real objects of pity,' White wrote. 'Conscious of the punishment that awaited so imprudent and improper an experiment, they had stayed out as long as the cravings of nature would permit and were nearly half starved.'[15]

The most common escape attempts were as stowaways by sea. In some cases this involved hiding on a ship ready to leave Sydney, often with the help of a sympathetic captain or crew member. From the very early days in the life of the colony Governor Phillip warned the British government that convicts were being helped to get away: 'I enclose a list of those convicts who have absconded . . . and some of them are supposed to have been secreted on board the ships and carried from the settlement.'[16]

Phillip complained that a number of convicts had escaped on the *Neptune* after it left Sydney having delivered many sick and dying convicts to the colony as part of the Second Fleet in 1790. According to Phillip the convicts went into hiding before the ship sailed but a search found only one of them, Joseph Sutton, hidden in the hold. Phillip believed 'there is little doubt that more convicts are concealed on board' that got away undetected and he wanted the ship's master, Donald Trail, prosecuted.[17] Trail was already under investigation for the maltreatment of convicts brought to Sydney on the Second Fleet and would be tried—and acquitted—when he reached England. He was not charged with aiding the escape of convicts.

From the early days of the settlement, thorough searches were made of all ships before they could leave Sydney and convicts were often found secreted below decks. Phillip admitted in a dispatch to England that while every effort was being made the practice 'cannot be prevented by any steps which can be taken at present'.[18] One precaution taken was to post guards aboard ships while they were in Sydney. Also, before they left, the ships were 'smoked' for some hours, which was designed to deny anyone hiding below decks fresh air to breathe—but smoking did not always work.

In 1795 Captain William Wilkinson of the *Indispensable* reported how he became aware of escapees on his ship after he left Sydney. He said that when the ship had reached Sydney in May 1794, he had agreed to a request by Lieutenant Governor Grose to keep a guard on the ship the whole time it was in port. The day before it left the ship was smoked for 'six or seven hours' and they found one convict who was taken ashore. After the ship left with the *Halcyon* and was 'a considerable distance' from shore Wilkinson said one of his officers brought a 'strange man out of his cabin'—it was a convict named Richard Hayes. A short time later, Wilkinson said, Captain Page on the *Halcyon* 'hailed me' to say that he, too, had a stowaway and asked what to do.

They considered turning back but the 'wind being strong off the land it was impossible', so they pressed on with the intention of handing over the escapees to the authorities at the next port. Four days later, another convict named Thomas Scott was discovered. However, when they reached China, Wilkinson said Hayes 'ran from the ship' and Captain Page of the *Halcyon* took Hayes 'up to Canton as a servant', where he was handed over to the British authorities.[19]

In the early days the opportunity for convicts to stow away on ships leaving Sydney was limited by the very small number that came to the colony. After the First Fleet it was to be more than two years before more ships arrived with supplies and more convicts as part of the Second Fleet in 1790. Throughout the 1790s more than 100 ships arrived, averaging around ten a year, mostly bringing more convicts and supplies. But by the end of the eighteenth century many more ships were calling in at Sydney, which created more opportunities for convicts to escape, often with the assistance of a sympathetic captain or ship's crew.

In 1799 Governor John Hunter issued a general order aiming to discourage anyone thinking of escape:

> This public notice is given that none of those concerned in concealing such worthless characters may plead ignorance; that any man belonging to ships who shall be known to have countenanced or assisted convicts in making their escape shall be taken out of the ship, detained, and punished with the utmost severity of the law; and as the most strict and scrupulous search will take place on board for every convict who may be concealed or suffered to remain on board without regular permission, so many of the ship's company shall be taken out and detained for daring to encourage such escape.[20]

From the beginning of the nineteenth century there was an increase in the number of commercial shipping calling in to sell their wares, particularly grog. There was also a big increase in the number of whaling ships using Sydney as a port for repairs and fresh provisions. At the time whale oil was high in demand as a source of lighting in America and Europe. The whalers' expeditions typically lasted two or three years, and they were often pleased to boost their crews when calling in to Sydney.

In 1805 Governor King, believing most whalers were aiding the escape of convicts, introduced a scheme whereby visiting ships had to lodge a security bond that was forfeited if convicts were found in their ships:

> [I]t is becoming necessary to restrain the practice of several vessels carrying the American flag, who having received assistance and relief according to their wants, have with very few exceptions, taken persons from hence who are under sentence of the law . . . who have been secreted on board those ships . . . The master of every ship or vessel, whether English or foreign, before they are allowed any communication

> with the settlement, shall give security [of] £500 . . . not to carry off any person whatsoever without the Governor's certificate.[21]

In 1807 and almost twenty years after the settlement had been established, Governor Bligh complained that convicts were still escaping on ships that were calling in at Sydney:

> Although the practice of merchant ships taking prisoners from the colony is much abated, yet it still exists, when opportunity offers, notwithstanding the masters of the ships are, here, under heavy bonds to prevent it. After the ships have sailed no proof can be got of their taking such convicts away . . . and therefore no punishment can attach to them before they arrive in England.[22]

In the settlement's early days many convicts simply escaped into the surrounding bush. Most prominent among these was 25-year-old John 'Black' Caesar, who became a notorious outlaw in the first decade of the colony.[23] Of unknown African parentage—possibly from Madagascar—he had come to England from the West Indies, where he had been a slave on a sugar plantation. In 1786, having been sentenced in Maidstone, Kent, to seven years' transportation for stealing £12, he sailed on the *Alexander* in the First Fleet.

Caesar was a giant of a man and, according to David Collins, needed more food to survive than he received in his rations: 'His frame was muscular and well calculated for hard labour; but in intellect he did not differ widely from a brute; his appetite was ravenous for he could in one day devour the full rations for two days. To gratify this appetite, he was compelled to steal from others; all of his thefts were directed to that purpose.'[24]

Caesar's lust for food would get him into endless trouble. He was first convicted in the colony for stealing 4 pounds (1.8 kilograms) of bread from the tent of another convict, Richard Partridge, and sentenced to life imprisonment. A few weeks later he made his first escape into the bush. Finding it difficult to survive he spent more than a month living on the outskirts of the settlement, periodically raiding it for food.

In June 1789 he was captured while trying to steal food from the shack of the assistant commissary for stores, Zachariah Clark. He was again tried and this time sentenced to death—but he was spared by Governor Phillip and sent instead in irons to work on the vegetable farm on Garden Island in Sydney Harbour. Later in the year, when he was allowed to work without being chained, Caesar escaped in a stolen canoe with some food, an iron pot and a musket, and he lived again on the periphery of the Sydney settlement, robbing settlers' gardens and stealing from the local Indigenous people. He eventually lost the musket, was wounded by Aboriginal people and finally surrendered to a marine officer at Rose Hill west of Sydney.[25]

At the time Governor Phillip was preparing to send 200 convicts to Norfolk Island and took the opportunity to rid Sydney of the 'troublesome and incorrigible Caesar, on whom he had bestowed a pardon'.[26] But after three years on the island Caesar was allowed back to Sydney and soon absconded once more into the bush from where he plundered the farms and huts on the edge of the settlement. When caught he was again severely flogged but remained defiant, leading Collins to the belief that the lashing was of little value and 'would not make him better'.[27]

A little over a year later Caesar teamed up with some other escaped convicts to form what is believed to have been Australia's first gang of bushrangers. By then Captain John Hunter, who had replaced Phillip as governor, said Black Caesar had become responsible for practically every theft in the colony and on 29 January 1796 offered a reward to anyone who could capture him, dead or alive:

> The many robberies which have lately been committed render it necessary that some steps should be taken to put a stop to a practice so

> destructive of the happiness and comfort of the industrious. And as it is well known that a fellow known as Black Caesar has absented himself for some time past from his work, and has carried with him a musquet, notice is hereby given that whoever shall secure this man Black Caesar and bring him in with his arms shall receive as a reward five gallons of spirits.[28]

On Monday, 15 February 1796, a fortnight after the posting of the reward, Caesar—having been in the colony for eight years, most of them as an outlaw—was shot dead on the Liberty Plains (near current-day Strathfield) by a bounty hunter named John Wimbow.[29] According to a later report, Wimbow and a colleague had managed to track Caesar down before setting an ambush:

> Information was received that Black Caesar had that morning been shot by one Wimbow. This man and another, allured by the reward, had been for some days in quest of him. Finding his haunt, they concealed themselves that night at the edge of a brush which they perceived him enter at dusk. In the morning he came out, when, looking around him and seeing his danger, he presented his musket; but before he could pull the trigger Wimbow fired and shot him. He was taken to the hut of Rose, a settler at Liberty Plains, where he died in a few hours. Thus, ended a man, who certainly, during his life, could never have been estimated at more than one removed above the brute, and who had given more trouble than any other convict in the settlement.[30]

There were also a number of cases where convicts attempted to mutiny—although it was only on the rarest occasions that they got away with an entire ship.[31] One of the most daring early attempts by convicts to seize their transports occurred on the *Albemarle*, part of the Third Fleet, which left England in early 1791.[32] The *Albemarle* had been a French merchant ship captured by the British in the Caribbean in 1779 and converted to a Royal Navy warship. For a short time in 1781, its captain was 23-year-old Horatio Nelson, the future hero of the Battle of Trafalgar. In 1784 the *Albemarle* was sold back into merchant service and became a convict transport in 1791.

The *Albemarle* left Portsmouth on the morning of 27 March with 252 male and six female convicts. Two weeks later, on 9 April, when they were clear of the other convict ships and the English Channel, the attempted mutiny took place:

> A number of convicts were admitted upon deck early for the benefit of fresh air. In a favourite opportunity (when the principal part of the watch was aloft about the rigging) they made an attempt to take the ship from us, having previously prepared themselves overnight for that purpose. They began with knocking down the sentinels and taking their arms from them, which they easily effected, and were actually making their way aft to the cabin, the principal ringleader going to the helm with a cutlass in his hand he had just taken from one of the sentinels to cut down the helmsman and take possession of the wheel.[33]

An account of the event, believed to have been written by the commander of the *Albemarle*, Lieutenant Robert Parry Young, claims he was able to help thwart the uprising:

> But, very fortunate for us all, I was upon deck at the time they began their insurrection, and immediately ran to the cabin for my blunderbuss, met and shot the ringleader in the right shoulder; feeling the smart of the wound, he downed cutlass and run; the others seeing their principal hero flying, immediately followed his example, and flew to the prison room and forehold and left me in possession of the deck.[34]

Young then said that he organised for the arrest of the attempted mutineers, including the ringleaders Owen Lyons and William Sydney:[35]

> I then mustered all hands under arms, and sent a party below to search for those that had secreted themselves; found three of the principals; the first we got up instantly confessed the whole plot, and that the other two were the ringleaders and the original instigators of this horrid scene.[36]

An example was made of the rebels:

> [I]t was unanimously thought proper for the future preservation of the ship and our lives, and to strike terror in the convicts, immediately to hang the two last at the fore-yard-arm; this had the desired effect upon the convicts in general, who immediately sent us a letter confessing all their horrid intentions, and of taking the ship to America.[37]

Over the next few years, uprisings were plotted on a number of ships, but all were ruthlessly crushed by the officers and crew, with the plotters executed or severely flogged.

Most convicts were ignorant of the geography of New South Wales and many thought there were settlements that would grant them sanctuary only a short trek away. As Governor Phillip pointed out in an early dispatch to London: 'Such is their ignorance that some have left the settlement to go to China, which they supposed to be at the distance of only one hundred and fifty miles.'[38]

Occasionally a group of convicts would take some provisions and disappear, only to come back to the settlement starving when their food was exhausted. In 1791, surgeon Peter Cunningham wrote of

21 Irish convicts who set off for China, which they believed was only a short distance and on the other side of a fordable river: '[T]hrough want of sign-posts, or some other essentials, on the way, they became bewildered in the woods and returned to the settlement so squalid and lean that the very crows would have declined the proffer of their carcases.'[39]

Overwhelmingly the convict escapees wanted to go home to Britain but many found their way to countries around the world. Some ended up in India, having escaped on trading ships that the government had chartered from the East India Company to carry convicts to Sydney before sailing to India to pick up cargo and return to England. In 1794 Jacob Nagle, the veteran seaman of the First Fleet who later worked a merchant ship to India, wrote that he met up with two escaped convict women he knew from Sydney, who had set up a high-class brothel in Calcutta:

> I fell in with two ladies that knew me. They had made their escape from Port Jackson. They rejoiced to see me and invited me home. I was astonished to see the grand situation they were in, sedans and chairs at all calls. They treated me handsomely, I suppose that I might keep my tongue to myself, as they keep no company except mates and captains of ships or those that appeared as gentlemen, though sailors when they are all gentlemen. The weather being hot, they must have a sedan with two Negroes to carry them wherever they wish to go and a boy a long side to fan them.[40]

So many convicts were escaping and reaching India that officials of the East India Company wrote in November 1799 to demand that the authorities in Sydney take steps to prevent it because the convicts were a threat to the 'good order of the territory'.[41] The situation worsened with the arrival of a number of convicts on the East India ship *Minerva*. The *Minerva* had sailed from Cork on 24 August 1799 with 191 Irish convicts—165 men and 26 women—reaching Sydney on 11 January the following year. The ship left Sydney in April 1800 bound for Bengal; unknown to the authorities, it carried many escaped prisoners, as the East India Company officials wrote:

> Not having received from your Excellency a reply to that letter, and a considerable number of people who have been convicts having been landed from the *Minerva*, a ship lately arrived from Port Jackson, we presume that our letter had not reached your Excellency before the departure of that ship . . . and we are persuaded that your Excellency will lose no time in taking such measures as you may judge best calculated for preventing the resort to India of [these convicts].[42]

Convicts also escaped from New South Wales by stealing small boats and sailing thousands of kilometres to freedom. One of the most spectacular instances involved a convict woman, her husband and two children, and seven other convict men.

Mary Bryant (nee Broad or Braund) was a 21-year-old who in 1786 was convicted in a Devon court with two other women for highway robbery. They had stolen a silk bonnet and other goods valued at a little more than £11.12s. Mary was sentenced to be hanged, but the sentence was later commuted to seven years' transportation.

Twenty-seven-year-old William Bryant was an experienced fisherman from Cornwall when he was convicted in 1784 for embezzlement. He, too, was sentenced to be hanged before the sentence was commuted to seven years' transportation. He was originally to go to America but the War of Independence prevented him from being sent there, so he languished in the increasingly overcrowded prisons and prison hulks until he was included in the First Fleet to go to New South Wales. By the time he sailed he had served three years of his sentence.

Mary and William were both assigned to the *Charlotte*, one of the First Fleet ships that carried male and female convicts. During the voyage to Sydney, Mary gave birth to a daughter, whom she named Charlotte, after the ship. Since the baby was born in September, a few weeks before the ship reached Cape Town, she had probably become pregnant in December 1786 before she was put aboard the *Charlotte* in Devon.

Mary and William were married in Sydney and in April 1790 Mary gave birth to a second child, whom they named Emanuel. William Bryant became a trusted convict and because of his experience as a fisherman he was put in charge of Governor Phillip's fishing boat.

In 1791 and after more than three years in the convict settlement William Bryant's prison term was almost completed but he was one of many prisoners whose records were not sent to Australia, and so, according to Phillip, could not be released. Another frustration for the Bryants and other convicts was the growing shortage of food in the colony, which led to their 'dread of starving'.[43]

There is some conjecture about how he did it but William managed to secure a single-masted, six-oared boat with a 'lug' sail, a quadrant, a compass and a chart of the east coast of Australia and the Torres Strait. In addition to the nine adults, three-year-old Charlotte and one-year-old Emanuel, the escapees loaded aboard their five-metre boat 100 pounds (45 kilograms) of flour, the same of rice, 14 pounds (6.3 kilograms) of pork and a 10-gallon (38-litre) cask of drinking water.

The seven convict men who accompanied the Bryant family included two who had come out on the First Fleet; the other five had arrived on the Second Fleet. All had been convicted of theft in England of items of small value, including handkerchiefs, a watch, three pigs, two silver spoons, some fish nets and some lead and iron. Of the eleven who escaped, only five would survive and reach England.

The party made their getaway at 10 p.m. on 28 March 1791, sailing down Sydney Harbour and out into the ocean in one of the most remarkable voyages in seafaring history. The little boat was to travel 5000 kilometres over nearly three months along the east coast of Australia and through the Great Barrier Reef, where Captain Cook's *Endeavour* had been badly damaged. Passing through the Torres Strait, they headed for the Dutch-controlled port of Kupang, on the island of Timor, another 2000 kilometres away, following a similar route taken by Captain William Bligh after he was deposed in the mutiny on the *Bounty* a little more than two years earlier.

Shortly after they made their escape, Judge Advocate David Collins claimed Bryant had been assisted by the captain of a Dutch ship that had recently brought supplies to Sydney:

> So soon as it was known in the settlement that Bryant had got out of reach, we learned that Detmer Smith, the master of the *Waaksamheyd*, had sold him a compass and a quadrant, and had furnished him with a chart, together with such information as would assist him in his passage to the northward. On searching Bryant's hut, cavities under the boards were found, where he had secured the compass and such other articles as required concealment: and he had contrived his escape with such address, that although he was well known to be about making an attempt, yet how far he was prepared, as well as the time when he meant to go, remained a secret.[44]

Initially the escapees kept close to the coast, landing where it was possible and eating fish and edible plants. Three hundred and twenty miles (515 kilometres) north of Sydney, roughly off the coast of Port Stephens, the little boat was blown out to sea. For several weeks in heavy rain they were only rarely able to reach the shore and light a fire. When they did so they were frightened of 'being murdered and ate by the savage natives'.[45] According to one of the escapees, James Martin, they were forced on one occasion to hastily return to the open sea, having been threatened by the locals: 'There came natives in vast numbers with spears and shields . . . we . . . made signs to pacify them . . . we fired a musket thinking to frighten them but they took not the least notice.'[46]

When they reached the Torres Strait, they were chased by hostile locals in canoes before they reached the open water and sailed across the Gulf of Carpentaria and into the Timor Sea. On 5 June they reached Kupang after a voyage of almost three months.[47]

Initially they succeeded in masquerading as English travellers shipwrecked on their way to New South Wales and were given clothes and food while they waited for the next passing ship that could take them back towards England.[48] They were treated kindly by the local Dutch governor until he 'happened one day to overhear a conversation among them' and discovered they were escaped convicts.[49] According to James Martin, it was William Bryant who blew their cover:

> We went on shore to the Governor's house where he behaved extremely well to us . . . filled our bellies and clothed double . . . [We] were very happy . . . for two months before Will Bryant had word with his wife, went and informed against himself, wife and children and all of us, which was immediately taken prisoner and was put in the castle.[50]

The convicts were unlucky in that the next English officer to arrive at the port of Kupang was Captain Edward Edwards, the notoriously cruel commander of HMS *Pandora*, which had been sent from England in November 1790 following the arrival of news of the mutiny on the *Bounty*, to hunt down the mutineers. The pursuers had reached Tahiti in 1791 and captured fourteen of the mutineers, whom Edwards ordered be confined in a box on the deck of the *Pandora*. He did not capture the other mutineers who had sailed further to the east with Fletcher Christian, where they sank the *Bounty* and remained undetected on Pitcairn Island.

Returning to England with the captured mutineers the *Pandora* hit the northern end of the Great Barrier Reef in the Torres Strait.

The ship was wrecked and 31 of the crew and four of the convicts drowned, while the others made it to shore. Edwards, pitiless even in this time of crisis, denied the mutineers shelter from the sun in tents, leaving them to suffer sunstroke.

Following the shipwreck Edwards and the surviving crew and convicts embarked on their own epic voyage in three small open boats for some 3000 kilometres, heading westward towards Kupang. They arrived in September 1791 about three months after the Bryants and their fellow escapees, who had been in custody for a month in the local prison.

Edwards clapped the convicts from New South Wales in irons and chartered a Dutch East Indiaman to take them to Batavia along with the captured mutineers and the surviving crew of the *Pandora*. In December they arrived at Batavia, where the convict escapees were imprisoned while Edwards waited for a ship to take them back to England. Shortly before Christmas William Bryant and his infant son Emanuel died in their disease-ridden Batavian gaol.

Captain Edwards then took Mary Bryant, her daughter Charlotte and the other convicts on a chartered Dutch ship, the *Rambang*, to Cape Town.[51] Shortly after leaving Batavia one of the convicts was believed to have drowned when trying to swim to freedom in the Sunda Strait. Two others also died during the voyage, including the navigator, William Morton.[52] At Cape Town, Mary, Charlotte and the remaining convicts were transferred to an English ship, the *Gorgon*, which was on its way back to London with the First Fleet marine detachment from Sydney, having delivered a new marine corps to relieve them. According to James Martin, the surviving convicts were 'well known to all the marine officers which was all glad we had not perished at sea'.[53]

Marine Captain Watkin Tench, on his way home on the *Gorgon*, was impressed by the achievements of the escapees. 'Among them were a fisherman, a carpenter and some competent navigators,' he wrote, 'so little doubt was entertained that a scheme so admirably planned would be adequately executed . . . after the escape of Captain Bligh, which was well known to us, no length of passage or hazard of navigation seemed above human accomplishment.'[54] But on 5 May 1792 Mary Bryant's daughter Charlotte, by now four and a half, died and was buried at sea when the *Gorgon* was off the African coast, only a month away from reaching England.

When the escapees finally reached London their story captured the public imagination. There was considerable public sympathy for them, which led to the eventual pardon of Mary Bryant and the four other survivors in May 1793, although by that time their original sentences had either been served or were nearly expired. Well-known London diarist James Boswell took up Bryant's cause and campaigned for her release. There were rumours that Boswell and the ex-convict were lovers, perhaps fuelled by the fact that he agreed to pay her an annuity of £10. Whatever the truth she eventually went back to live with her family in Cornwall.

Of the freed convicts Samuel Broom (alias John Butcher) immediately enlisted as a volunteer with the New South Wales Corps and returned to the colony that same year. Two years later in 1795, he was granted 25 acres (10.1 hectares) of farming land in Petersham, now one of Sydney's inner-western suburbs.

The stealing of boats as a means of escape continued long after Mary Bryant's adventure. In late 1797 a group of convicts made their getaway in the *Cumberland*, which Governor Hunter described as the colony's 'largest and best boat'. The *Cumberland* was carrying supplies to the Hawkesbury River when a group of convicts hijacked the vessel and 'threatened the life of the coxswain and all who dared to oppose them'.[55] The convicts put the crew ashore and then sailed in the *Cumberland* and a smaller boat 'we know not whither'.[56]

Having no suitable boat left in which to chase the escapees, Hunter 'dispatched two row boats, well-armed'—one along the north coast, where the *Cumberland* was believed to have headed, and the other to the south in pursuit of the smaller boat. The search to the north was led by Lieutenant John Shortland, whose father had been commander of the *Supply* on the First Fleet. Shortland junior did not find the *Cumberland* but he discovered and named the Hunter River, later the site of the city of Newcastle. Shortland also confirmed significant deposits of coal, which had been first noticed by fishermen two years before.

The search boat that went south encountered such rough weather that it was forced to abandon the chase and seek refuge on shore. Hunter thought that of the escapees who had headed south there was 'every reason to believe that the party have perished, as the vessel was very feeble'.[57] However, it seems that at least some of the convicts on this smaller boat survived. The following year George Bass was exploring the south coast in an open boat when he unexpectedly found some escaped convicts:

> On passing a small island laying off the coast he discovered smoke, and supposed it was made by some natives . . . on approaching the shore he found the men were white, and had some clothing on and when he came near he observed two of them take to the water and swim off. They proved to be seven of a gang of fourteen who escaped from hence in a boat on 2 October last . . . and who had been treacherously left on this desolate island by the other seven, who returned northward . . . these poor distressed wretches, who were chiefly Irish, would have endeavoured to have travelled northward and thrown themselves upon His Majesty's mercy, but were not able to get from this miserable island to the mainland.[58]

Bass's little boat was too small to take all the men back to Sydney but he took the two who were in the poorest health. He took all the others over to the mainland and urged them to walk north to Sydney, which was 'not less than five hundred miles' (800 kilometres) to the north. To help them on their long trek he gave them a musket, ammunition, a pocket compass, fishing lines and hooks—but there is no record of any of the men surviving.

So frequent were escape attempts in small boats that Governor Hunter issued a public notice warning convicts of the dangers of fleeing in small, unreliable open boats, which he described as 'pregnant with infinite danger'. Hunter's general order said that too often escapees were unaware that they would be sacrificed by the escape ringleaders to save the few, either by being forced to live on shore, exposed to 'savage people' where 'death is inevitable', or 'thrown overboard to lighten their miserable vessel'. He urged those contemplating escape to 'reflect' on the risk of 'such wicked and ill-judged enterprises'.[59]

One of the most adventurous but ultimately tragic escapes from the penal colony was made by Thomas Muir, one of the five so-called 'Scottish martyrs', men convicted of sedition and sentenced to seven or fourteen years' transportation. They were political radicals who were influenced by the French Revolution and advocated widespread parliamentary and constitutional reforms in Britain. All were well-educated, came from prosperous families and were considered by the British establishment to be traitors not only to their country but also to their class.

Thomas Muir was born in 1765, the son of a wealthy Glasgow merchant, and attended the local grammar school before going to Glasgow and then Edinburgh universities, where he entered the law aged 22 in 1787. He became a strong advocate of political reform, including universal male suffrage and freedom of speech. In December 1792 at a convention of the Scottish Societies of the Friends of the People held in Edinburgh, Muir read an 'inflammatory address' from the United Irishmen of Dublin. This action together with evidence that he had distributed an allegedly seditious pamphlet led to his arrest in 1793.[60] Released on bail he went to France with the bizarre idea of interceding to save Louis XVI who was then awaiting execution. In his absence from Scotland he was struck off as a lawyer and declared an outlaw. In Paris he was able to secure a French passport with the intention of going to America but, landing at Belfast on his way there, he rashly crossed to Scotland to make a clandestine visit to family and friends.[61] He 'was pounced on by the minions of the law' within an hour of arriving.[62]

In August 1793 Muir was tried and convicted for sedition and sentenced to fourteen years' transportation. During his trial the prosecution described his conduct as 'diabolical and mischievous', and described him as 'the pest of Scotland' and a 'demon of sedition' who was 'spinning his filthy web to entrap the unwary'. The judge in the case, Lord Braxfield, told the jury that Muir was 'poisoning the minds of the common people and preparing them for rebellion'.[63]

There was widespread shock at the severity of the sentences given to Muir and his four colleagues as this was the first time a sentence of transportation had been imposed for sedition. Muir was held for the next eight months on a prison hulk on the Thames before being shipped on the *Surprize* to New South Wales with his fellow 'Scottish martyrs', 45-year-old William Skirving, 46-year-old Reverend Thomas Fyshe Palmer and 45-year-old Maurice Margarot. The fifth member of the group, 30-year-old Joseph Gerrald, was sent the following month.

The British wanted the five to be treated just as severely as all other convicts in New South Wales. They were not to be given pardons by the governor, but were to remain prisoners 'until the times for which they have been respectively sentenced are elapsed'.[64] But they were given special treatment when they reached Sydney. In his journal, Judge Advocate David Collins described them as 'gentlemen', who were not expected to live with other convicts in crude wood and branch huts on the west side of Sydney Cove. Instead, 'set apart for each gentleman [was] . . . a brick hut, in a row on the east side of the cove'.[65] They were not expected to work but neither were they entitled to government stores—which was not a problem because they had all brought money with them. They all had servants and bought land. Governor Hunter wrote to a friend in Leith, Scotland, to say he was impressed with the Scotsmen. 'On the whole,' he said, 'I have to say that their general conduct is quiet, decent and orderly; if it continues so, they will not find me disposed to be harsh or distressing to them.'[66]

After sixteen months in the colony, however, Muir made a daring escape. In January 1796 an American sealing ship, the *Otter*, called in at Sydney for repairs and supplies before returning to North America. While the *Otter* was in Sydney, Muir met with its captain, Ebenezer Dorr, who was sympathetic to his plight and agreed to help him escape. The day after the *Otter* left Port Jackson, Muir was rowed out of Sydney Heads in a small boat with two servants. After some difficulty the following day they were spotted by the *Otter*, which was waiting to take them aboard. There are differing accounts of how many other escapees were on board the *Otter* but Captain Dorr later claimed there were 35 when they reached the north-west coast of America—suggesting Dorr was either extremely altruistic or, more likely, well paid for the risk he had taken to help so many escape.

Sailing north-east via the Friendly Islands the *Otter* crossed the Pacific and reached Nootka Sound, on Vancouver Island, four months later, at the end of May 1796. Nootka by then had become a thriving area for the trading of seal hides, and England and Spain were clashing over their respective territorial claims.

Dorr was keen to offload some of his human cargo, claiming he was short of food 'being burdened with thirty-five men stowaways from

New Holland'.[67] No doubt he was also concerned about being caught with Muir and the other escapees on board by the Royal Navy warship HMS *Providence*, which was patrolling the area. Dorr managed to persuade a Spanish gunboat, *Sutil*, which was sailing south to the Spanish port of Monterey (south of current-day San Francisco), to take some of the escapees, including Muir, as extra crew members.

Arriving in Monterey in July 1796 Muir was initially hospitably received by the governor, Don Diego Borica.[68] It was while he was enjoying the hospitality of the Spanish that Muir wrote to the American president, George Washington, seeking permission to come to the United States to work as a legal advocate. But the Spanish confiscated the letters and they were never delivered.[69]

By now Muir had no choice but to go where the Spanish viceroy dictated; he was out of money and 'without clothes, or money, or jewels, or any article which could be worth ten pesos'.[70] Muir was allowed to go by sea to San Blas, and thence by land to Mexico City and Vera Cruz, on the Atlantic side of Mexico, which he reached on 22 October 1796. He was then put onto a Spanish warship bound for Havana, Cuba, where he was imprisoned by the local authorities for four months. His original intention of reaching Philadelphia was now long gone.

In early 1797 Muir was allowed on board the frigate *Ninfa*, sailing for Spain. Four months later in April 1797, the *Ninfa* and another ship, the *Santa Elena*, were intercepted off the coast of Cadiz by two British warships, the *Irresistible* and the *Emerald*. In the fierce sea battle that ensued, the Spanish ships were captured. It was during the battle that a British naval officer described how Muir was badly wounded and lost his left eye: 'One of his eyes was literally carried away, with the bone and lower part of the cheek and the blood about him was deep.'[71]

Believing Muir was dead, the English were about to throw his body overboard 'when he uttered a deep sigh'. The naval officer said nothing to his superiors and Muir was allowed to be taken ashore to a hospital in Cadiz, where he made a slow recovery. Eventually, after the intervention of French foreign minister Charles Maurice de Talleyrand, Muir travelled from Spain to revolutionary France, reaching Bordeaux in November 1797; here the locals 'welcomed, treated and received him as a martyr of liberty'.[72]

In 1798 he finally arrived in Paris where he joined other British exiled radicals and 'enjoyed many of the comforts of civilised life that had so long denied him', provided by his hosts the French revolutionary government.[73] However, by May 1798 'the first flush of his welcome had faded and the problems of money became insistent'.[74] 'Neglected by friends, pursued by poverty and enfeebled by his wounds', Muir drifted into obscurity and died at Chantilly, near Paris, on 26 January 1799. He was 33 years old.[75]

11

The Irish Uprising of 1804

'I am much concerned to inform your Grace that the rumours of a troublesome spirit among the Irish lately sent [to] this colony for sedition (which existed before my arrival here) has lately proceeded to a very great height, and according to much corroborating evidence . . . there is much reason for apprehending that the principal people among them have been irritating the restless dispositions of these people.'

Governor Philip Gidley King

After more than fifteen years of struggle the settlement faced another serious threat to its survival in March 1804, when hundreds of Irish political prisoners in Sydney attempted to overthrow British rule and return to Ireland, where they could continue to fight for an Irish republic.

From the time of the First Fleet there had been Irish prisoners who had been sentenced in courts in England and sent to New South Wales but only two years later in February 1790 it was decided to start 'exporting' convicts directly from Irish gaols.[1] At the time the Irish prisons and hulks were every bit as overcrowded as those in

England—filled beyond capacity and typically with little natural light, fresh air or running water and sanitation.[2] Ultimately, the Irish made up about a quarter of the 160,000 convicts sent by Britain to Australia during more than 75 years of convict transportation between 1788 and 1865.

From the beginning, many Irish convicts were political prisoners who had been part of the growing movement that led to the establishment of the Society of United Irishmen in October 1791. Inspired by the French Revolution and admiring the new democracy of the United States, a number of prominent Irishmen came together in an attempt to unite Protestants, Catholics and dissenters in support of an independent Irish nation. From 1791 until 1800 a total of 850 Irish prisoners (645 male and 205 female) were sent to New South Wales on five ships.[3]

Once in Sydney the Irish felt they were treated with the same suspicion and derision by the British authorities as they had been at home. To many of the colony's officials the Irish were 'religiously regressive, racially inferior and culturally backward'.[4] Prominent among those hostile to the Irish was the colony's leading chaplain and magistrate Samuel Marsden who had first arrived in New South Wales in 1794. It was in his role as magistrate that Marsden developed a fearsome reputation for ordering extreme and excessive punishments, including torture, to extract confessions from suspects. Known as 'the Flogging Parson', he bore a particular hatred for the Irish.

> The number of Catholic convicts is very great in the settlement; and these in general composed of the lowest Class of the Irish Nation, who are the most wild, ignorant and savage Race that were ever favoured with the Light of Civilization: men that have been familiar with robberies, murders and every horrid crime from their Infancy . . . [they are] governed entirely by the Impulse of passion and always alive to rebellion and mischief they are very dangerous members of

> Society . . . They are extremely superstitious, artful and treacherous, which renders it impossible for the most watchful and active Government to discover their real Intentions.[5]

From as early as 1796, the colony's Judge Advocate David Collins claimed many of the Irish arriving in Sydney were 'desperate, and ripe for any scheme from which danger and destruction were likely to ensue'.[6] Later that year Governor Hunter wrote to the Duke of Portland warning that he had evidence that the Irish planned to defy the local authority: 'I have at this moment an information upon oath before me of a very serious nature, and in which the turbulent and worthless characters called Irish Defenders are concerned; they have threatened resistance to all orders but they have not yet carried far their threats; a few of them have been punished . . . I will continue to watch narrowly.'[7] Shortly afterwards, Hunter advised the British government that he was building 'a strong log prison' for 'turbulent and disobedient persons' such as the Irish.[8]

In 1798 Hunter asked Britain not to send so many Irish convicts, as they posed a threat to the security of the settlement. He complained that the arrival of convicts from Ireland also made the earlier Irish convicts from England more difficult to manage:

> I mean to observe my Lord that if so large a proportion of these lawless and turbulent people, the Irish convicts, are sent to this country, it will scarcely be possible to maintain that order so highly essential to our well-being. Those whom we have received from that country within the last year have completely ruined those we had formerly received from England, who, although extremely bad, were by no means equal in infamy and turbulence until mixed with them . . . Permit me my hope, My Lord, that your grace will consider this evil, and, as far as possible, have it corrected by a less proportionate supply of such characters.[9]

Barely a month later Hunter was again complaining to London that the Irish would not work: 'I have to inform your grace that the Irish convicts are become so turbulent, so dissatisfied with their situation here, so extremely insolent, refractory, so troublesome, that, without the most rigid and severe treatment, it is impossible for us to receive any labour whatever from them.'[10]

Rather than a reduction in the number of Irish sent to Australia there was a big increase following the Irish Rebellion of 1798 when rebels rose against British rule in Ireland. Political dissent in Ireland had steadily grown since the Society of United Irishmen had been established. The British initially viewed the movement with suspicion but this quickly evolved into hostility. For several years the authorities cracked down on the movement, infiltrated its ranks and introduced repressive legislation in the Irish parliament, including the 1796 *Insurrection Act*, which prescribed the death penalty for anyone 'administering a seditious oath'.[11]

On the night of 23 May 1798 a planned uprising across Ireland began involving thousands of Irish rebels. After weeks of fighting the Irish suffered a severe setback on 21 June when they were crushed at the Battle of Vinegar Hill in County Wexham, during which hundreds were killed and many of the leaders executed. The battle involved about 13,000 British soldiers and a similar or even larger number of rebels—but the British were better trained, better organised and better armed.

By September the uprising was effectively over. It had been one of the most violent episodes in Irish history, with a death toll on all sides of around 30,000 people.[12] Between May and November the following year over 1000 men were tried under the *Insurrection Act*. Eighty-five per cent of those charged were convicted; about 20 per cent of these were executed and hundreds were transported to New South Wales.[13] Between 1800 and 1806 a further 1196 Irish convicts (1023 male and 173 female) were sent to Sydney.[14] When they arrived in Sydney the rebelliousness continued as many harboured a passionate desire to escape and rejoin the Irish Rebellion.

Philip Gidley King took over the governorship from John Hunter in September and was soon writing to London expressing similar concerns as his predecessor about the threat posed by the Irish convicts to the security of the settlement:

> I am much concerned to inform your Grace that the rumours of a troublesome spirit among the Irish lately sent [to] this colony for sedition (which existed before my arrival here) has lately proceeded to a very great height, and according to much corroborating evidence . . . there is much reason for apprehending that the principal people among them have been irritating the restless dispositions of these people, which has not a little been aggravated by the artifices of [Father] Harold, the priest and several others.[15]

King believed that there were now several hundred 'seditious' Irish convicts in the colony and reported that he had found it necessary to form and arm loyalist organisations for added protection.[16]

Two and a half years later in May 1803, King reported that fifteen Irish convicts at Castle Hill west of Sydney went on a rampage, 'committing every possible enormity, except murder', although they had nearly killed a man when they fired a musket in his face. After four days at large they were all captured and tried, with fourteen being sentenced to death. Governor King commuted twelve of these sentences to life imprisonment but insisted that the two 'most wicked and desperate' be hanged in the first public execution in the colony for over a year.[17]

Also in May 1803, and after having earlier assured London that the Irish appeared to have quietened down, King reported that he had banished a number of them to Norfolk Island on hearing of a planned uprising:

> Notwithstanding what I have stated in my earlier letters [about the Irish] sent here for sedition, and being principally concerned with rebellion in that country, yet I am much concerned the same restless and diabolical spirit still pervades them. It was but very lately some of their leaders very incautiously discovered what their intentions were, of which I had the most corroborating proof.[18]

London was aware of the growing tensions in Sydney and ordered King to take great care: 'The behaviour of the Irish convicts, and particularly those transported for the crime of sedition, show how necessary it is to watch over them with all possible vigilance.'[19]

The uprising that occurred in Sydney in March 1804 was carefully planned and had been in preparation for at least a month. The plot appears to have been formulated by a small group of convicts around Castle Hill. Their security was good—perhaps too good because when the uprising started their liaison with other convict groups turned out to be ineffective so that only a few hundred insurgents joined the rebellion.[20]

At 7 p.m. on Sunday, 4 March, as darkness fell, the signal for the rebellion to begin was given by an Irish convict who set fire to his small hut at Castle Hill, about 8 kilometres north of Parramatta.[21] The plan was that hundreds of mainly Irish convicts from west of Sydney would march and take Parramatta, and then proceed to Sydney, steal a ship and escape back to Ireland. It was hoped that more than 600 convicts at the start of the rebellion would be joined by more than a thousand others when they reached Sydney.

The 'moving spirit' behind the uprising was Phillip Cunningham, one of the most prominent veterans of the Irish rebellion of 1798.[22] Cunningham had been born at Glenn Liath, County Kerry, around 1770. He was not from a position of great social standing, and had worked in the 1790s as a stonemason and publican.[23] He was believed to have been involved in rescuing prisoners and conducting armed raids in Ireland in the lead-up to the Battle of Vinegar Hill in 1798. He first came to the notice of the Irish police when he helped reorganise the United Irish network in the south of Ireland. Based on the evidence of an informer he was charged with sedition at Clonmel in October 1799. On a legal technicality he avoided the death penalty and was transported for life to New South Wales.

In 1800 he was placed aboard the *Anne*, the third transport to carry rebel prisoners to New South Wales in the aftermath of the rebellion. On 29 July when the *Anne* was off the Brazilian coast the prisoners attempted to take control the ship. The mutiny was 'quickly quelled', with the ringleaders shot dead and the others flogged.[24] Cunningham escaped severe punishment for his participation but when he reached Sydney he was sent to Norfolk Island, where the worst offending convicts were sent. However, his skills as a stonemason were in high demand and he was returned to Sydney and assigned to work at Castle Hill, west of Sydney, where he became the overseer of the government stonemasons.

At the start of the 1804 uprising, Cunningham and between 200 and 300 others began breaking into government stores and stealing weapons and ammunition. They were joined by others at Castle Hill, many of whom were 'enthused by rum'. At the beginning, Cunningham gave a speech in which he said they planned to join other convict groups in Toongabbie, Parramatta and the Hawkesbury, and then march and take Sydney with more than 1000 men.[25]

In the first hours of the uprising, the rebels raided homes around Castle Hill and nearby Toongabbie for arms, and as far away as Pennant Hills, 6 kilometres to the east, and Seven Hills, 8 kilometres to the west.[26] At Seven Hills settler William Joyce was pulled from his bed at his farmhouse while the Irish stole his firearms. Able to get to a horse, he galloped 10 kilometres to Parramatta, where he raised the alarm.[27]

By this stage some of the rebels had reached houses near Parramatta but they had not yet attacked the township, which included the barracks and Government House. When Joyce reached town he went straight to Samuel Marsden's house where the cleric and his family were hosting dinner for Elizabeth Macarthur and her children. According to Macarthur, Joyce persuaded them to flee in a small boat on the Parramatta River for Sydney:

> We had a fortunate escape . . . about 5 o'clock when we were sitting at supper our servant burst into the parlour pale and in violent agitation. 'Sir,' says he, looking wildly at Mr Marsden, 'Come with me, and you too Madam,' looking at me. Then half shutting the door he told us that the Croppies had risen, that they were at my Seven Hills farm and that numbers were approaching Parramatta. Mr Marsden, myself and the children repaired to the Barracks. We then learnt that Castle Hill was in flames. The fire was discernible from Parramatta. It was recommended that as many ladies as chose should go to Sydney, as constant intelligence was brought into the Barracks of the near approach of the Irishmen who were expected every minute to enter the Town. The number reported to be 300. Mrs Williamson, Mrs Abbott, Mrs Marsden, myself and all our children took leave of our few friends and about eleven at night departed for Sydney. The Irishmen were at that moment at the Park Gate.[28]

After raising the alarm at Parramatta William Joyce was dispatched to report to Governor King. He reached Sydney at around midnight, where the news was greeted 'with a firing of cannon and the beating of drums'. On hearing the news King headed immediately to Parramatta where he intended taking control of the situation: 'On receiving the information and verbal accounts brought, I considered no time ought to be lost, but hasted immediately to where my information led me as the place where these tumults were going on.'[29]

The same evening in Sydney the colony's senior military officer, William Paterson, called out the guard, including 140 men from the *Calcutta*, which was then in Sydney Harbour, along with members of the Sydney Loyal Association. Also urgently assembled were 56 members of the New South Wales Corps, with Lieutenant William Davies and Quartermaster Sergeant Thomas Laycock, who would play a significant role in the events that followed.

To lead the hastily assembled troops Provost Marshal Thomas Smyth was sent ahead to Annandale to alert Major George Johnston on his family farm, a little more than 5 kilometres from Sydney on the way to Parramatta, which lay a further 22 kilometres west. As it turned out Governor King had already called in and alerted Johnston a short time before as he made for Parramatta.

The Scottish-born Johnston was one of the colony's most experienced officers, having served with distinction in New York, Halifax and the East Indies before going to New South Wales as a 23-year-old lieutenant on the First Fleet in 1788. A 'handsome and popular officer', he jealously protected the honour of the New South Wales Corps; at one point he'd been charged, but not tried, for his involvement in the illegal rum trade.[30] On being told of the convict uprising Johnston swung into action:

> About half past one o'clock on Monday morning . . . I took command of the detachment marched from head-quarters [in Sydney] . . . consisting of two officers, two sergeants and fifty-two rank and file of the New South Wales Corps . . . I proceeded immediately to Parramatta where we arrived at the dawn of day.[31]

Throughout the night the rebels continued raiding farms across a wide area to the west and north of Parramatta but never attacked the town itself. At some point just before dawn and with the failure of more convicts joining the uprising the rebels abandoned their plan to take Parramatta. Instead, they headed on the road to the north-west, towards the Hawkesbury settlement where they hoped more convicts would join their ranks.

The fact that Parramatta was still in loyalist hands when King and then Johnston got there was probably the turning point. As soon as he arrived Johnston secured the perimeter of Government House—where rebels had been seen earlier—and posted sentries. At around 5.30 a.m., according to Johnston, he 'refreshed' his party before heading west in pursuit of the rebels.[32]

At his disposal Johnston had 36 members of the Parramatta Loyal Association, about 50 men from the local reserve militia and his force of New South Wales Corps soldiers. Unsure where the rebels might be he split his force into two, taking his own troops directly to Toongabbie and leaving a subaltern, Davies, with a second force to head west on the more northerly Castle Hill Road.

Meanwhile in Parramatta, on the morning of 5 March, Governor King issued a proclamation of martial law:

> Whereas a number of labouring convicts of Castle Hill and other parts in this district have assembled and in a rebellious and daring manner have attacked and robbed several of His Majesty's peaceable and loyal subjects of property and arms, and proceeded therewith to great acts of outrage . . . I do therefore proclaim the districts of Parramatta, Castle Hill, Toongabbie, Prospect, Seven and Baulkham Hills, Hawkesbury and Nepean to be in a state of rebellion, and do establish martial law throughout those districts.[33]

In his proclamation King also promised: 'If . . . any of them give up the ring leaders to justice it may be an effectual means of procuring them that amnesty it is so much my wish to grant.'[34]

By mid-morning it was becoming clear that the rebels' plans were in disarray. Samuel Humes, who was organised to bring with him around 70 reinforcements, got lost during the night and did not arrive as planned. The rebels' plans were further compromised when James Griffin failed to alert other convicts in the Windsor area that the uprising had begun. As their leaders, Phillip Cunningham and William Johnston, ordered their forces into drill practice, they were unaware that they had lost the advantage of surprise.

When further planned reinforcements failed to appear and with his intentions now well known to the authorities, Cunningham decided against attacking Parramatta and withdrew to Toongabbie to 'reassess strategy' and, he hoped, attract some additional convicts to the cause. As he withdrew to the west he met and recruited a number of convicts heading east from Green Hill (Windsor) and today's Rouse Hill and Kellyville. These men later claimed they had been 'pressed' into the rebel army, which had now grown to around 230 men.

Meanwhile, Major George Johnston rode ahead towards the rebels with a small mounted party while the bulk of his force followed on foot. As he neared Toongabbie, Johnston said he was told that 'the rebels, in number about 400, were on the summit of the hill'.[35] 'I immediately detached a corporal with four privates and about six inhabitants, armed with muskets, to take them in flank,' he later recorded, 'while I proceeded with the rest up the hill, where I found the rebels had marched for the Hawkesbury.'[36]

Johnston rode ahead in pursuit of the rebels, and about 16 kilometres later 'got sight of them'. Showing 'a white handkerchief' Johnston called on the rebels to stop and negotiate:

> I immediately rode forward, attended by the trooper and Mr [James] Dixon, the Roman Catholic priest, calling them to halt, that I wished to speak to them. They desired that I would come into the middle of them, as their captains were there, which I refused,

> observing to them that I was within pistol shot and that it was in their power to kill me, and that their captains must have very little spirit if they would not come forward to speak to me, upon which two persons C [Cunningham] and J [Johnston] advanced towards me as their leaders.[37]

The commander of the redcoats said he told the two rebel leaders that they should surrender and that if they did, he would 'mention them in as favourable terms to the Governor'. The Major said Cunningham rejected this offer, claiming they would 'have death or liberty'.[38] At that point, according to George Johnston, the balance of his troops who had followed on foot arrived. Notwithstanding that he had met the rebels under the flag of truce he took the opportunity of the arrival of reinforcements to arrest Phillip Cunningham and William Johnston: 'Quartermaster Laycock with the detachment just then appearing in sight . . . I clasped my pistol to [Johnston's] head', he later reported, 'whilst a trooper did the same to [Cunningham] and drove them with their swords in their hands . . . to the detachment.'[39]

Cunningham attempted to attack George Johnston but was cut down and seriously wounded by Laycock, who hit him with a sword. The Major said he then ordered his troops to form a line and fire on the rebels. The redcoats were well armed and well organised, and they quickly broke up the Irish:

> The detachment immediately commenced a well-directed fire, which was but weakly returned, for the rebels' line being soon broken they ran in all directions. We pursued them a considerable way, and have no doubt but that many of them fell. We have found 12 killed, six wounded, and have taken 26 prisoners.[40]

Much has since been claimed about the numerical superiority of the rebels over the New South Wales Corps. Johnston reported that the rebels numbered more than 400, when his own force was less than 60.[41] However, after the battle it was confirmed that the rebels had only a few weapons; most carried only wooden staffs or pikes. The official report of 'arms taken from the rebels' included 'twenty-six musquets, one fowling piece, four bayonets on poles, one pitched fork, one pistol, eight reaping hooks, two swords'.[42]

In his official dispatch to London sent a week after the event Governor King painted a vastly more threatening picture of the rebel force:

> The whole number of those who were armed, by plundering the settlers etc., amounted to 333, of which the two parties of 50 men each lost their way and did not join the main body. Had time been allowed them . . . it is certain their force would have been increased to upwards of three hundred more from among Irish labourers of the Hawkesbury, which would have caused much trouble . . .[43]

Now leaderless the rebels returned fire but soon broke and ran. During the battle at least fifteen were killed. Several more convicts were killed or captured by the pursuing troops that night and the following day as they fled towards Windsor. Over the next few days 230 of the rebels were brought in. Governor King's retribution was swift and targeted the leaders, who, he believed, had persuaded the others to follow.

Phillip Cunningham was badly injured but still alive when he was tried under martial law. He was publicly hanged in front of the Commissariat Store at Windsor on 6 March. The rest of the leaders were brought before a judicial panel. William Johnston, who had surrendered to the authorities, pleaded guilty; John Neale admitted he was in the rebel group; Jonathon Place denied all charges; and the rest claimed they had been forced to participate in the rebellion.

William Johnston and Samuel Humes, as leaders of the rebellion, were ordered to be hanged in a public place, and their bodies to be left hanging in chains. Nine of the remaining leaders were flogged with as many as 500 lashes each, and then sent to a new colony at Coal River, near Newcastle, along with 50 other convicts implicated in the rebellion. There, they would work in extremely harsh and oppressive conditions in the coalmines.

Father Dixon, for his perceived part in the rebellion, was made to put his hands on the raw and bloodied backs of the rebels flogged at Sydney, as a macabre reminder of his role in the uprising. Others suspected of involvement were sent into exile to the dreaded Norfolk Island, so as to break up the concentration of the Irish convict population in New South Wales.

Initially the military officers wanted to hang a large number of the captured rebels but this was stopped by Governor King, who feared it would make martyrs of the Irish and provoke vengeful repercussions. The land on which the rebellion was crushed was given as a grant to the loyalist Richard Rouse deliberately to prevent it becoming a significant site for dissident Irish convicts. Thirty-year-old Rouse had arrived as a free settler three years before, in 1801, with his wife and two young children, and had been granted land at north Richmond, on the Hawkesbury River, where he operated a successful farm.

Martial law was eventually lifted on 10 March 1804 but this did not end the insurgency. Irish plots continued to develop, keeping the government and its informers vigilant, and military call-out rehearsals continued over the next three years. Governor King remained convinced that the real drivers of the revolt had kept out of sight and had some suspects sent to Norfolk Island as a preventive measure.

All these suppression measures were effective: after the uprising in 1804 there was no further serious Irish insurrection in the colony.

12

The Military Rise against Governor Bligh

> 'I am called to execute a most painful duty. You are charged by the respectable inhabitants of crimes that render you unfit to exercise the supreme authority another moment in this colony; and in that charge all the officers under my command have joined.'
>
> Major George Johnston

Three years after the Irish uprising, the colony faced another crisis. This time insurrection came not from the convicts but from the officers of the marine corps when they were involved in Australia's only coup d'etat and overthrew the colony's governor.

In August 1806 Philip Gidley King was replaced as governor of New South Wales by William Bligh, a naval captain who was already well known for having survived a mutiny on HMS *Bounty.* Short in stature and possessing a fierce temper, Bligh had a reputation for determination and toughness that was believed to make him just the man to clean up the corruption of the colony of New South Wales.

Bligh was born in Plymouth in 1754, the son of a customs officer. At the age of seven, with the help of family connections he signed on as a captain's servant, which was a common method for young gentlemen to begin their naval careers. At fourteen years of age he became an able seaman and was later promoted to midshipman. In 1776, aged 22, Bligh was appointed sailing master on Captain Cook's *Resolution*, which, along with the *Discovery*, made Cook's fateful last voyage. It was in the third year of the four-year expedition to the Pacific that Bligh witnessed the murder of Cook in Hawaii on 14 February 1779. Bligh and the other survivors of the Cook expedition arrived back in England more than a year later, in October 1780.

After serving with Cook, Bligh was assigned to a number of warships, as England was at war with Spain, the Netherlands and France. When hostilities declined in Europe and North America, he signed off from the navy at half-pay (which was the standard arrangement for navy officers) and with the approval of the Admiralty sailed merchant ships for the next four years.

In 1787 and with the support of Sir Joseph Banks, the now 33-year-old Bligh was given the job as commander of the *Bounty* to sail to the South Pacific to collect samples of the breadfruit that grew there.[1] The breadfruit is a large, round, starchy fruit that Banks and others believed might be cultivated in the West Indies as a cheap source of food for slaves on the sugar plantations there. The English had first been made aware of breadfruit by the pirate explorer William Dampier 100 years before, and later by Captain Cook on his first voyage to the Pacific, in 1768.

Bligh left Spithead on the *Bounty* with a crew of 46 men on 23 December 1787, some seven months after Arthur Phillip departed with the First Fleet. At the time Bligh was leaving England, the First Fleet was rounding Van Diemen's Land. Bligh was trying to reach the Pacific from the east around Cape Horn but, after struggling against strong headwinds for several weeks in early April 1788, he abandoned that route and sailed the other way—around the Cape of Good Hope. The *Bounty* crossed the southern Indian Ocean and reached Adventure Bay in the south of Van Diemen's Land in August, seven months after Arthur Phillip reached Botany Bay.

Bligh did not call in at Sydney but headed north-east to Tahiti, which he reached in October 1788. Over the next five months more than 1000 breadfruit plants were loaded above and below the decks on the *Bounty*, including in the great cabin, which had been converted to serve as a plant nursery. Like the crews of earlier French and English ships that had landed at Tahiti, the men of the *Bounty* enjoyed the beauty of the Tahitian women and their sexual freedom. Before landing there Bligh claimed that medical examinations revealed no venereal disease among his crew but when they left, eighteen—including the master's mate, Fletcher Christian—had to be treated for the infection.

Now loaded with breadfruit the *Bounty* left Tahiti on 5 April 1789 and a little over three weeks later the crew mutinied under the leadership of Christian. Bligh later wrote an account of what happened in a letter to his wife, Betsy:

> On the 28 April at day light in the morning Christian having the morning watch, he with several others came into my Cabin while I was asleep, and seizing me, holding naked bayonets at my breast, tied my hands behind my back, and threatened instant destruction if I uttered a word. I however called loudly for assistance, but the conspiracy was so well laid that the officer's cabin doors were guarded by sentinels, so Nelson, Peckover, Samuels or the Master could not come to me. I was now dragged on deck in my shirt and closely guarded—I demanded of Christian the case of such a violent act, and severely degraded for his villainy but he could only answer—'not a word sir or you are dead.' I dared him to the act and endeavoured to rally someone to a sense of their duty but to no effect.[2]

After the arrest, Bligh said that 'with a tribe of armed ruffians about me' he was forced over the side of his ship into a 7-metre-long cutter with eighteen of the crew who had remained loyal.[3] They were given food, water, a sextant, compass and a map. The boat, designed to carry a maximum of fifteen people over short distances, was so overloaded that the sea water was only inches from the top. Over the next six weeks, 'cast adrift in the open ocean', Bligh managed to steer the tiny boat 6000 kilometres to the Dutch port of Kupang in current-day East Timor.[4] There he bought a small schooner and sailed to the Dutch East India Company capital of Batavia (current-day Jakarta), where he took the next passing ship to the Cape of Good Hope. He reached Portsmouth almost a year after the mutiny on 14 March 1790.

After deposing Bligh and throwing the breadfruit saplings overboard the mutineers sailed the *Bounty* back to Tahiti, where sixteen of the crew decided to leave the ship and settle into what they saw as a wonderful lifestyle. Fletcher Christian and the remaining eight mutineers correctly believed that the English would try to hunt down the mutineers, so they sailed the *Bounty* another 1400 kilometres to the east through unchartered waters to settle on the remote Pitcairn Island. They took with them eighteen Tahitian women and six men and later burned and sank the *Bounty*, which Christian thought might be seen by any British ship sent to search for them.

When news of the mutiny reached England the Royal Navy sent Captain Edward Edwards on the *Pandora* to hunt down the mutineers. Arriving in Tahiti in April 1791 Edwards captured fourteen of the crew (two had died on Tahiti) and imprisoned them on the deck of the *Pandora*. Although four of the prisoners were drowned during the boat's shipwreck on the Great Barrier Reef, the *Pandora*'s crew and the surviving mutineers managed to reach Batavia in small open boats, before eventually reaching England—however, 60 of the original 134 men died on the way. Of the surviving mutineers three were hanged, four were acquitted and three were pardoned but Fletcher Christian and the others on Pitcairn Island were never caught.

When Bligh reached England following the mutiny he was subjected to the normal process of court martial. He suggested the main reason for the uprising was that the seamen did not want to be dragged away from the women and a happier life on Tahiti than they 'could possibly enjoy in England':

> The women . . . are handsome, mild and cheerful . . . possessed of great sensitivity, and have sufficient delicacy to make them admired and beloved . . . it is . . . scarcely possible to have foreseen, that a set of sailors, most of them void of [family] connections, should be led away . . . to such powerful inducements.[5]

After being cleared by the court, Bligh was sent on a second expedition to collect breadfruit, again with the support of Sir Joseph Banks. This time he was given two ships, the *Providence* and the *Assistant*, as well as a marine detachment to ensure the crew was kept in order. On a voyage that lasted two years, Bligh collected and delivered breadfruit that were successfully replanted and grown in the West Indies.

It was after returning to active naval service and seeing action under Lord Nelson at the Battle of Copenhagen against the Danish and Norwegian fleets in 1801 that Bligh was offered the position as governor of the troublesome New South Wales colony.

Yet again it was the influential Sir Joseph Banks who played a critical role in the appointment—as he had done in the choice of both of Bligh's predecessors, John Hunter and Philip Gidley King. With Britain totally preoccupied with war against France it made sense for the government to defer for advice to Banks who by now had had 35 years of experience dealing with New South Wales and had followed its fortunes closely. By the beginning of the nineteenth century he had become the accepted authority on an amazing range of subjects relating to the development of the colony, including its exploration, geography, botany, agriculture and plant diseases. As a result, he was invariably consulted on who should be its governor.

In 1805 Banks had been asked by the colonial secretary the Earl of Camden to recommend a new governor for the colony, a man 'who had integrity unimpeached . . . firm in discipline, civil in deportment and not subject to whimper and whine when severity is wanted to meet emergencies'.[6] Banks had no hesitation in recommending the 51-year-old Bligh, who took the offer of the appointment at the reasonably comfortable £2000 a year and the promise of a pension of £1000 a year. (By way of comparison, an ordinary seaman at the time earned around £12 a year.)

Bligh left England in February 1806 with his 23-year-old daughter Mary and her husband Lieutenant John Putland, whom Bligh had appointed to his staff. Bligh's wife Betsy stayed in England with the couple's other daughters. She was 52 and had an 'extreme horror of the sea', which Bligh thought 'would be her death'.[7]

Bligh's written instructions included the explicit order to clean up the grog trade, which was still largely controlled by the colony's military officers:

> It hath been represented to us that great evils have arisen from the unrestrained importation of spirits into our said settlement from vessels touching there, whereby both the settlers and the convicts have been induced to barter and exchange their livestock and other necessary articles for the said spirits, to their particular loss and detriment, as well as our said settlement at large, we do, therefore strictly enjoin you, on pain of our utmost displeasure, to order and direct that no spirits be landed from any vessel coming to our said settlement without your consent . . . You are to signify to all captains or masters of ships immediately on their arrival.[8]

Arriving in Sydney in August 1806 Bligh was well received by the locals as was Mary, who became the colony's first lady in the absence of her mother. The *Sydney Gazette* reported that the colony was 'extremely happy [that Bligh] is accompanied by his amicable daughter . . . [it is] a circumstance which conveys the greatest pleasure'.[9]

Bligh began his term with some highly questionable land grants involving the outgoing governor Philip Gidley King, from which both their families personally benefited. Shortly after Bligh arrived in Sydney and before King handed over responsibility, King granted Bligh 240 acres (97 hectares) of land near Sydney at Camperdown, 105 acres (42 hectares) near Parramatta and 1000 acres (405 hectares) on the Hawkesbury River. On being sworn in as the new governor, Bligh immediately granted King's wife, Anne, 790 acres (320 hectares) of land, which she tactlessly named 'Thanks'.[10] These were unusually large land grants and it was a poor way to launch a campaign against the corrupt use of public office for private gain that had afflicted the colony for many years.

At the time of Bligh's arrival there were almost 7000 non-Indigenous people living in the colony. Of these around 1400, or 20 per cent, were convicts and 685, or around 10 per cent, were members of the New South Wales Corps. There were 66 civil officers, and the balance of around 4800 people were civilians. Many of these were ex-convicts although some, like John Macarthur, were former members of the military.

After nearly twenty years of settlement the economy was still not very well developed. There was little commerce other than farming, which meant the settlement still relied heavily on regular shipments of supplies from Britain. Manufacturing was limited to the production of a small quantity of coarse linen and sailcloth, some blanketing, a little pottery and the tanning of leather. Bligh said that the colony was now producing more of its own meat requirement but there would be a need 'to have salt meat sent out from England for at least another six years'.[11]

Bligh's opinion of most of the people in the colony was low. He said that the convicts were incapable of reform or rehabilitation and that it would take years for the settlement to be rid of these bad habits:

> It is to be deplored that by far the greater part of the prisoners remain, after their servitude, the same characters as by their vicious habits they have maintained in their career of life, notwithstanding the rewards and blessings offered to them to do well; but the road leading to it being honesty and industry. This melancholy truth has been proved by many of the emancipists and free pardons which have been given . . . if happily they leave off thieving, their habits of cheating and knavery seem to be increased by the giving up of the other vice. Fair and honourable principle they cannot admit . . . not until the next or after generations can be expected any considerable advances to morality and virtue.[12]

His assessment of the marines was also negative:

> As to the military, about 70 of the privates were originally convicts, and the whole are so very much ingrafted with that order of persons as in many instances have had a very evil tendency, as is to be feared may lead to serious consequences, more particularly from their improper connections with the women, by whom they have a number of children, and which lessens the respect due to the virtuous mothers and their families.[13]

Bligh's views of the 160 free settlers, who had come to New South Wales as migrant settlers and not as convicts, were mixed.[14] Some he said had laboured well 'to clear their land' for farming and others had worked 'with honest men' to do their utmost to achieve 'domestic tranquillity'. But many others, he said, were 'still addicted to liquor and disposed to get in to debt'.[15]

The new governor's biggest headache was still the military officers and former military officers—particularly John Macarthur, who by now had become even richer and more powerful. The free settlers were too few in number and had insufficient social weight to counter the power of the officers.

Bligh had been made aware that Macarthur was not universally popular in the colony. Only a month after his arrival in Sydney 137 free settlers wrote to Bligh after they had seen a reference in the *Sydney Gazette* to Macarthur claiming to be their representative. They informed the governor that Macarthur did not represent them. Many settlers felt Macarthur to be a greedy and ruthless businessman and blamed him for withholding the supply of sheep to the market so as to push up prices:

> We proclaim it (in our opinion) to be highly unconstitutional . . . the said John Macarthur taking a liberty that we never would have allowed, nor can or will sanction . . . and that had we denoted anyone, John Macarthur would not have been chosen by us, we considering him an unfit person to step forward . . . as we may chiefly attribute the rise in the price of mutton to his withholding the large flock of wethers he now has to make such price as he may choose to demand.[16]

Bligh was soon in dispute with Macarthur. Five years before Bligh's arrival Macarthur had been sent back to England to face the charges arising from his duel with Paterson. Not only were the charges dropped, but Macarthur also persuaded the British government to make a further massive land grant to him. By the beginning of Bligh's governorship, Macarthur was the colony's biggest farmer, as well as its most successful and richest entrepreneur.

Macarthur claimed that at one stage Bligh had threatened to cancel his land grant, shouting that the colony was under his command: 'What have I to do with your sheep, Sir? What have I to do with your cattle?'[17] When Macarthur protested that he had the grant from the Privy Council and the secretary of state, he alleged that Bligh had angrily replied: 'Damn the Privy Council and damn the Secretary of State, too, he commands at home, I command here.'[18]

According to Macarthur, the governor clashed with him a number of times on a number of issues. Elizabeth Macarthur shared her husband's dislike of Bligh, and wrote in a letter to a friend, Miss Kingdon back in England, that the governor was 'violent', 'rash' and 'tyrannical'.[19]

Increasingly, Bligh was at odds with the powerful military, including its chief, Major George Johnston. After more than a year of growing tension between the colony's two most senior officials Johnston wrote to his superior in London, complaining that Bligh was improperly meddling in the affairs of the New South Wales Corps:

> His interfering in the interior management of the Corps by selecting and ordering both officers and men on various duties without my knowledge, his abusing and confining the soldiers without the smallest provocation, and without ever consulting me as their commanding officer; and again, his casting the most undeserved and opprobrious censure on the Corps at different times in company at Government House.[20]

Others were also privately communicating with London to express their concerns about Bligh. Surgeon John Harris wrote to former governor Philip Gidley King, describing Bligh as 'a tyrannical villain':[21] 'He has been every day getting worse and worse . . . and if some steps are not soon—nay, very soon—taken, the place is ruined. Caligula himself never reigned with more despotic sway.'[22]

Things came to a head in June 1807, when Bligh became aware of the escape from Sydney of the convict John Hoare on the *Parramatta*, one of Macarthur's ships bound for Tahiti. It was alleged that the master of the *Parramatta*, John Glenn, had 'allowed' the escape and in Tahiti helped Hoare to hide on another ship, the *General Wellesley*, bound for India.[23] As a result of this lapse in security Bligh ordered that when the *Parramatta* returned to Sydney the ship be impounded and the bond of £900 be forfeited to the government.

Rather than pay the fine Macarthur declared that he had abandoned the vessel, its contents and crew. At this, the colony's senior judge Richard Atkins called on Macarthur to explain what he was going to do about his impounded ship and crew. Macarthur, who by now was an arch enemy of Atkins, replied that he no longer had any involvement with the ship and the 'summons' had been improperly issued.[24]

Atkins was a poor choice to judge the case and even Bligh acknowledged his incompetence. Several months before the case against Macarthur, Bligh had written to William Windham, the colonial secretary, with a scathing assessment of the judge:

> He has been accustomed to inebriety; he has been the ridicule of the community; sentences of death have been pronounced in moments of intoxication; his determination is weak; his opinion floating and infirm; his knowledge of the law insignificant and subservient to private inclination; and confidential cases of the Crown, where due secrecy is required, he is not to be trusted with.[25]

It was a view widely shared. Surgeon John Harris said that the alcoholic Atkins lived 'worse than a dog' in a squalid dwelling described as 'a perfect pigsty'. Lieutenant Governor William Paterson remarked on 'his character for low debauchery and every degrading vice as well as a total want of every gentlemanly principle'.[26]

Atkins ordered Macarthur to appear before the court on 15 December but Macarthur failed to attend. He was duly arrested and charged then released on bail to appear at the court's next sitting day, 25 January 1808. Again Macarthur refused to appear, claiming in a letter to Bligh that Atkins was unfit to convene the court:

> I have been apprized by a letter from the Judge-Advocate . . . that I am to be brought before a Criminal Court, on Monday, the 25th instant . . . I should . . . be wanting in justice to myself if I neglected to protest against Richard Atkins, being suffered to sit as the judge at the impending trial . . . because that gentleman is deeply interested to gain a verdict against me . . . On this ground . . . I require, as is my legal right, that an impartial judge may be appointed . . .[27]

The new year of 1808 had begun stressfully for Bligh, but he was also facing personal tragedy. His daughter Mary's husband, John Putland, who had been suffering for more than a year from tuberculosis, died on 4 January and was buried in Sydney 'with full military honours'.[28]

The night before the court hearing, the head of the marines, George Johnston, hosted a large dinner in Sydney and invited John Macarthur, his close friend, as a special guest along with a number of other prominent civilians, all of whom shared a dislike for Bligh. The dinner was a powerful gesture of support for Macarthur and a symbol of defiance against Bligh.

The next morning the court hearing began with chief judge Atkins sitting with six other judges, all of them serving officers in the New South Wales Corps. However, the trial could not proceed when the six officers, all of whom supported Macarthur, sent a letter to Bligh saying that they wanted Atkins thrown off the case and a new chief judge appointed:

> We the officers composing the court of Criminal Jurisdiction . . . beg leave to state to your Excellency that a right of challenge . . . has now been demanded by the prisoner now before us to Richard Atkins Esq. sitting as judge on his trial, which we have, after mature and deliberate consideration, agreed to allow as a good and lawful objection. We, therefore, submit to your Excellency to determine on the propriety of appointing another Judge-Advocate to preside on the present trial.[29]

The trial then fell into farce when Atkins withdrew and the other judges released Macarthur on bail. On hearing this news Bligh was enraged and responded in writing the same day rejecting the challenge of the officers. He ordered the Provost Marshal William Gore to rearrest Macarthur the next day. Bligh also summoned Major Johnston to Government House but Johnston said he was unwell at his farm in Annandale having fallen off his horse on the way home from the dinner two nights before. At the same time, the six officers who had made up the court for Macarthur's trial met and reapplied to Bligh to have someone other than Atkins hear the case. Bligh refused and ordered the six to answer for their conduct.

Throughout the day there was an exchange of letters between the six officers and Bligh, but neither side conceded any ground. Meanwhile, Major Johnston—having miraculously recovered from his injuries—arrived back at the Sydney barracks on 26 January and, instead of going to Government House, went to the lockup and ordered the release of Macarthur.

Johnston was given a handwritten letter written by John Macarthur calling for Bligh to be arrested and replaced as governor. The letter was signed by other prominent citizens, including surgeon D'Arcy Wentworth and farmer Gregory Blaxland, who a few years later would become famous for being in the first exploration party to successfully cross the Blue Mountains. The letter had more than 100 signatures, although it has been suggested that many of the locals added theirs *after* Bligh was arrested.[30]

> Sir, the present alarming state of this colony, in which every man's property, liberty, and life is endangered, induces us most earnestly to implore you instantly to place Governor Bligh under an arrest and to assume the command of the colony. We pledge ourselves, at a moment of less agitation, to come forward to support the measure with our fortunes and our lives.[31]

The die was cast. Johnston immediately ordered several hundred of his troops to arms and directed four officers to accompany him to arrest Bligh, who at the time was eating dinner with his daughter and several guests at Government House. When the marines reached the house having marched to the band playing 'The British Grenadiers', Bligh's daughter Mary, 'brandishing her parasol', blocked their path at the front gate.[32] As an eyewitness reported:

> Regardless of her own safety and forgetful of the timidity peculiar to her sex, her extreme anxiety to preserve the life of her beloved father prevailed over every consideration . . . she dared the traitors to stab her in the heart but spare the life of her father. The soldiers themselves, appalled by the greatness of her spirit hesitated and that principle of esteem and respect which is present in the breast of every man . . . deterred them from offering any violence to her.[33]

After taking the governor captive soldiers marched on either side of him, their muskets at the ready. Bligh's clothing was covered with dust, which Mary tried to wipe off, while another soldier, Captain Sims, took his naval sword.

During the arrest, Johnston gave a letter to Bligh that outlined the reasons behind his dismissal: 'I am called to execute a most painful duty. You are charged by the respectable inhabitants of crimes that render you unfit to exercise the supreme authority another moment in this colony; and in that charge all the officers under my command have joined.'[34]

The same evening, Macarthur wrote to his wife to assure her he was safe and no longer in prison but advised that he would not be returning to their Rose Hill home that evening:

> My dearest Love,
> I have been deeply engaged all this day in contending for the liberties of this unhappy colony, and I am happy to say I have succeeded beyond what I expected. I am too much exhausted to attempt giving you particulars; therefore I must refer you to Edward [their son] who knows enough to give you a general idea of what has been done. The tyrant is now, no doubt, gnashing his teeth with vexation at his overthrow. May he often have cause to do the like.[35]

For several days after the coup soldiers and others opposed to Bligh celebrated. Throughout Sydney sheep were roasted, liquor flowed, bonfires were lit and 'musket and canon volleyed in salute' as Bligh was burned in effigy.[36]

Major Johnston took three months to write to the British government and inform it of the coup and the 'incredible circumstances' that had led him to overthrow Bligh. The cause of the delay he told the home secretary was the need to 'prepare and arrange the detail' of the 'connected chain of evidence'.[37] In a long letter to Lord Castlereagh, Johnston claimed John Macarthur was a 'model citizen' and Bligh a danger to the colony:

> Governor Bligh has betrayed the high trust and confidence reposed in him by his sovereign, and acted on a predetermined plan to subvert the laws of his country, to terrify and influence the courts of justice,

> and to bereave those persons to be obnoxious to him for their fortunes, their liberty, and their lives.[38]

Much has been argued about Bligh's immediate reaction to his arrest. Johnston implied that he was hiding in the toilet, and said that four officers carried out a search of the house and he 'was nowhere to be found'—and that after a 'rigid search [he] was in a situation too disgraceful to mention.'[39] Shortly after the arrest a political cartoon showed Bligh being pulled out from under a bed by a red-coated marine. However, there is no solid evidence that he acted in a cowardly manner.

After the coup Bligh was held by the marines under house arrest. In April 1808, Bligh was able to send his own written account of the arrest to Lord Castlereagh in London. The letter was smuggled out of Sydney on a merchant ship, the *Brother*, disguised as a bill of exchange. In Bligh's letter he describes how Johnston staged the arrest with hundreds of infantry and with the guns of the artillery aimed at Government House:

> This rebellious act was done so suddenly that in about five minutes from the first time we knew of it, Government House was surrounded with troops, Major Johnston having brought up in battle array above three hundred men under martial law, loaded with ball to attack and seize my person and a few friends, some of whom were magistrates, that had been at dinner with me. Their colours were spread, and they marched to the tune of 'The British Grenadiers', and, to render the spectacle more terrific to the townspeople, the field artillery on parade was presented against the house where I became arrested.[40]

Bligh added that he believed Macarthur had duped the locals and was the main cause of the coup:

> The archfiend, John Macarthur, so inflamed their minds as to make them dissatisfied with the government, and tricked them in to misfortune, which they now, at too late a period, acknowledge . . . this Macarthur began his career with endeavours to delude the settlers and landholders but who execrated him for the attempt, as they have always done . . .[41]

Bligh reminded the British government that Macarthur had a terrible record going back to the time of the first governor, Arthur Phillip, two decades earlier:

> [Macarthur] stands sufficiently notorious in all the accounts which have been sent to your Lordship's office since the colony began, and whose very breath is sufficient to contaminate a multitude, and who has been a disturber of public society and a venomous serpent to His Majesty's Governors.[42]

Johnston assumed command of the colony using the title of lieutenant governor, and a regime of reprisal followed. Senior Bligh advisers were sacked, including magistrates Robert Campbell and John Palmer and stores commissariat James Williamson, along with Judge Advocate Richard Atkins and the Reverend Henry Fulton, who was suspended as chaplain. In 'malevolent acts of revenge', show trials were staged, which resulted in the sentencing to hard labour of Provost Marshal William Gore and emancipist George Crossley, who had given legal advice to Bligh.[43] Johnston then appointed a raft of military officers and other supporters to fill the vacant public offices. Supporters of the rebels were also rewarded with land grants, trading licences and allotments of convict labourers and servants.

Johnston's most controversial decision was to appoint John Macarthur to the powerful position of colonial secretary. The settlers may have disliked Bligh and there was little protest at his dismissal but they were alarmed at Macarthur's rise in power. Disregarding the risk of reprisal more than twenty settlers wrote to Johnston protesting Macarthur's promotion to such a powerful position in the colony:

> The whole government seems to have been put into the hands of John Macarthur . . . who seems a very improper person, he having been a turbulent and troublesome character, constantly quarrelling with His Majesty's Governors, and other principal officers, from Governor Phillip to Governor Bligh; and we believe him to be the principal agitator and promoter of the present alarming and calamitous state of the colony.[44]

In a subsequent protest letter to Johnston from a number of settlers on the Hawkesbury and Nepean rivers the petitioners accused Macarthur of having 'violated the law, violated public faith, and trampled on the most sacred and constitutional rights of British subjects'.[45]

In July 1808, six months after the coup, control of the colony passed into the hands of Joseph Foveaux, who was senior in rank to Johnston and had recently arrived in Sydney to take up the position of lieutenant governor. 'Astonished' to find Bligh overthrown Foveaux had to decide what to do with the governor, who was still under house arrest at Government House.[46] The 41-year-old bachelor Foveaux was no stranger to New South Wales, or the military control of the settlement. He had first arrived in Sydney as a 25-year-old lieutenant in 1792, and was promoted to captain in 1796. Between 1796 and 1799 he acted as head of the marine corps at a time when officers were making fortunes from trading and their expanding farming properties.

Foveaux took less than two hours to decide not to release Bligh after consulting with Johnston and other senior officers—but not

Bligh. Two months later he wrote to Lord Castlereagh, saying that the people had been so tyrannised by Bligh 'that nothing but his removal from the Government could have prevented an insurrection':

> My mind was fully satisfied of the unavoidable necessity of the measures which had been taken, and that I had no choice left me but to maintain the Government in the way it was resigned into my hands.[47]

Not relishing the awkward situation he found himself in, Foveaux also wrote to Lieutenant Colonel William Paterson in Van Diemen's Land, appealing to him, as the most senior officer in the colony, to return to Sydney and take command. Paterson had now been head of the tiny settlement at Port Dalrymple for almost five years. He was a weak man who had earlier avoided calls from Major George Johnston to return to Sydney but now at last he returned, arriving on New Year's Day 1809.

Paterson offered to release Bligh provided he agreed to leave the colony immediately and return to England. This Bligh initially refused to do, insisting that he was still legally the governor and could only be relieved of office by order of the British government. Then in February 1809 he did agree to the conditions—but on boarding the *Porpoise*, he reneged and claimed that the commitment he made had been extracted by force. Instead, he ordered the *Porpoise* to sail him and his party—which included his daughter Mary—to Hobart Town, hoping for the support of David Collins.

Collins had now been lieutenant governor of Hobart Town for more than five years. At first he treated Bligh courteously but he could only offer him the most modest accommodation. Government House in Hobart was a tiny dwelling, which Bligh described as a 'miserable shell, with three rooms, the walls a brick thick, and neither wind nor water proof, lately built, without conveniences'.

Mary stayed there but, after only a short stay, Bligh decided to return each night to sleep on the *Porpoise*. Bligh said that he also kept away because 53-year-old Collins was living there with seventeen-year-old Margaret Eddington.

Bligh complained to London that Collins had ceased to cooperate with him after receiving an instruction from Paterson in Sydney. '[Collins] acknowledged my authority,' Bligh wrote; 'he was very happy to see me, and we remained on the very best terms a week or a fortnight; when a gazette containing a proclamation was sent down from Colonel Paterson at Head Quarters, proscribing me and my family, and prohibiting all descriptions of persons from having any communication with me.'[48]

For the next ten months Bligh stayed on the *Porpoise* at the mouth of the Derwent River. He stopped all ships approaching Hobart so he could read any messages they were carrying from London and also to restock his own ship with food. Finally in January 1810, almost two years after the coup, he sailed for Sydney when he heard that Lachlan Macquarie was due to arrive as the colony's new governor.

Macquarie arrived in Sydney on 28 December 1809 carrying orders that Bligh was to be reinstated for 24 hours 'to confirm the King's writ', before Macquarie was to assume the governorship for himself and Bligh was to return to England. In the instructions from Lord Castlereagh is the first suggestion that the British government believed that Bligh's conduct contributed to his overthrow:

> Upon your arrival at Port Jackson, I am to signify to you His Majesty's command, that if Captain Bligh be still in the settlement you forthwith liberate him from arrest, and replace him in the government; but at the same time intimate to him that as from the circumstances

> which have taken place, and the number of complaints against him his continuance in the colony might keep alive dissatisfaction, it is His Majesty's pleasure that he do give up the government into your hands immediately and return to England.[49]

Macquarie was also instructed to declare void all the appointments made after Bligh's arrest and to restore all of Bligh's officials to their posts, except for the drunken Judge Advocate Richard Atkins.

Bligh arrived back in Sydney three weeks after Macquarie on 17 January 1810. At first Macquarie offered Bligh 'every respect and attention', but he refused to become involved in arguments about Bligh's overthrow. Macquarie complained in his journal that when Bligh came ashore with his daughter Mary, Macquarie invited them for dinner but they declined. In a letter to his brother, Macquarie was more direct:

> Bligh certainly is a most disagreeable person to have dealings, public or business to transact with; having no regard to his promise or engagements, however sacred, and his natural temper in uncommonly harsh, and tyrannical in the extreme . . . and he is certainly generally detested by high, low, rich and poor, but more specifically by the higher classes of people.[50]

News of Bligh's overthrow had reached London nine months after the event and three months after Major Johnston had handed over power to Foveaux. At the time the British government was preoccupied with war against Napoleonic France and confronted at home with rising prices, falling employment, poverty, strikes and civil disorder. The turmoil in the tiny distant penal settlement of Sydney did not dominate the Westminster political agenda. Nevertheless, the arrest of Bligh was a rare and unacceptable occurrence in the orderly British Empire, where a military insurrection against the civil power established by authority of the Crown constituted an act of treason.

It was not until November 1809—nearly two years after the coup—that Lord Castlereagh received comprehensive legal advice advocating that Johnston be court-martialled,[51] by which time the new governor of New South Wales, Lachlan Macquarie, was already five months into his voyage to Australia.

Having been ordered to do so by the British government, Bligh agreed to return to London in April 1810 for Johnston's trial, which he was eager to do.

The mutiny trial against George Johnston began on 7 May 1811 at Chelsea, where it was charged that he did '[b]egin, excite, cause, and join in a mutiny, by putting himself at the head of the New South Wales Corps . . . seizing and causing to be seized and arrested, and imprisoned and causing to be imprisoned, by means of the aforementioned military force, the person of William Bligh . . . Governor in Chief in and over the territory of New South Wales'.[52]

In a statement defending his decision to sack Bligh, Major Johnston told the court that he feared there would be an insurrection and Bligh would be murdered that night by an angry mob if he did not act: 'I was anxious . . . to prevent a massacre and the plunder and ruin of an infant colony.'[53] He claimed to have acted in the nick of time because the people with the support of the soldiers were on the brink of an uprising:

> The military . . . I am perfectly sure . . . were with the people, and inflamed by the feelings of wrongs and insults affecting them all, they would have before the night was past have joined with them, or at least refused to act against them, while vengeance would have been

> urged to its greatest degree of acrimony, and produced on one side or the other deplorable excesses. If the people, joined by the military, had broken out, terror and devastation would have marked their course, and His Majesty's fine flourishing infant colony would have been reduced to a state of distress and dissolution.[54]

The trial lasted thirteen days and finished on 4 June after evidence had been taken from 42 witnesses. At the end of the evidence the judges took less than an hour to reach a verdict. Johnston was 'guilty of an act of mutiny' but rather than being sentenced to death he was simply 'cashiered'—dismissed from the army. The court acknowledged that the sentence was 'inadequate to the order of the crime' but justified it by referring to the 'novel and extraordinary circumstances, which . . . may have existed during the administration of Gov. Bligh, both as affecting the tranquillity of the colony, and calling for some immediate decision'.[55]

However, it was a military court and most of the judges were, like Johnston, senior army officers—while Bligh was a navy man. The president of the judges was Lieutenant General William Keppel, five of the others were also lieutenant generals, two were major generals and two were lieutenant colonels.

After being dismissed from the army, Johnston, now aged 47, was free to return to Sydney. He owned considerable farmland in the colony, which he had acquired from land grants while still on active service in the New South Wales Corps. For more than a decade he lived a successful and wealthy life as a farmer in Annandale and Bankstown. He died in January 1823 at the age of 58, and was buried in a family vault at Annandale Farm.

John Macarthur had travelled to the trial to defend himself but also to support Johnston. However, he yet again avoided facing court by arguing that as a civilian he could not be charged with mutiny. Earlier the secretary of state for war and the colonies, Lord Castlereagh, had written to Governor Macquarie in Sydney saying that, if Macarthur returned to Sydney, he should be tried before the criminal court in the settlement:

> As Governor Bligh has represented that Mr. Macarthur has been the leading promoter and instigator of mutinous measures . . . you will, if examinations be sown against him . . . have him arrested thereupon and brought to trial before the criminal court of the settlement.[56]

To avoid the risk of being arrested and charged if he went back to the colony, Macarthur remained in England for eight years while his wife Elizabeth managed the family affairs in Sydney. Macarthur was finally given permission to return after protracted negotiations in London and on condition that he should in no way participate in public affairs. In 1817 he returned to Sydney where he successfully presided over the further expansion of his wool-growing empire. In 1825 he was among the first appointed to the colony's new Legislative Council but in 1832 he became mentally ill and was 'pronounced a lunatic'.[57] He died in 1834 and was buried at the family farm at Camden.

Bligh was angry that Macarthur escaped any real punishment. He felt vindicated by the guilty verdict given to George Johnston but 'damned' the court for the leniency of its sentencing.[58] Aged almost 57 at the time of Johnston's trial, Bligh had been due for promotion from senior captain but this had been held back pending the court hearing. Four weeks after Johnston's guilty verdict, Bligh was promoted to rear admiral in the blue, backdated to July 1810—this was the first step towards becoming a full admiral.

When Bligh left Sydney for London, his daughter, Mary, did not return to England with her father for the trial of his usurper. She had been by his side nearly every day for more than four years, from the date he sailed from England in February 1806 until he sailed on the *Hindustan* back to England in May 1810. She had been with him as the colony's first lady when he was governor. She had shared a year of house arrest with him in the small Government House in Sydney—and then more than a year on the *Porpoise* and in the tiny Government House in Hobart. When Bligh was due to return to England after Macquarie arrived to take over as governor she planned to go back with him and had reached the stage of having her luggage stored aboard the *Hindustan*.

Only days before sailing, however, she told her father that she planned to remarry and that she would not be going home with him. In the short time they had been back in Sydney from Hobart the now 27-year-old widow had met and fallen in love with Colonel Maurice Charles O'Connell. The 42-year-old bachelor was in command of Governor Lachlan Macquarie's 73rd Regiment, which had arrived in New South Wales only weeks before the Blighs returned from Hobart.

In a letter Bligh sent to his wife Betsy in London, he explained that he had been taken by surprise and felt he had no say in the matter:

> I at last found what I had least expected—Lt Col O'Connell commanding the 73rd Regiment had, unknown to me, won her affections . . . a few days before I sailed when everything was prepared for her reception, and we had even embarked, he then opened the circumstances to me—I gave him a flat denial for I could not believe it—I retired with her, when I found she had approved of his and given her word to him . . . I could only make the best of it . . . on many proofs of the honour, goodness and high character of Colonel O'Connell and his good sense . . . I did . . . having no alternative, consent to her marriage.[59]

Bligh was never again in active office. He lived in Lambeth and was promoted to the rank of vice admiral in 1814. After the death of his wife in 1812, he moved to Farningham, in Kent, where he died on 7 December 1817, aged 63. His six daughters inherited his estates, which included land granted in the colony of New South Wales that had gained substantially in value.[60]

13

The Father of Australia

'At my first entrance into this colony . . . I certainly did not anticipate any intercourse . . . with men who were, or had been convicts; a short experience showed me, however, that some of the most meritorious men of the few to be found, and who were more capable and most willing to exert themselves in the public service, were men who had been convicts!'

Governor Lachlan Macquarie

It was Governor Lachlan Macquarie who steadied the colony after the turbulent Bligh years, when the legitimate governor of New South Wales had lost control and been driven into exile. It is somewhat ironic that Macquarie would become such a successful governor, because he was only selected for the job as a last-minute replacement for the man originally appointed.

The job as Governor Bligh's replacement had been given to 40-year-old General Sir Miles Nightingall, who had served in the army with distinction in India and the West Indies, and had recently returned from the Peninsular War against Napoleon. However, only a month before the ship sailed for Australia, Nightingall withdrew citing rheumatism that was so crippling he complained he could not even hold a pen to write.[1]

Macquarie had already been given the job as Nightingall's second in command, taking with him his 73rd Regiment of Marines to replace the troublesome New South Wales Corps, which was being recalled after years of controversy and corruption, and its involvement in the overthrow of Bligh.[2] By taking his own regiment with him Macquarie was more fortunate than his predecessors because it made him both the head of the military and governor of the colony. All his predecessors—Phillip, Hunter, King and Bligh—were naval officers who had to deal with an uncooperative and at times outright hostile marine corps that was commanded independently by a senior army officer.

At the time of his appointment Lachlan Macquarie was approaching 50 years of age. After a military career spanning more than 30 years he must have thought himself destined for retirement. The idea that he would serve a record of nearly twelve years as New South Wales governor would have been unthinkable.

Macquarie was born in 1762 on the island of Ulva off the west coast of Scotland, into a landowning family. He joined the army at fourteen, was promoted the following year to ensign, and at nineteen was serving in North America and Jamaica before being posted to India, where he would serve for the next sixteen years.

In 1787, while still in the Indian army, Macquarie was in Egypt and present at the capture of Alexandria and the final expulsion of the French army from the country. In 1793, the 31-year-old married twenty-year-old Jane Jarvis, the daughter of the former chief justice of Antigua, but within a year his new bride was diagnosed with tuberculosis. On medical advice Macquarie took his sick wife on a long sea voyage to China but she died fifteen days after arriving in July 1796. Devastated, he brought her remains back to India where she was buried in Bombay's European cemetery the following January.

After several more years in India during which time he became commander of the regiment Macquarie finally returned home to England in March 1807. Later the same year, and now aged 45, he married for a second time, to 29-year-old Elizabeth Campbell. Macquarie had met Elizabeth ten years earlier and he met her again in 1804 when he was home on leave from India. He was so taken by her that he recorded in his diary at the time that she would make an 'excellent soldier's wife' and it would be a fortunate man who became her husband.[3] Macquarie arrived with his wife and the 73rd Regiment in Sydney on 28 December 1809, after a seven-month voyage on the HMS *Dromedary* via Rio de Janeiro and Cape Town.

A House of Commons report provides an interesting snapshot of the state of the New South Wales colony in March 1810, three months after Macquarie's arrival.[4] After more than twenty years of settlement it had not developed much either economically or socially. The total population was less than 12,000 people. Of these almost 10,500 lived in an area of barely 100 square kilometres around Sydney 'bounded on the north, west and south by a ridge of hills, known by the name Blue Mountains, which no one has yet been able to penetrate'.[5] Most of these people lived in or around Sydney Town (6158). The others lived at Parramatta (1807), the Hawkesbury (2389) and Newcastle (100).

Of those living around Sydney about 5500 or over 50 per cent, were men, a little more than 20 per cent were women, and the rest were children. Around 40 per cent of the people were still being 'victualled' from the public stores. The remainder either fended for themselves by farming or working for pay—or living from crime.

Another 1321 people lived in the two settlements of Dalrymple (later Launceston) and Hobart Town, which were 200 kilometres apart in the north and south of Van Diemen's Land. The only other centre with British settlers was Norfolk Island; a decision had already been made to close it, but there were still 177 people living on the island.

The total area for farming around Sydney stretched for only about 150 kilometres—from Port Stephens in the north to Port Jervis (later known as Jervis Bay) in the south—but half of that land was described as 'absolutely barren'. Only 21,000 acres (or 84 square kilometres) of the available farmland was under cultivation, and 74,000 acres (300 square kilometres) was held in pasture. Much of the most fertile land was around the Hawkesbury River, which was subject to violent and sudden floods.

The total farm livestock included only a little more than 500 horses, 6000 cows, 1700 goats and nearly 9000 pigs. The largest number of animals was 33,000 sheep, which reflected the rapidly growing, but still infant, Australian wool industry.

When Macquarie was sworn into office on 1 January 1810, he carried with him detailed instructions from Lord Castlereagh ordering him to clean up the colony. After revoking most of the actions of the rebel government he organised for Judge Advocate Richard Atkins to be sent back to England and replaced by 37-year-old Ellis Bent, who had arrived with his wife and son on the *Dromedary* with Macquarie.

At a New Year's Day ceremony in front of the lines of the newly arrived regiment, Macquarie made clear His Majesty's 'utmost regret and displeasure on account of the late tumultuous proceedings' and 'mutinous conduct' towards his predecessor Bligh.[6] At the same time Macquarie was careful to avoid becoming involved with the mess of his predecessor or give any public sign of the parlous state of the colony. Nor did he publicly offer any clue to his own view of Bligh. Instead, before Bligh left for England in April 1810 he was given a splendid farewell party, as reported in the *Sydney Gazette*:

> On Monday last a last farewell Fete was given by His Excellency in honour of Commodore Bligh and his daughter, on which occasion a numerous party of ladies and Gentlemen were invited . . . Government House was neatly decorated, and brilliantly lighted; the ballroom hung round with festoons of flowers . . . In the evening a ball was given . . . a handsome firework was also displayed . . . and no circumstance was omitted that could convey an idea of respect entertained by His Excellency for the distinguished person . . . to whom the entertainment had been given.[7]

Macquarie sent his first dispatch to Lord Castlereagh on 30 April, saying he had already sacked all those appointed to jobs when the Bligh government was overthrown and 'reinstated those gentlemen who had been removed'.[8] Macquarie also said that all the land grants 'by the usurped Government have been revoked' and that 'no grants or leases made to any officer of the New South Wales Corps have been renewed'.[9]

He then said he wanted to introduce social reforms 'to improve the morals of the colonists, to encourage marriage, to provide for education, to prohibit the use of spirituous liquors'.[10] To this end he issued a general order: 'I have recommended in the strongest manner to the inhabitants of this colony a strict and regular attendance on Divine worship . . . and the necessity of morality, virtue and temperance.'[11]

Macquarie objected to the 'unlawfulness and immorality of the two sexes cohabitating together in an unmarried state'[12] and issued a public proclamation emphasising the importance of marriage:

> Whereas his Excellency the Governor has seen with great regret the immorality and vice so prevalent among the lower classes of the colony . . . feels himself called upon . . . to check . . . the scandalous and pernicious custom so generally and shamelessly adopted throughout the territory of persons of different sexes cohabiting and

> living together. The consequences of this immoral and illicit intercourse . . . [are] not only highly injurious of the society at large . . . but also . . . the innocent offspring of their conduct.[13]

Reducing the excessive alcohol consumption in New South Wales was another priority for Macquarie. 'The very great and unnecessary number of licenced houses for retailing wines and spirituous liquors,' he wrote, 'have been allowed . . . the most mischievous and bane full effects on the morals and industry of the lower part of the community, and must inevitably end to a profligacy of manners, dissipation, and idleness.'[14]

As well as increasing the duty on alcohol the governor announced that the number of pubs would be cut by more than half to a total of twenty in the town of Sydney, one at the halfway house between Sydney and Parramatta, three in Parramatta, one at the halfway house on the road between Sydney and the Hawkesbury, and six at the Hawkesbury and 'surrounding districts':[15]

> I have reduced the number of licensed public houses in the town of Sydney from seventy-five (the number I found here on my arrival) to twenty and I have made a similar reduction in the same proportion in all the smaller towns and districts in the colony . . . it would be good and sound policy of . . . a high duty of not less than three or four shillings per gallon.[16]

It was in this first long dispatch, which was sent four months after he was sworn in as governor, that Macquarie outlined his extraordinarily liberal view about the possibility for convicts to be rehabilitated. None of his predecessors had ever expressed views like this. All had held the prevailing view that once a convict, always a convict, never to be cleansed of the criminal taint. The view that convicts could become respectable and acceptable members of society would isolate Macquarie from many in the colony and ultimately put him on a collision course with the British government:

> I was very much surprised and concerned, on my arrival here, at the extraordinary and illiberal policy I found had been adopted by all the persons who had proceeded me in office respecting those men who had been sent out to this country of convicts, but who, by long habits of industry and total reformation of manners, had not only become respectable but by many degrees the most useful members of the community. Those people have never been countenanced or received into society.[17]

Macquarie then added, without asking permission, that he would introduce a radically new policy regarding the treatment of ex-convicts:

> I have, nevertheless, taken upon myself to adopt a new line of conduct, conceiving that emancipation, when united with rectitude and long tried good conduct, should lead a man back to that rank in society which he had forfeited, and do away, in as far as the case will admit, all retrospect of former bad conduct. This appears to me to be the greatest inducement that can be held out towards the reformation of the manners of the inhabitants, and I think it consistent with the gracious and humane pretentions of His Majesty and his Ministers in favour of this class of people.[18]

Macquarie assured the British government that he would exercise 'great caution and delicacy', but went on to tell Lord Castlereagh he had already 'admitted to the Governor's table' three men who had been convicts.[19]

One was William Redfern, who had been a 23-year-old ship's surgeon on the *Standard* when the crews of a number of Royal Navy ships mutinied while the fleet was anchored at Nore in the Thames

Estuary in 1797. Redfern had been sentenced to death, which was commuted to transportation for life. In New South Wales he worked as a surgeon on Norfolk Island, where he was pardoned by Governor King in 1803. In 1808 he returned from Norfolk Island to Sydney and continued to work as a surgeon at the Sydney Hospital.

The second was Scottish-born Andrew Thompson, who was nineteen when sentenced to fourteen years' transportation for theft and arrived on the *Pitt* in 1792. After working in the government stores, he was allowed to become a policeman at Toongabbie west of Sydney. He was pardoned in 1798 and quickly rose to the position of chief constable. Over the next ten years he distinguished himself by 'investigating crimes, capturing runaway convicts, acting as intermediary between whites and blacks and rescuing settlers from disastrous floods'.[20] Thompson also became a businessman and ship-builder and one of the colony's richest farmers.

The third, Yorkshire-born Simeon Lord, was also nineteen when sentenced for theft and sent to New South Wales in 1791. Assigned as a servant to a marine captain he was emancipated early and by 1798 had acquired warehouses, which he used for retailing grog and other merchandise with the military.[21] He eventually became one the richest men in the colony as a successful wholesaler, retailer, auctioneer, sealer, pastoralist, timber merchant and manufacturer.[22]

In his first year as governor, Macquarie began to transform Sydney into an orderly town. Sydney's streets had previously been called 'rows', or had odd names such as Sergeant Major's Row, or no names at all. Macquarie named George Street after King George III, who was still alive but too ill to reign, and York, Gloucester, Kent, Clarence, Cumberland and Sussex streets after the royal dukes. He named Pitt Street after the prime minister who had served for over 25 years and died in 1806, and Castlereagh Street after the colonial secretary. He named Phillip, Hunter, King and Bligh streets after former governors, and Macquarie and Elizabeth streets after himself and his wife.

Macquarie also ordered the building of the main road to Parramatta and the main road to South Head, and he named new towns that had sprung up along the Hawkesbury and Nepean rivers to the west of Sydney, including Wilberforce, Pitt Town, Windsor, Castlereagh and Richmond.

The governor faced an almost total absence of public infrastructure at a time when convict numbers were continuing to increase. At the end of his term he listed a total of 265 public works built during his tenure, some of which survive today, including the Mint (1811–16) and the Hyde Park Barracks (1819), both on Macquarie Street, and St James Church (1819–24) close by.

London was highly critical of Macquarie's spending on public works. Early in his term as governor he was told that Britain, financially exhausted by the continuing war against France, could not afford to pay for the convict colony's public buildings. In May 1812 Lord Liverpool pointed out that Governor King in his last year in the colony drew only £13,873 against the British government. In Bligh's first year it had been £31,110. By contrast, Lord Liverpool pointed out, the expenditure by Macquarie in his first year of £72,600 was totally unacceptable:

> I am to repeat to you the positive commands of His Royal Highness that while you remain in charge of the colony of New South Wales you use the most unremitting exertions to reduce the expense at least within its former limits, that you undertake no public buildings or works of any description without having the previous sanction of His Majesty's Government for their construction, or without being enabled to prove most clearly that and satisfactorily that the delay of reference would be productive of serious injury to the public service.[23]

Macquarie's largest and most controversial project was the building of the new Sydney Hospital on Macquarie Street, which, at 95 metres long, 9 metres deep and 12 metres (two storeys) high, was to be the colony's largest building. The money to build the hospital was provided by three merchants who in return were given an exclusive three-and-a-half-year monopoly to sell rum in the colony. It was this arrangement that gave the building its popular name: the 'Rum Hospital'. As well as a rum licence the contractors were given the services of a large number of convict labourers and a number of cattle from the government stores.

By acceding to the terms of this contract Macquarie was guilty of the biggest deal in spirits the colony had known.[24] The arrangement was difficult to understand and impossible to defend. The governor entered the contract only months after receiving specific instructions to strictly prohibit all bartering of spirits—and only months after advising London that he had dramatically cut the number of grog shops in the colony.

All three contractors were shrewd businessmen. The most prominent was 50-year-old D'Arcy Wentworth, the colony's most senior medical officer. Wentworth came from an old and well-to-do Irish family that had fallen on hard times. In 1789 he was twice found not guilty of armed robbery at the Old Bailey and on another charge he was acquitted through lack of evidence. Before the court could consider further charges he took the position of assistant surgeon and headed for New South Wales, arriving in 1790.[25] Over the next twenty years Wentworth became a prominent businessman and member of the colony. He sired a number of children to convict women, starting the Wentworth dynasty that would be a dominant feature of the Australian political landscape for the next century and a half. He had been a major player in the overthrow of William Bligh.

Thirty-three-year-old Garnham Blaxcell had been in the colony for eight years, having arrived as a Royal Navy bursar in 1802 and then been given a number of government posts by Governor King. A close associate of John Macarthur, Blaxcell became successful in a number of businesses, including farms, a windmill, warehouses, hotels and a number of merchant ships.[26]

Thirty-two-year-old Alexander Riley became one of the early free settlers to the colony when in 1809 he followed his two sisters, who had both married officers of the New South Wales Corps.[27] With some generous land grants and a good grasp of commerce he rapidly became one of the colony's richest merchants and pastoralists.

Macquarie's deal with the three contractors enabled them to make enormous profits and they all became very much richer as a result of the deal. They purchased the spirits at around 3 shillings a gallon and sold them at around 40 shillings per gallon.[28] (The only exception to the monopoly was a provision for the government to import its own spirits for 'special purposes' and for the officers and military ration.[29])

Macquarie was a prolific writer of dispatches to England but he could only provide a limp and unconvincing explanation for not having provided earlier advice on this matter. The deal with the three merchants was struck in November 1810 but it took him nearly a year to tell the new colonial secretary, Lord Liverpool, about it on 18 October 1811. Included with the letter was an attractive architectural drawing of the large hospital.

> Previous to the present time I have not had an opportunity of reporting to your lordship that, finding it absolutely necessary to build a general hospital, the old one being in so wretched a state of decay as to threaten a tumbling down, and being also inadequate in size to the increased population of this place, I received proposals for building one by contract, and the terms offered by Messieurs Wentworth, Blaxcell and Riley appearing highly advantageous . . . I have sanctioned a contract [with] . . . those gentlemen for their erecting a

> general hospital at Sydney . . . sufficiently large to accommodate, comfortably, at least two hundred sick persons.[30]

Macquarie included a copy of the contract, the provisions of which must have alarmed the British government.

> On perusal of the contract itself, your Lordship will perceive that a spacious, elegant and indispensable necessary public building will be erected . . . The contractors have engaged to perform the whole work . . . for . . . the exclusive privilege of purchasing spirits . . . to the amount of forty-five thousand gallons at the Government price, no other spirits being permitted within that time to be imported into the colony by private individuals . . .[31]

The government was livid. It had already written to Macquarie, who would not yet have received the letter, ordering him to curtail spending on public works.[32] Its criticism of Macquarie was the most severe ever handed out to a governor of New South Wales. In a scathing letter, Lord Liverpool said that the deal was an embarrassment to the government and should not have been entered into without prior approval.

> Many objections might be urged to an engagement of this nature under any circumstances . . . I am surprised that you did not foresee the embarrassment which would inevitably be occasioned in the execution of this contract . . . It would have been advisable that an engagement of this kind had not been entered into, until you had an opportunity of learning the sentiments of His Majesty's Government.[33]

Macquarie was 'depressed and discouraged' by such a severe reprimand, and wrote back to Lord Liverpool expressing his 'sincere sorrow and mortification'.[34] Macquarie was spared further censure because by the time his apology reached London Lord Liverpool was no longer colonial secretary; he had become prime minister following the assassination of Spencer Perceval in the House of Commons on 11 May 1812. Luckily for Macquarie, Liverpool's successor as colonial secretary was Lord Bathurst, who proved to be 'more equitable and reasonable'.[35] A tragedy in England may have saved Macquarie in Sydney.

In November 1811 Macquarie became the first governor of New South Wales to visit Hobart Town. The governor and his party, which included his wife Elizabeth, left Sydney on 4 November and after nineteen days' sailing and much seasickness reached the Derwent, where they were welcomed by 'cheering crowds and saluting guns'.[36] Macquarie was appalled at what he thought was a run-down and neglected settlement and quickly set about designing the layout of the city, including a major street named after Hobart's founder, David Collins, who had died the previous year. The Macquarie plan remains the outline of the city of Hobart today.

Three kilometres outside Hobart in the district of New Norfolk Macquarie ordered the building of the town named Elizabeth. As he toured of the rest of Van Diemen's Land the governor had no qualms about naming sites and landmarks after himself, as he had done on the mainland, including Macquarie Street, Governor Macquarie's Resting Place, Macquarie River, Macquarie Springs and Macquarie Plains. Macquarie and his party then travelled overland north to Launceston, where the *Lady Nelson* had sailed round to pick them up for the return voyage to Sydney. They celebrated Christmas in Bass Strait where Macquarie recorded that they had 'a good dinner with some drink for the sailors'.[37]

It was in the fourth year of Macquarie's governorship that a way was finally found through the mountains west of Sydney to the great pastoral lands beyond. While the local Aboriginal peoples may have known of ways to cross the mountains, the settlers had generally agreed that they were impassable. The crossing of the 'divide' would lead to the dramatic opening up of farmlands that enabled much of Australia's future agricultural prosperity.

Earlier attempts to cross the range had been thwarted by 'sheer cliffs, deep gorges, thick scrub and river rapids'.[38] In the second year of settlement, in December 1789, officers William Dawes and George Johnston reported that they were 'obliged to relinquish' after finding 'the difficulty of walking excessive' and advancing only 24 kilometres in three days.[39] Three years later, Johnston unsuccessfully tried again in a party that included fellow officer William Paterson. In August 1794 quartermaster Harry Hacking claimed to have gone 32 kilometres further than any other European but he turned back when reaching 'an impossible barrier which seemed fixed to the westward'. In 1796 George Bass tried and then abandoned an attempt, acknowledging 'the impossibility of going beyond those extraordinary ramparts'.[40]

The best of the failed attempts was by French-born Francis Barrallier, whose family were royalists who had escaped France in 1793. Barrallier arrived in Sydney in 1800 with Governor King, who appointed him as an ensign in the New South Wales Corps and employed him as an architect.

In 1802 and aged 29, Barrallier made his attempt at crossing the mountains. Leaving Prospect in western Sydney on 5 November with four soldiers and five convicts he established a base camp at Nattai on the Nepean River, where they would twice return to replenish their provisions. Barrallier penetrated 161 kilometres into the mountains, much further than any earlier European, sighting Byrne's Gap and the Tonalli and Burragorang Valleys, but he was then stopped by a waterfall that seemed impassable. Barrallier decided to turn back as his provisions were running low and his men were becoming despondent. He was very close to the Kanangra Plateau and did not know that a further day's march would have taken him across the main divide between Oberon and the Jenolan Caves.[41]

Other attempts followed, including by botanist George Caley in 1804 who complained later to Sir Joseph Banks that 'the roughness of this country' was 'beyond description'.[42] However, the failure of the Barrallier expedition did much to deter further attempts on the mountains for some years.[43] In November 1805 Governor King reported to London that he thought they would never be crossed:

> I cannot help thinking that persevering in crossing those mountains, which are a confused and barren assemblage of mountains with impassable chasms between, would be as chimera as useless . . . As far as respects the extension of agriculture beyond the first range of mountains, that is an idea that must be given up.[44]

Only the year before the mountains were successfully crossed, the great explorer Matthew Flinders told a House of Commons committee that 'numerous' attempts had failed to penetrate the mountains that existed 'in every direction from Port Jackson'. Flinders also claimed that the 'exceedingly mountainous range' was not fit for agriculture, and that the only land in New South Wales 'capable of being inhabited and cultivated' was 'not more than 50 miles' (80 kilometres) of coastal strip, and only 'half of that was suitable'.[45]

In May 1813 the mountains were finally crossed by three colonists—William Lawson, Gregory Blaxland and William Charles Wentworth—who found a passage through the range.

Thirty-five-year-old Gregory Blaxland was born in Kent to wealthy English landowners and had been encouraged by Sir Joseph Banks to migrate to New South Wales in 1805 with his family. A man with a 'moody personality', Blaxland had a testy relationship with Governor Macquarie—as he'd had with Bligh, and would have with Macquarie's successor, Sir Thomas Brisbane.[46]

At 23 years old, William Charles Wentworth was the youngest of the three explorers. The son of the prominent D'Arcy Wentworth and a convict mother, young Wentworth was sent to England for schooling but returned to Sydney in 1810, keen to explore. Over the next half-century the journalist, politician and author would become a leading figure in the colony of New South Wales, and a successful campaigner for self-government by the Australian colonies.

The third member of the team was 39-year-old William Lawson, who was born in Middlesex, England, to Scottish parents. He had trained as a surveyor before buying a commission in the New South Wales Corps in 1799 and being posted to Norfolk Island. Returning to Sydney in 1806 he rapidly rose in the ranks, acquiring land and becoming a successful farmer.

Blaxland, Wentworth and Lawson, together with four servants, four horses and five dogs, set off from Blaxland's farm on 11 May 1813. The three men were aware of the routes taken by earlier explorers and knew that those who had kept to the ridges rather than the valleys had penetrated the furthest. It took them 21 days to reach the other side. During their epic journey, Wentworth described the awesome nature of the landscape:

> A country of so singular a description could in my opinion only have been produced by some mighty convulsion in nature—Those immense unconnected perpendicular masses of mountain which are to be seen towards its eastern extremity towering above the country around, seem to indicate that the whole of this tract has been formed out of the materials of the primitive mountains of which these masses are the only parts that have withstood the violence of the concussion.[47]

On Monday, 31 May, when they could see the vast open country on the other side of the mountains, Blaxland described in his journal 'all around, forest or grass land', which was 'sufficient in extent . . .

to support the stock of the colony for the next thirty years'.[48] Notably, the route the three men discovered is, with some slight exceptions, the road across the mountains still used today.

Five months after Blaxland, Wentworth and Lawson's find, Macquarie sent government surveyor George Evans to confirm the route through the mountains, and to find the best place for settlement and farming on the other side.[49] Evans's party left Sydney on 20 November 1813 and was away 49 days before returning on 8 January. Governor Macquarie was then able to announce the discovery and the availability of 'plenty of good farming land, and with various streams of water, in the richest soil' at what was to become Bathurst, on the Lachlan River.[50]

To access the interior, Macquarie commissioned the building of a road from the edge of Sydney to Bathurst. The construction was overseen by 50-year-old former marine lieutenant William Cox, who had come to the colony fourteen years earlier with his wife and six children before being ordered to London in 1807 to answer charges of missing money in the regimental accounts.[51] He seems to have avoided a trial and resigned from the army before returning to Sydney in 1810 to become a successful builder and businessman. From July 1814 and in only six months, with just 30 convict labourers and the protection of eight soldiers, Cox supervised the building of 160 kilometres of road, including six bridges, through the rugged mountains and on to the western plains.

Cox was given the first grant of 2000 acres (809 hectares) of land near Bathurst and the convicts earned their freedom as a reward. Only four months later Governor Macquarie and an official party that included his wife were able to travel in horses and coaches along the length of the road to officially open the new town of Bathurst on 7 May 1815.

The crossing of the Blue Mountains began the opening of the vast Australian inland for farming, and would have great consequences for the Indigenous people of the area. In the first twenty or so years of European settlement the dispossession of traditional hunting lands had been limited to the coastal area around Sydney but after the spread of farming to the west, the savage treatment of Aboriginal people became more widespread. For more than a century the spread of the British settlers led to widespread abductions, rapes and indiscriminate killings of Aboriginal people across the hinterland.

As new farms spread, the Aboriginal people were robbed of their traditional sources of food, and increasingly they raided settlements as their only means of survival. Since the authorities were unable to provide all the frontier territories with order and protection, farmers were left to defend themselves and their newly acquired lands with guns—in much the same way as was occurring at about the same time on the North American frontier.

While an increasing number of humanitarians and missionaries were highlighting the plight of Aboriginal peoples in the colonies, it would be many years before there was any official inquiry into the matter. On 9 February 1836 the House of Commons ordered a select committee be appointed to review the state of affairs with respect to the treatment of indigenous peoples by British subjects throughout the Empire. The committee was to inquire into and propose measures that would secure justice for aboriginal peoples, protect their rights, promote the spread of 'civilisation' among them, and 'lead them to the peaceful and voluntary reception of Christianity'.

The committee published an interim report in 1836, and a final report was presented to the British House of Commons in 1837. While the report did not cause any great changes to British colonisation practices, it provided a devastating assessment of the impact of British colonisation on indigenous peoples.[52]

> Too often, their territory has been usurped, their property seized, their numbers diminished; their character debased; the spread of civilisation impeded, European vices and diseases have been introduced amongst them, and they have been familiarised with the use of our most potent instruments for the subtle and the most violent destruction of human life, viz, brandy and gunpowder.[53]

The report acknowledged that aspects of Britain's program of colonisation were at odds with its claims to be an enlightened country that valued freedom and liberty:

> The injuries we have inflicted, the oppression we have exercised, the cruelties we have committed, the vices we have fostered, the desolation and utter ruin we have caused, stand in strange melancholy contrast with the enlarged generous exertions we have made for the advancement of civil freedom, for the moral and intellectual improvement of mankind, and the furtherance of the sacred truth, which alone can permanently elevate and civilise mankind . . . Every law of humanity and justice has been forgotten or discarded. Through successive generations the work of spoliation and death has been carried on . . .[54]

Most damaging was the report's catalogue of evil that had been inflicted on the Australian Aboriginal peoples by the British:

> The inhabitants of New Holland, in their original condition, have been described by travellers as the most degraded of the human race; but it is to be feared that intercourse with Europeans has cast over their original debasement a yet deeper shade of wretchedness . . . from the planting amongst them of our penal settlements . . . very little care has since been taken to protect them from the violence of the contamination of the dregs of our countrymen. The effects have

> consequently been dreadful beyond example, both in the diminution of their numbers and in their demoralisation.[55]

Of all Macquarie's reforms and initiatives, the most controversial—and the one that would ultimately lead to his downfall—was his liberal view about convicts who had completed their sentences or earned pardons.

When Macquarie arrived in the colony convicts who had finished their sentences, or been given 'tickets of leave', were free to work in any endeavour of their choice. However, they were rarely appointed to government posts and were never accepted into higher colonial society. By offering ex-convicts greater opportunity and social acceptance, Macquarie was defying the rigid British class system, which ultimately put him out of step with his London superiors.

Macquarie had not always held such radical views and later explained that he had changed his opinions after arriving in Sydney:

> At my first entrance into this colony, I felt as you do, and I believe I may add, everyone does; at that moment I certainly did not anticipate any intercourse but that of control with men who were, or had been convicts; a short experience showed me, however, that some of the most meritorious men of the few to be found, and who were more capable and most willing to exert themselves in the public service, were men who had been convicts! I saw the necessity and justice of adopting a plan on a general basis which had always been partially acted upon towards these people, namely, that of extending to them generally the same consideration and qualifications, which they would have enjoyed from the merits and situations in life, had they never been under the sentence of the Law, and which had been partially or rather individually adopted towards them by my predecessors.[56]

Macquarie's promotion of ex-convicts not only put him at odds with the government in England, but increasingly alienated him from the colony's 'exclusives', who were totally opposed to his appointment of ex-convicts to government posts without regard to their criminal background or social origins. The exclusives were composed of local officials, military and civil officials, and a number of gentlemen squatters. They felt threatened by the prospect of large numbers of ex-convicts becoming full members of society.

The most persistent critic of Macquarie was the Reverend Samuel Marsden, who had already been in the colony sixteen years when the new governor arrived, serving as a magistrate as well as a churchman. Born in Farsley, Yorkshire, in 1765, the son of a blacksmith, Marsden was a man of strong personality and deep religious conviction. After limited schooling, he was apprenticed to his father, and by adulthood was said to have developed the 'ox-like features' of many blacksmiths.[57] Young Samuel developed a strong interest in religion and, under the guidance of Christian and social reformer William Wilberforce, attended the University of Cambridge before becoming ordained.

Marsden was 29 when he arrived in the colony with his wife Elizabeth on 10 March 1794 as assistant to the colony's chaplain, Richard Johnson. When Johnson returned to England in 1802 Marsden became the senior clergyman in the colony. By then he had also become a rich and successful sheep, cattle and pig farmer, which brought financial security for his large family of six children, as well as a raised social status and power he could not have aspired to in England. He had become so successful at farming that Governor Philip King described him as 'the best practical farmer in the colony'.[58]

Marsden's first serious clash with Macquarie came within a few months of the Macquaries' arrival, in early 1810. Marsden was alarmed to read in the *Sydney Gazette* that he had been appointed by Macquarie to become a director of the new toll road to Parramatta and that two of his co-directors were ex-convicts. Marsden later wrote of his opposition to Macquarie's policy of promoting former convicts: 'To unite the free and convict populations [was to] raise one class and lower another, and to bring bond and free to a common level.'[59]

In 1814 Marsden found himself again at odds with Macquarie when the governor issued an order that magistrates should refrain from excessive flogging: 'The governor recommends in the strongest manner to the magistrates, to inflict corporal punishment as seldom as possible, but to substitute in its stead confinement to the stock for petty crimes, and either solitary confinement or hard labour in gaol gang, according to their judgement of the degree of the offence, still keeping in view the conduct and character of the delinquents.'[60] Macquarie further upset Marsden by insisting that no magistrate sitting alone could inflict more than 50 lashes. Marsden regularly ordered several hundred lashes.

The hostility between the two men continued for several years. By 1817 Macquarie had come to believe that Marsden was sending reports back to London criticising the colony's administration and wrote to Lord Bathurst to complain:

> Although the author of these gross calumnies is withheld, I have good reason to suppose it proceeded from the pen of the Reverend Samuel Marsden, as I firmly believe he is the only person, in the character of a gentleman in the whole of the colony, capable of writing and making such unfounded and malicious representations with a view to injure me in the opinion of His Majesty's Ministers.[61]

On 8 January 1818, Macquarie summoned Marsden to Government House and in front of witnesses presented him with a letter accusing him of disloyalty and undermining the governor's reputation in England:

> I have long known, Mr Marsden, that you are a secret enemy of mine and as long as you continue only a secret one, I despised too

> much your malicious attempts to injure my character to take any notice of your treacherous conduct, but now you have thrown off your mask, and have openly and publicly manifested your hostile and factious disposition towards me I can no longer . . . pass over unnoticed, [your] recent most daring act of insolence, and insubordination, of which you have been guilty.[62]

Undeterred, Marsden and other exclusives continued to complain to London about Macquarie's liberal attitude towards convicts.

Like most of the governors before him Macquarie's noble ideas were undermined by the harsh reality of constant opposition. Eventually the British government was convinced that there was a problem in the colony and decided to conduct an inquiry. The man chosen to travel to Australia and undertake the task was 32-year-old judge John Thomas Bigge. Not only was Macquarie criticised for being too autocratic, it was also widely believed that his humanitarianism had gone too far—that among the criminal classes it was held that being sent as a convict to New South Wales was preferable to being unemployed in England.[63] Before Bigge left England Lord Bathurst made it clear to him that the primary purpose of the convict colony was to impose severe punishment and terror as a deterrent:

> You will . . . constantly bear in mind that transportation to New South Wales is intended as a severe punishment . . . and as such must be rendered an object of real terror to all classes of the community . . . if . . . by ill-considered compassion for convicts, or from what might . . . be considered a laudable desire to lessen their sufferings, the situation in New South Wales be divested of all salutary terror, transportation cannot operate as an effectual example on the community at large, and as a proper punishment for those crimes . . . against . . . which His Majesty's subjects have a right to claim protection.[64]

Bigge arrived in Sydney on 26 September 1819, took thousands of pages of evidence in New South Wales and Van Diemen's Land, and then returned to England in 1821. In his three reports he made it clear that he was largely in agreement with the complaints of the exclusives criticising Macquarie's emancipist policy and his public works program.

Macquarie had tried to resign a year before Bigge was appointed. In December 1817 he had qualified for the pension he had been promised if he completed eight years as governor, and he offered his resignation the following month. At first it was not accepted but after repeated requests and some major differences with Bigge, who was then in the process of preparing his reports, Macquarie finally received notice from Lord Bathurst on 31 January 1820 that his resignation had been accepted.

At the beginning of 1821 and after eleven years in the job, Macquarie began preparing to return to Britain but he had to wait until June to discover who his replacement would be. The man chosen was Sir Thomas Brisbane, who had been recommended by the Duke of Wellington, with whom Brisbane had been in service.

Despite the disapproval of sections of Sydney society and from London, Macquarie and his family were widely liked in New South Wales. They were given a splendid farewell on 12 March 1822 when they finally left Sydney on the *Surry* to sail to London.

Arriving in England on 5 July 1822, for much of the next year the family undertook a grand tour of France, Italy and Switzerland. The following year, while in London defending himself against Bigge's charges, Macquarie had a recurrence of a bowel illness that had troubled him since his army service in India. He died in his London lodgings on 1 July 1824, with Elizabeth at his side.

Macquarie's reputation continued to grow after his death, especially among emancipists and their dependents who had become the majority of the Australian population. Macquarie is still recognised for his public building and town-planning programs, and for establishing some solid infrastructure for the colony.

Lachlan Macquarie was also responsible for the official adoption of the name 'Australia'. Matthew Flinders had wanted to use this name rather than 'Terra Australis', but he did not have enough influence to persuade the British authorities. Flinders' chart, which included a reference to the name 'Australia', was not published until 1814, and copies did not reach Macquarie in Sydney until 1817. On 21 December 1817 Macquarie first used the name 'Australia' in an official dispatch to the British under-secretary for war and the colonies, Henry Goulburn. Gradually the appellation replaced 'Terra Australis' and in 1824 the name 'Australia' became official when the Lords of the Admiralty used it on their maps.

Today Macquarie is regarded as the most enlightened and progressive of all the early colonial governors, the man responsible for ending the colony's decades of struggle for survival and for transforming Australia from a prison camp to a fledgling nation. His grave in Mull, Scotland, is inscribed with the words 'The Father of Australia'.

When Macquarie left Sydney to return to Scotland the colony was a little more than 30 years old. In the early decades it had battled against the odds and had encountered almost every conceivable challenge, including prolonged shortages, near starvation, the threat of foreign invasion, a corrupt and exploitative military, a convict uprising and the overthrow of its government.

But after a struggling start its future now looked more secure. In a little over a decade during the Macquarie era its population increased almost four-fold to nearly forty thousand. During the next quarter of a century it grew to four hundred thousand as more and more settlers came to seek the opportunities at what would eventually become the prosperous new country of Australia.

ACKNOWLEDGEMENTS

In addition to the array of available historical material for researching and writing about the early decades of colonial Australia, I am yet again especially grateful for the *Historical Records of New South Wales* (HRNSW). First published in 1893, the eight volumes of the HRNSW include copies of many thousands of original documents dating from Captain James Cook's first great voyage in 1768 to 1811. (The later *Historical Records of Australia*, which were published between 1914 and 1925, cover much the same material in the years from 1788 to 1848.) Including more than 6000 pages of primary source material, the HRNSW provides an account of the foundation and progress of the early colony and allows us to follow many of the stories—great and small—in minute detail. The records include copies of the plans for the first convict fleet, instructions to the early governors, all of the governors' dispatches to England, all of the letters sent by the British government, proclamations and orders, official letters, vast amounts of statistics about the early colony, contemporary newspaper and magazine articles, private letters, diaries, journals and even some accounts of convicts.

I would also like to thank everyone at Allen &Unwin, particularly Richard Walsh, Elizabeth Weiss and Samantha Kent, for her help and guidance. And, as always, I have to thank my dear friend Linda Atkinson, who has for many years helped with research and advice on the books I have written and on a raft of other projects and adventures.

NOTES

Introduction

1 'Trial of Ruth Baldwin, otherwise Bowyer', *The Proceedings of the Old Bailey*, <www.oldbaileyonline.org/browse.jsp?div=t17861025-1>.

Chapter 1

1 G. Menzies, *1421: The year China discovered the world*, London: Bantam, 2003.
2 Letter from Dundas to Phillip, 15 June 1792, *Historical Records of New South Wales* (HRNSW), vol. 1, pt. 2, p. 622.
3 P. Colquhoun, *A Treatise on Police of Metropolitan London*, London: Gillet, 1805, p. 53.
4 Lord Dover (ed.), *Letters of Sir Horace Walpole, Earl of Orford to Sir Horace Mann, British Envoy at the Court of Tuscany*, London: Richard Bentley, 1833, p. 55.
5 L. Radzinowicz, *A History of the English Criminal Law and Its Administration from 1750, Vol. 1*, London: Stevens and Sons, 1948–50, p. 4.
6 Radzinowicz, *A History*, p. 29.
7 J. Hall, *Theft, Law and Society*, Michigan: Little, Brown, 1937, p. 254.
8 Radzinowicz, *A History*, p. 147.
9 B. Field (ed.), *Memoirs of James Hardy Vaux: A Swindler and a Thief. Now Transported to New South Wales for the second time, and for life. Written by himself and signed 18 May 1817.* London: Whittaker, Treacher, and Arnot, 1830, p. 124.
10 The Atheneum; or Spirit of the English Magazines, vol. V, *Memoirs of the First Thirty-Two Years of the Life of James Hardy Vaux, a Swindler and a Pickpocket, now transported to New South Wales for the second time, and for life. Written by*

Himself. London 1819 in 2 Volumes. From the Literary Gazette. Boston: Munroe and Francis, 1819, p. 194.

11 Field (ed.), *Memoirs of James Hardy Vaux*, p. 262.

12 T. Watling, *Letters from an Exile at Botany Bay to his Aunt in Dumfries, 1784*, with an Introduction by George Mackaness, Australia: Review Publications, 1945, p. 23.

13 J. Howard, *The State of Prisons in England and Wales: With preliminary observations, and an account of some foreign prisons and hospitals*, Warrington: William Eyres, 1777, p. 9.

14 Howard, *The State of Prisons*, pp. 8–9.

15 R. Hughes, *The Fatal Shore: The epic of Australia's founding*, New York: Vintage Books, 1986. Refer to *An Act for Punishment of Rogues, Vagabonds and Sturdy Beggars*, 1597. Eliz. 39. p. 40.

16 *Journal of the House of Commons*, Public Records Office, RB F342.4206/1.

17 *Journal of the House of Commons*, Public Records Office, RB F342.4206/1.

18 J. Banks, *The Endeavour Journal of Sir Joseph Banks*, 1 May 1770, Project Gutenberg, <http://gutenberg.net.au/ebooks05/0501141h.html>.

19 Banks, *The Endeavour Journal.*

20 C. de Brosses, *History of Navigation to Southern Lands*, 1756, New York: Da Capo Press, 1967, p. 29

21 Banks, *The Endeavour Journal.*

22 Banks, *The Endeavour Journal.*

23 J. Cook, *The Journal of HMS Endeavour 1768–1771*, Adelaide: Rigby, 1977. See entry for 6 May 1770.

24 Sir John Fortesque (ed.), *The Correspondence of King George III*, London: Macmillan, 1928, vol. 6, p. 415.

25 UK National Archives HO47/3 Pt. 5.

26 *Journal of the House of Commons*, vol. 40, Co 1161, 20 April 1785.

27 Letter from Arden to Sydney, 13 January 1785, HRNSW, vol. 1, pt. 2, p. 10.

28 Sir George Young's Plan, HRNSW, vol. 1, pt. 2, p. 11.

29 M. Clark, *A History of Australia, Vol. 1, From the Earliest Times to the Age of Macquarie*, Melbourne: Melbourne University Press, 1962, p. 67.

30 Clark, *A History of Australia, Vol. 1*, p. 68.

31 Letter from Sydney to Treasury, 18 August 1786, HRNSW, vol. 1, pt. 2, p. 14.

32 Heads of a Plan HRNSW, 18 August 1786, HRNSW, vol. 1, p. 2, p. 30.

33 Heads of a Plan HRNSW, 18 August 1786, HRNSW, vol. 1, p. 2, p. 30.
34 *The Times*, 21 October 1786.

Chapter 2

1 Letter from Howe to Sydney, 3 September 1786, HRNSW, vol. 1, pt. 2, p. 22.
2 L. Becke & W. Jeffery, *Admiral Phillip: The founding of New South Wales*, London: T. Fisher Unwin, 1897, p. 22.
3 *Phillip's Views on the Conduct of the Expedition and the Treatment of Convicts*, HRNSW, vol. 1, pt. 2, p. 50.
4 *Phillip's Views*, HRNSW, vol. 1, pt. 2, p. 50.
5 *Phillip's Views*, HRNSW, vol. 1, pt. 2, p. 52.
6 *Phillip's Views*, HRNSW, vol. 1, pt. 2, p. 52.
7 *Phillip's Views*, HRNSW, vol. 1, pt. 2, p. 53.
8 *Phillip's Views*, HRNSW, vol. 1, pt. 2, p. 53.
9 *Phillip's Views*, HRNSW, vol. 1, pt. 2, p. 53.
10 *Phillip's Views*, HRNSW, vol. 1, pt. 2, p. 53.
11 Letter from Sydney to Treasury, 18 August 1786, HRNSW, vol. 1, pt. 2, p. 14.
12 Letter from Sydney to the Admiralty, 31 August 1786, HRNSW, vol. 1, pt. 2, p. 20.
13 *Report from the Select Committee on Transportation*, House of Commons, July 10 1812, p. 28.
14 P. King, *The Journal of Philip Gidley King, Lieutenant R.N. 1787–1790*, Sydney: Australian Documents Library, 1980, p. 4.
15 C. Bateson, *The Convict Ships*, Glasgow: Brown and Son, 1959, p. 11.
16 King, *The Journal of Philip Gidley King*, p. 5.
17 'Return of the Botany Bay Detachment', 15 April 1787, HRNSW, vol. 1, pt. 2, p. 79.
18 Ordinance Stores, HRNSW, vol. 1, pt. 2, p. 33.
19 A. Frost, *The First Fleet: The real story*, Collingwood: Black Inc., c. 2011, p. 102.
20 Letter from Phillip to Sydney, 15 May 1788.
21 Plan of Transportation, HRNSW, vol. 1, pt. 2, p. 18.
22 Plan of Transportation, HRNSW, vol. 1, pt. 2, p. 18.
23 A. Phillip, *The Voyage of Governor Phillip to Botany Bay with and Account of the Establishment of the Colonies*, London: Stockdale Piccadilly, 1789, pp. 58–60.
24 Plan of Transportation, HRNSW, vol. 1, pt. 2, p. 18.
25 Plan of Transportation, HRNSW, vol. 1, pt. 2, p. 18.

26 Plan of Transportation, HRNSW, vol. 1, pt. 2, p. 18.
27 Phillip's Instructions, 25 April 1787, HRNSW, vol. 1, pt. 2, p. 90.
28 J. Cobley, *The Crimes of the First Fleet Convicts*, Sydney: Angus & Robertson, 1970, p. 85.
29 Cobley, *The Crimes of the First Fleet Convicts*, p. 241.
30 'Elizabeth Haywood', *Convict Records*, <https://convictrecords.com.au/convicts/haywood/elizabeth/57080>.
31 Oliver Twist was first published as a serial between February 1837 and April 1839. The first edition was subtitled *The Parish Boy's Progress.*
32 R. Holden, *Orphans of History: The forgotten children of the First Fleet*, Melbourne: Text Publishing, 2000, p. 73.
33 J. Nicol, *The Life and Adventures of John Nicol, Mariner*, Edinburgh & London: W. Blackwood & T. Cadell, 1822, p. 116.
34 Letter from George Barrington to his wife, March 1791, HRNSW, vol. 2, p. 771.
35 W. Tench, *A Complete Account of the Settlement at Port Jackson, in New South Wales, concluding an Accurate Description of the Situation of the Colony*, London: G. Nicol and J. Sewell, 1793; W. Tench, *A Narrative of the Expedition to Botany Bay: With an Account of New South Wales. Its Productions, Inhabitants, Etc: to which is Subjoined a List of Civil and Military Establishments at Port Jackson*, London: Debrett, 1789 (reprinted by Angus & Robertson, in association with the Royal Australian Historical Society, Sydney, 1961), chapter 1.
36 Frost, *The First Fleet*, p. 54.
37 D.S. Macmillan, 'Robert Ross', *Australian Dictionary of Biography*, <http://adb.anu.edu.au/biography/ross-robert-2608>.
38 D.S. Macmillan, 'Robert Ross', *Australian Dictionary of Biography*, <http://adb.anu.edu.au/biography/ross-robert-2608>.
39 Letter from Ross to Stephens, 9 July 1788, HRNSW, vol. 1, pt. 2, p. 145.
40 Letter from Phillip to Nepean, 18 March 1787, HRNSW, vol. 1, pt. 2, p. 58.
41 Letter from Ross to Stephens, 19 April 1787, HRNSW, vol. 1, pt. 2, p. 78.
42 A. Bowes Smyth, *A Journal of a Voyage from Portsmouth to New South Wales and China—in the Lady Penrhyn, Merchantman—William Cropton Sever, Commander by Arthur Bowes Smyth, Surgeon—1787-1788-1789*, April 1787, <http://archival-classic.sl.nsw.gov.au/_transcript/2017/D36405/a1085.html>.
43 Bowes Smyth, *A Journal of a Voyage*, April 1787.
44 Tench, *A Complete Account of the Settlement at Port Jackson*; Tench, *A Narrative of the Expedition to Botany Bay*, chapter 1.

45 Letter from White to Nepean, 27 February 1787, HRNSW, vol. 1, pt. 2, p. 49.
46 King, *The Journal of Philip Gidley King*, p. 6.
47 J.C. Dann (ed.), *The Nagle Journal: A Diary of the Life of Jacob Nagle, Sailor, from the Year 1775 to 1841*, New York: Weidenfeld & Nicolson, 1988, p. 77.
48 L. Becke & W. Jeffery, *The Naval Pioneers of Australia*, London: John Murray, 1899, pp. 94–5.

Chapter 3

1 Dann (ed.), *The Nagle Journal*, p. 85.
2 Tench, *A Narrative of the Expedition to Botany Bay*, chapter 2.
3 J. White, *Journal of a Voyage to New South Wales*, Piccadilly: J. Debrett, 1790.
4 J. Hunter, *An Historical Journal of the Transactions at Port Jackson and Norfolk Island with the Discoveries which have been made in New South Wales and the Southern Ocean since the Publication of Phillip's Voyage compiled from the official papers, including the Journals of Governors Phillip and King and Lieut. Ball and the Voyages of the first sailing of the Sirius in 1787 to the return of that Ship's Company to England in 1792*, Piccadilly: John Stockdale, 1793, p. 5.
5 R. Clark, *The Journal and Letters of Lieutenant Ralph Clark 1787–1792*, Sydney: Australian Documents Library in association with the Library of Australian History Pty Ltd, University of Sydney, 1981.
6 Dann (ed.), *The Nagle Journal*, p. 86.
7 White, *Journal of a Voyage to New South Wales*, November 1787.
8 White, *Journal of a Voyage to New South Wales*, November 1787.
9 Hunter, *An Historical Journal.*
10 White, *Journal of a Voyage to New South Wales.*
11 Letter from Phillip to Nepean, 5 June 1787, HRNSW, vol. 1, pt. 2, p. 106.
12 Letter from Phillip to Nepean, 2 September 1787, HRNSW, vol. 1, pt. 2, p. 110.
13 White, *Journal of a Voyage to New South Wales.*
14 Clark, *The Journal and Letters of Lieutenant Ralph Clark*, July 1787.
15 White, *Journal of a Voyage to New South Wales.*
16 Clark, *The Journal and Letters of Lieutenant Ralph Clark*, July 1787.
17 White, *Journal of a Voyage to New South Wales.*
18 Clark, *The Journal and Letters of Lieutenant Ralph Clark*, July 1787.
19 Clark, *The Journal and Letters of Lieutenant Ralph Clark*, July 1787.
20 Clark, *The Journal and Letters of Lieutenant Ralph Clark*, July 1787.

21 Clark, *The Journal and Letters of Lieutenant Ralph Clark*, July 1787.
22 Bateson, *The Convict Ships*, p. 107.
23 D. Collins, *An Account of the English Colony of New South Wales, Vol. 1*, London: T. Cadell Jun. and W. Davies, 1798, p. xvii.
24 Phillip, *The Voyage of Governor Phillip to Botany Bay*, p. 28.
25 Collins, *An Account of the English Colony of New South Wales, Vol. 1*, p. xviii.
26 Hunter, *An Historical Journal*, p. 19.
27 Collins, *An Account of the English Colony of New South Wales, Vol. 1*, p. xvi.
28 Dann (ed.), *The Nagle Journal*, p. 89.
29 Collins, *An Account of the English Colony of New South Wales, Vol. 1*, p. xvii.
30 White, *Journal of a Voyage to New South Wales.*
31 White, *Journal of a Voyage to New South Wales.*
32 Bowes Smyth, *A Journal of a Voyage.*
33 White, *Journal of a Voyage to New South Wales.*
34 Letter from Phillip to Nepean, 2 September 1787, HRNSW, vol. 1, pt. 2, p. 113.
35 White, *Journal of a Voyage to New South Wales.*
36 Collins, *An Account of the English Colony of New South Wales, Vol. 1*, p. xxviii.
37 Letter from Phillip to Nepean, 2 September 1787, HRNSW, vol. 1, pt. 2, p. 112.
38 Letter from Phillip to Nepean, 2 September 1787, HRNSW, vol. 1, pt. 2, p. 113.
39 Letter from Ross to Stephens, 10 July 1788, HRNSW, vol. 1, pt. 2, p. 173.
40 White, *Journal of a Voyage to New South Wales.*
41 Letter from Phillip to Nepean, 2 September 1787, HRNSW, vol. 1, pt. 2, p. 113.
42 White, *Journal of a Voyage to New South Wales.*
43 J. Easty, *Journal, November 1786–May 1793.*
44 White, *Journal of a Voyage to New South Wales.*
45 Clark, *The Journal and Letters of Lieutenant Ralph Clark,* August 1787.
46 King, *The Journal of Philip Gidley King*, p. 19.
47 Clark, *The Journal and Letters of Lieutenant Ralph Clark,* August 1787.
48 Phillip, *The Voyage of Governor Phillip to Botany Bay*, p. 18.
49 Bowes Smyth, *A Journal of a Voyage.*
50 White, *Journal of a Voyage to New South Wales.*
51 Collins, *An Account of the English Colony of New South Wales, Vol. 1*, p. xxvi.
52 Letter from Phillip to Stephens, 10 November 1787, HRNSW, vol. 1, pt. 2, p. 118.
53 Letter from Phillip to Stephens, 10 November 1787, HRNSW, vol. 1, pt. 2, p. 118.

54 Letter from Daniel Southwell to his mother, in D. Southwell, *Journal and Letters of Daniel Southwell*, Sydney: Charles Potter, 1893, <http://gutenberg.net.au/ebooks12/1204411h.html>.

55 White, *Journal of a Voyage to New South Wales.*

56 White, *Journal of a Voyage to New South Wales.*

57 C. McDowall, 'Fantastic Flora in Australia—First Fleet to Federation', *The Culture Concept Circle*, 31 May 2014, <www.thecultureconcept.com/fantastic-flora-in-australia-first-fleet-to-federation>.

58 Letter from Worgan to his brother, State Library of New South Wales, <www.sl.nsw.gov.au/collection-items/collection-10-george-bouchier-worgan-letter-written-his-brother-richard-worgan-12>.

59 Letter from Daniel Southwell to his mother, 11 November 1787.

60 T. Dalton & E. Lobbecke, 'Part 4. Day of Destiny. First Fleet—A Graphic Journal', *Weekend Australian*, 23 January 2018.

61 White, *Journal of a Voyage to New South Wales,* November 1787.

62 Collins, *An Account of the English Colony of New South Wales, Vol. 1*, p. lxxxvi.

63 White, *Journal of a Voyage to New South Wales.*

64 White, *Journal of a Voyage to New South Wales.*

65 *Phillip's Views,* HRNSW, vol. 1, pt 2, p. 50.

66 Letter from Phillip to Nepean, 2 March 1787, HRNSW, vol. 1, pt. 2, p. 55.

67 Letter from Sydney to Phillip, 20 April 1787, HRNSW, vol. 1, pt. 2, p. 82.

68 King, *The Journal of Philip Gidley King*, p. 24.

69 King, *The Journal of Philip Gidley King*, p. 27.

70 Easty, *Journal.*

71 King, *The Journal of Philip Gidley King*, p. 29.

72 King, *The Journal of Philip Gidley King.*

73 Hunter, *An Historical Journal*, p. 33.

74 White, *Journal of a Voyage to New South Wales.*

75 Bowes Smyth, *A Journal of a Voyage*, January 1788.

76 J. Scott, *Remarks on a Passage to Botany Bay, 1787–1792*, December 1787.

77 Hunter, *An Historical Journal*, p. 36.

78 Bowes Smyth, *A Journal of a Voyage*, January 1788.

79 Bowes Smyth, *A Journal of a Voyage*, January 1788.

80 Bowes Smyth, *A Journal of a Voyage,* January 1788.

81 King, *The Journal of Philip Gidley King*, p. 32.

Chapter 4

1 King, *The Journal of Philip Gidley King*, p. 32.

2 Letter from Phillip to Sydney, 15 May 1788, HRNSW, vol. 1, pt. 2, p. 123.

3 Tench, *A Complete Account of the Settlement at Port Jackson*; Tench, *A Narrative of the Expedition to Botany Bay*, chapter VIII.

4 Bowes Smyth, *A Journal of a Voyage*, January 1788.

5 Letter from Phillip to Sydney, 15 May 1788, HRNSW, vol. 1, pt. 2, p. 124.

6 Cook named Port Jackson in honour of Sir George Jackson (1725–1827), a member of parliament, the Judge Advocate of the fleet, and a friend and patron. Cook would also name Jackson Head and Jackson Bay on New Zealand's South Island after him.

7 Dann (ed.), *The Nagle Journal*, p. 94.

8 Letter from Phillip to Sydney, 15 May 1788, HRNSW, vol. 1, pt. 2, p. 122.

9 Letter from Phillip to Sydney, 15 May 1788, HRNSW, vol. 1, pt. 2, p. 124.

10 White, *Journal of a Voyage to New South Wales.*

11 Tench, *A Complete Account of the Settlement at Port Jackson*; Tench, *A Narrative of the Expedition to Botany Bay*, chapter VIII.

12 G.B. Worgan, *Journal of a First Fleet Surgeon*, Sydney: Library Council of New South Wales in association with the Library of Australian History, 1978.

13 Worgan, *Journal of a First Fleet Surgeon.*

14 Clark, *The Journal and Letters of Ralph Clark*, January 1788.

15 Clark, *The Journal and Letters of Ralph Clark*, January 1788.

16 Bowes Smyth, *A Journal of a Voyage*, January 1788.

17 Collins, *An Account of the English Colony in New South Wales, Vol. 1,* p. 5.

18 Bowes Smyth, *A Journal of a Voyage*, January 1788.

19 Bowes Smyth, *A Journal of a Voyage*, January 1788.

20 Tench, *A Complete Account of the Settlement at Port Jackson*; Tench, *A Narrative of the Expedition to Botany Bay*, chapter VIII.

21 White, *Journal of a Voyage to New South Wales*, January 1788.

22 Clark, *The Journal and Letters of Ralph Clark*, February 1788.

23 King, *The Journal of Philip Gidley King*, p. 31

24 Letter from Phillip to Nepean, 9 July 1788, HRNSW, vol. 1, pt. 2, p. 152.

25 Worgan, *Journal of a First Fleet Surgeon.*

26 Tench, *A Complete Account of the Settlement at Port Jackson*; Tench, *A Narrative of the Expedition to Botany Bay*, chapter XVII.

27 Letter from Phillip to Sydney, 15 May 1788, HRNSW, vol. 1, pt. 2, p. 127.

28 White, *Journal of a Voyage to New South Wales*, March 1788.
29 Collins, *An Account of the English Colony in New South Wales, Vol. 1*, p. 79.
30 Collins, *An Account of the English Colony in New South Wales, Vol. 1*, p. 14.
31 Memoranda by Convict Davis, Servant to Mr Foster, Superintendent of Convicts, Norfolk Island—1843—Relating principally to Macquarie Harbour, Dixon Library, State Library of NSW, Sydney. DLMS Q168.
32 Collins, *An Account of the English Colony in New South Wales, Vol. 1*, p. 26.
33 Letter from Phillip to Sydney, 15 May 1788, HRNSW, vol. 1, pt. 2, p. 124.
34 White, *Journal of a Voyage to New South Wales*, July 1788.
35 Letter from Phillip to Sydney, 9 July 1788, HRNSW, vol. 1, pt. 2, p. 146.
36 Letter from Phillip to Sydney, 28 September 1788, HRNSW, vol. 1, pt. 2, p. 188.
37 Letter from Phillip to Stephens, 10 July 1788, HRNSW, vol. 1, pt. 2, p. 168.
38 Letter from Phillip to Nepean, 9 July 1788, HRNSW, vol. 1, pt. 2, p. 155.
39 Letter from Ross to Stephens, 10 July 1788, HRNSW, vol. 1, pt. 2, p. 173.
40 Letter from Phillip to Sydney, 28 September 1788, HRNSW, vol. 1, pt. 2, p. 188.
41 Letter from Phillip to Nepean, 28 September 1788, HRNSW, vol. 1, pt. 2, p. 182.
42 Letter from Phillip to Sydney, 28 September 1788, HRNSW, vol. 2, pt. 1, p. 188.
43 J. Hunter, *Journal Kept on Board the Sirius During a Voyage to New South Wales, May 1787–March 1791*, State Library of New South Wales, <http://acms.sl.nsw.gov.au/_transcript/2015/D06318/a1518.html>.
44 Letter from Hunter to Stephens, 3 January 1789, HRNSW, vol. 2, pt. 1, p. 224.
45 Letter from Hunter to Stephens, 3 January 1789, HRNSW, vol. 2, pt. 1, p. 224.
46 Hunter, *An Historic Journal*, p. 101.
47 Dann (ed.), *The Nagle Journal*, p. 102.
48 Letter from Hunter to Stephens, 3 January 1789, HRNSW, vol. 2, pt. 1, p. 224.
49 Dann (ed.), *The Nagle Journal*, p. 112.
50 Dann (ed.), *The Nagle Journal*, p. 106.
51 Letter from Fowell to his father, 31 July 1790, HRNSW, vol. 1, pt. 2, p. 374.

Chapter 5

1 Letter from Lord Sydney to the Admiralty, 29 April 1789, HRNSW, vol. 1, pt. 2, p. 230.

2 E. Riou, *The Journal of the Proceedings on Board His Majesty's Ship the Guardian, Commanded by Lieutenant Riou, Bound for Botany Bay from 22 December 1789 to the 15th of January, 1790*, London: Ridgeway, 1790, p. 6.
3 T. Clements, *Guardian: A Journal of Proceedings on Board the Above Ship, Lieutenant Riou, Commander; as Delivered into the Admiralty Board by Mr. Clements*, London: Charles Stalker, 1790, p. 9.
4 Riou, *The Journal of the Proceedings on Board His Majesty's Ship the Guardian*, p. 22.
5 Clements, *Guardian*, p. 15.
6 Clements, *Guardian*, p. 15.
7 Riou, *The Journal of the Proceedings on Board His Majesty's Ship the Guardian*, p. 16.
8 Clements, *Guardian*, p. 16.
9 Clements, *Guardian*, p. 19.
10 Letter from Riou to the Admiralty, 26 December 1789, HRNSW, vol. 1, pt. 2, p. 286.
11 Letter from Riou to the Admiralty, 26 December 1789, HRNSW, vol. 1, pt. 2, p. 286.
12 Clements, *Guardian*, p. 23.
13 Riou, *The Journal of the Proceedings on Board His Majesty's Ship the Guardian*, p. 32.
14 Clements, *Guardian*, p. 35.
15 Clements, *Guardian*, p. 37.
16 *The Times*, 29 April 1790.
17 Letter from Riou to Stephens, 20 May 1790, HRNSW, vol. 1, pt. 2, p. 326.
18 Letter from Grenville to Phillip, 16 November 1790, HRNSW, vol. 1, pt. 2, p. 414.
19 Letter from Phillip to Sydney, 11 April 1790, HRNSW, vol. 1, pt. 2, p. 326.
20 Letter from Phillip to Sydney, 11 April 1790, HRNSW, vol. 1, pt. 2, p. 326.
21 Letter from White to Skill, 17 April 1790, HRNSW, vol. 1, pt. 2, p. 332.
22 Tench, *A Complete Account of the Settlement at Port Jackson*; Tench, *A Narrative of the Expedition to Botany Bay*, chapter VI.
23 Tench, *A Complete Account of the Settlement at Port Jackson*; Tench, *A Narrative of the Expedition to Botany Bay*, chapter VII.
24 Collins, *An Account of the English Colony in New South Wales, Vol. 1*, p. 96.
25 Letter from Johnson to Thornton, July 1790, HRNSW, vol. 1, pt. 2, p. 388.

26 Letter from Johnson to Thornton, July 1790, HRNSW, vol. 1, pt. 2, p. 388.

27 Collins, *An Account of the English Colony in New South Wales, Vol. 1*, p. 99.

28 Tench, *A Complete Account of the Settlement at Port Jackson*; Tench, *A Narrative of the Expedition to Botany Bay*, chapter VII.

29 Letter from Hill to Wathen, 26 July 1790, HRNSW, vol. 1, pt. 2, p. 366.

30 Letter from Johnson to Thornton, July 1790, HRNSW, vol. 1, pt. 2, p. 388.

31 *The Times*, 18 November 1791.

32 Letter from Phillip to Nepean, 13 July 1790, HRNSW, vol. 1, pt. 2, p. 354.

33 *The Times*, 9 June 1792.

34 Collins, *An Account of the English Colony in New South Wales, Vol. 1*, p. 130.

35 Collins, *An Account of the English Colony in New South Wales, Vol. 1*, p. 156, December 1791.

36 Collins, *An Account of the English Colony in New South Wales, Vol. 1*, p. 171, April 1792.

37 Collins, *An Account of the English Colony in New South Wales, Vol. 1*, p. 266, October 1793.

38 Collins, *An Account of the English Colony in New South Wales, Vol. 1*, p. 292.

39 Collins, *An Account of the English Colony in New South Wales, Vol. 1*, p. 57.

40 Collins, *An Account of the English Colony in New South Wales, Vol. 1*, p. 57.

41 Collins, *An Account of the English Colony in New South Wales, Vol. 1*, p. 142.

42 Letter from Hunter to Under-Secretary King, 1 November 1798, HRNSW, vol. 3, p. 503.

43 *Report from the Select Committee on Transportation*, House of Commons, 1812, p. 21.

44 Letter from Hunter to Portland, 10 July 1799, HRNSW, vol. 3, p. 691.

45 Letter from a female convict, 14 November 1788, HRNSW, vol. 2, p. 746.

46 J.L. Guy, 'Building Construction Practice in the Colony of New South Wales from the Arrival of the First Fleet to the End of the Primitive Era and Its Influence in Later Time', paper presented to the Second International Congress on Construction History, Queens College, Cambridge University, 2006, <www.arct.cam.ac.uk/Downloads/ichs/vol-2-1475-1500-guy.pdf>.

47 Phillip, *The Voyage of Governor Phillip to Botany Bay*, p. 70.

48 D. Collins, *An Account of the English Colony of New South Wales, Vol. 2*, London: T. Cadell Jun. and W. Davies, 1802, p. 281.

Chapter 6

1 Collins, *An Account of the English Colony of New South Wales, Vol. 1*, p. 292.
2 W. Dampier, *A New Voyage Round the World*, London: Argonaut Press, 1927, p. 464.
3 J. Cook, *Captain Cook's Journal During His First Voyage Round the World Made in H.M. Bark Endeavour 1768–1771*, London: Elliot Stock, 1893: April 1770.
4 Cook, *Captain Cook's Journal During His First Voyage Round the World*, May 1770.
5 J.C. Beaglehole (ed.), *The Endeavour Journal of Joseph Banks: 1768–1771*, Sydney: The Trustees of the Public Library of New South Wales, in association with Angus & Robertson, 1963, 4 May 1770.
6 J. Banks, 'House of Commons Inquiry. 1779', Journal of the House of Commons, State Library of New South Wales, RB F342.4206/1.
7 Phillip's Instructions, 25 April 1787, HRNSW, vol. 1, pt. 2, p. 89.
8 *Phillip's Views,* HRNSW, vol. 1, pt. 2, p. 53.
9 Watling, *Letters from an Exile at Botany Bay*, 13 December 1791.
10 Tench, *The Expedition to Botany Bay*, 10 July 1788, chapter XI.
11 Tench, *The Expedition to Botany Bay*, 10 July 1788, chapter XI.
12 Tench, *A Complete Account of the Settlement at Port Jackson*, p. 183.
13 White, *Journal of a Voyage to New South Wales.*
14 Tench, *A Complete Account of the Settlement at Port Jackson*, chapter 1.
15 Letter from Phillip to Stephens, 16 November 1788, HRNSW, vol. 1, pt. 2, p. 208.
16 Letter from Phillip to Stephens, 16 November 1788, HRNSW, vol. 1, pt. 2, p. 214.
17 Tench, *A Complete Account of the Settlement at Port Jackson*, chapter III.
18 Tench, *A Complete Account of the Settlement at Port Jackson*, chapter III.
19 Tench, *A Complete Account of the Settlement at Port Jackson*, chapter III.
20 Tench, *A Complete Account of the Settlement at Port Jackson*, chapter III.
21 Tench, *A Complete Account of the Settlement at Port Jackson*, chapter III.
22 Tench, *A Complete Account of the Settlement at Port Jackson*, chapter III.
23 Letter from Phillip to Sydney, 13 February 1789, HRNSW, vol. 1, pt. 2, p. 308.
24 Letter from Fowell to his father, 31 July 1790, HRNSW, vol. 1, pt. 2, p. 376.
25 Letter from Phillip to Nepean, 13 February 1790, HRNSW, vol. 1, pt. 2, p. 308.

26 Letter from Phillip to Sydney, 12 February 1790, HRNSW, vol. 1, pt. 2, p. 229.
27 Tench, *The Expedition to Botany Bay*, 10 July 1788, Chapter XI.
28 Tench, *A Complete Account of the Settlement at Port Jackson*, Chapter IV.
29 *Lloyd's Evening Post*, 29 May 1793.
30 Letter from Hunter to King, 25 January 1795, HRNSW, vol. 2, p. 281.
31 Collins, *An Account of the English Colony of New South Wales, Vol. 1*, p. 292.
32 Collins, *An Account of the English Colony of New South Wales, Vol. 1*, p. 326.
33 Collins, *An Account of the English Colony of New South Wales, Vol. 1*, p. 348.
34 Collins, *An Account of the English Colony of New South Wales, Vol. 1*, p. 329.
35 Letter from Paterson to Dundas, 15 June 1795, HRNSW, vol. 2, p. 306.
36 Collins, *An Account of the English Colony of New South Wales, Vol. 1*, p. 348.
37 Letter from Paterson to Dundas, 15 June 1795, HRNSW, vol. 2, p. 307.
38 Collins, *An Account of the English Colony of New South Wales, Vol. 1*, p. 371.
39 Hunter, General Order, 22 February 1796, HRNSW, vol. 3, pp. 24–5.
40 Collins, *An Account of the English Colony of New South Wales, Vol. 2*, p. 26.
41 Collins, *An Account of the English Colony of New South Wales, Vol. 2*, p. 66.
42 A.G.L. Shaw (ed.), *Gipps–La Trobe Correspondence 1839–1846*, Melbourne: Miegunyah Press, 1989, p. 40.
43 Letter from Hunter to Portland, 2 January 1800, HRNSW, vol. 4, p. 2.
44 Shaw (ed.), *Gipps–La Trobe Correspondence*, p. 40.
45 King, General Order, 1 May 1801, HRNSW, vol. 4, p. 369.
46 Letter from Caley to Banks, 25 August 1801, HRNSW, vol. 4, p. 514.
47 King, General Order, 22 November 1801, HRNSW, vol. 4, p. 628.
48 Letter from Hobart to King, 30 January 1802, HRNSW, vol. 4, p. 682.
49 P. Turbet, *The First Frontier: The occupation of the Sydney region 1788–1816*, Sydney: Rosenberg Publishing, 2011, p. 53.
50 Tench, *A Complete Account of the Settlement at Port Jackson,* Chapter XII.
51 Tench, *A Complete Account of the Settlement at Port Jackson,* Chapter XII.
52 Tench, *A Complete Account of the Settlement at Port Jackson,* Chapter XII.
53 Tench, *A Complete Account of the Settlement at Port Jackson*, Chapter XII.
54 Collins, *An Account of the English Colony of New South Wales, Vol. 1*, p. 349.
55 Collins, *An Account of the English Colony of New South Wales, Vol. 1*, p. 371.
56 Collins, *An Account of the English Colony of New South Wales, Vol. 2*, p. 20.
57 Collins, *An Account of the English Colony of New South Wales, Vol. 2*, p. 24.
58 Collins, *An Account of the English Colony of New South Wales, Vol. 2*, p. 70.
59 King, General Order, 1 May 1801, HRNSW, vol. 4, p. 362.

60 Letter from King to Hobart, 30 October 1802, HRNSW, vol. 4, p. 867.
61 King, General Order, 17 November 1801, HRNSW, vol. 4, p. 626.
62 J.L. Kohen, 'Pemulwuy', *Australian Dictionary of Biography*, Melbourne: Melbourne University Press, 2005, <http://adb.anu.edu.au/biography/pemulwuy-13147>.
63 Turbet, *The First Frontier*, p. 127.
64 Letter from King to Banks, 5 June 1802, HRNSW, vol. 4, p. 784.
65 *Report of the Parliamentary Select Committee on Aboriginal Tribes*, House of Commons, 1837, <https://catalogue.nla.gov.au/Record/2412631>.
66 Letter from George Murray to George Arthur, 5 November 1830, republished in the House of Commons report 'Colonies and Slaves', 1831.

Chapter 7

1 *General Statement of the Inhabitants in His Majesty's Settlement on the East Coast of Australia*, HRNSW, vol. 7, p. 502.
2 A. Summers, *Damned Whores and God's Police: The colonization of women in Australia*, Melbourne: Pelican, 2002, p. 313.
3 G. Thompson, *A Private Journal*, 1792, HRNSW, vol. 2, p. 793.
4 Letter from a female convict, 14 November 1788, HRNSW, vol. 2, p. 747.
5 M. Jokiranta (presenter), 'Esther Abrahams: Convict "first lady", *Earshot*, 27 January 2015, <www.abc.net.au/radionational/programs/earshot/podcasts/esther-abrahams---convict-27first-lady27/6031166>.
6 S. Marsden, *Essays Concerning New South Wales, 1807–18*, Mitchell Library, State Library of New South Wales, MLMSS 18, <http://acms.sl.nsw.gov.au/_transcript/2015/D06597/a2105.html>.
7 Letter from Bligh to Castlereagh, 10 June 1809, HRNSW, vol. 7, p. 181.
8 'Collins, David (1756–1810)', *Australian Dictionary of Biography*, National Centre of Biography, Australian National University, <http://adb.anu.edu.au/biography/collins-david-1912/text2269>, published first in hardcopy 1966 by Melbourne University Press.
9 J. Lynravn, 'Margaret Catchpole (1762–1819)', *Australian Dictionary of Biography*, volume 1, Melbourne: Melbourne University Press, 1966, <http://adb.anu.edu.au/biography/catchpole-margaret-1886>.
10 M. Steven, 'John Palmer', *Australian Dictionary of Biography*, volume 2, Melbourne: Melbourne University Press, 1967, <http://adb.anu.edu.au/biography/palmer-john-2533>.

11 Letter from Margaret Catchpole to Mrs Cobbold, 29 December 1801, State Library of New South Wales, <www.sl.nsw.gov.au/stories/transcript-catchpole-letters>.

12 Letter from Margaret Catchpole to Mrs Cobbold, 29 December 1801, State Library of New South Wales, <www.sl.nsw.gov.au/stories/transcript-catchpole-letters>.

13 Lynravn, 'Margaret Catchpole (1762–1819)'.

14 Lynravn, 'Margaret Catchpole (1762–1819)'.

15 Lynravn, 'Margaret Catchpole (1762–1819)'.

16 'Simon Mould', *Australian Royalty: A family tree of colonial Australians, their forbears and descendants*, <https://australianroyalty.net.au/individual.php?pid=I253&ged=purnellmccord.ged>.

17 'Simon Mould', *Australian Royalty.*

18 'Trial of Mary Wade Jane Whiting, Old Bailey Online, January 1789, <www.oldbaileyonline.org/browse.jsp?id=t17890114-58-off300&div=t17890114-58>.

19 *Phillip's Suggestions*, 1787, HRNSW, vol. 1, pt. 2, p. 793.

20 Letter from Phillip to Sydney, 15 May 1788, HRNSW, vol. 1, pt. 2, p. 127.

21 Hunter, General Order, 4 July 1799, HRNSW, vol. 3, p. 685.

22 Collins, *An Account of the English Colony of New South Wales, Vol. 2*, p. 121.

23 Letter from Hunter to Portland, 18 November 1796, HRNSW, vol. 3, p. 182.

24 Letter from Marsden to Cooke, 21 November 1807, HRNSW, vol. 6, p. 382.

25 Letter from King to Treasury Commissioners, 7 July 1800, HRNSW, vol. 4, p. 113.

26 Letter from King to Hobart, 1 March 1804, HRNSW, vol. 5, p. 331.

27 Tanner & Associates, *Female Orphan School, Rydalmere: Conservation management plan, prepared for University of Western Sydney*, Surry Hills: Tanner & Associates, 2000, p. 39.

28 B. Bubacz, 'The Female and Male Orphan Schools in New South Wales 1801–1850', PhD thesis submitted to the University of Western Sydney, 2007, <www.westernsydney.edu.au/__data/assets/pdf_file/0007/926188/FOS_Website_text_with_footnotes_UPDATED_19_Aug_15.pdf>, p. 67.

29 J. Ramsland, 'Children's Institutions in Nineteenth-century Sydney', *The Dictionary of Sydney*, 2011, <https://dictionaryofsydney.org/entry/childrens_institutions_in_nineteenth_century_sydney>.

30 *Report from the Select Committee on Transportation*, House of Commons, 1812, p. 13.

31 *Report from the Select Committee on Transportation*, House of Commons, 1812, p. 21.
32 *Report from the Select Committee on Transportation*, House of Commons, 1812, p. 21.
33 *Report from the Select Committee on Transportation*, House of Commons, 10 July 1812, p. 34.
34 *Report from the Select Committee on Transportation*, House of Commons, 10 July 1812, p. 34.
35 *Report from the Select Committee on Transportation*, House of Commons, 10 July 1812, p. 51.
36 *Report from the Select Committee on Transportation*, House of Commons, 10 July 1812, p. 56.
37 *Report from the Select Committee on Transportation*, House of Commons, 10 July 1812, p. 50.

Chapter 8

1 B.H. Fletcher, 'Francis Grose (1758–1814)', *Australian Dictionary of Biography*, volume 1, Melbourne: Melbourne University Press, 1966, <http://adb.anu.edu.au/biography/grose-francis-2130 >.
2 Clark, *A History of Australia, Vol. 1*, p. 132.
3 Letter from Bligh to Banks, 17 December 1791, Papers of Sir Joseph Banks, Mitchell Library, vol. 5, p. 166.
4 Letter from Phillip to Dundas, 4 October 1792, HRNSW, vol. 1, pt. 2, p. 651.
5 Letter from Grose to Phillip, 4 October 1792, HRNSW, vol. 1, pt. 2, p. 652.
6 Letter from Grose to Phillip, 4 October 1792, HRNSW, vol. 1, pt. 2, p. 652.
7 Letter from Grose to Dundas, HRNSW, vol. 2, p. 14 (note).
8 Clark, *A History of Australia, Vol. 1*, p. 133.
9 Clark, *A History of Australia, Vol. 1*, p. 135.
10 Agreement between officers, Sydney, 18 June 1798, HRNSW, vol. 3, p. 405.
11 K. Phillips, 'Alcohol in Australia: A history of drinking', *Rear Vision*, ABC Radio, 15 June 2008, <www.sarmy.org.au/Global/SArmy/Resources/training/SACi/news-items-and-report-summaries/alcohol-in-australia-abc-rear-vision.pdf>.
12 Collins, *An Account of the English Colony of New South Wales, Vol. 1*, p. 311.
13 Collins, *An Account of the English Colony of New South Wales, Vol. 1*, p. 220.
14 Collins, *An Account of the English Colony of New South Wales, Vol. 1*, p. 327.
15 Letter from Grose to Dundas, 16 February 1792, HRNSW, vol. 2, p. 15.

16 Fletcher, 'Francis Grose (1758–1814)'.
17 Letter from Grose to Dundas, 16 February 1792, HRNSW, vol. 2, p. 15.
18 M. Duffy, *John Macarthur: Man of honour*, Sydney: Pan Macmillan, 2003, p. 26.
19 J. Conway, 'Elizabeth Macarthur (1766–1850)', *Australian Dictionary of Biography*, volume 2, Melbourne: Melbourne University Press, 1967, <http://adb.anu.edu.au/biography/macarthur-elizabeth-2387>.
20 M.H. Ellis, *John Macarthur*, Sydney: Angus & Robertson, 1955, pp. 18–19.
21 H. King, *Elizabeth Macarthur and Her World*, Sydney: Sydney University Press, 1980, p. 12.
22 Duffy, *John Macarthur*, p. 35.
23 *Surgeon Harris's account of the quarrel between Captain Gilbert and Lieutenant Macarthur*, November 1789, HRNSW, vol. 2, p. 427.
24 *Mrs MacArthur's Journal of the Voyage from London to Sydney, in the Neptune Transport, 1789*, HRNSW, vol. 2, pp. 487–91.
25 Duffy, *John Macarthur*, p. 39.
26 King, *Elizabeth Macarthur and Her World*, p. 14.
27 M. Steven, 'John Macarthur (1767–1834)', *Australian Dictionary of Biography*, volume 2, Melbourne: Melbourne University Press, 1967, <http://adb.anu.edu.au/biography/macarthur-john-2390>.
28 Duffy, *John Macarthur*, p. 90.
29 Letter from Grose to Dundas, 16 February 1793, HRNSW, vol. 2, p. 14.
30 H. Heney, *Dear Fanny: Women's letters to and from New South Wales 1788–1857*. Canberra: Australian National University Press, 1985, p. 10.
31 Clark, *The Journal and Letters of Ralph Clark*, p. 134.
32 F.M. Bladen, 'Introduction', HRNSW, vol. 3, p. xxi.
33 Letter from Hunter to Dundas, 14 October 1793, HRNSW, vol. 2, p. 73.
34 Letter from Howe to Chatham, 15 October 1793, HRNSW, vol. 2, p. 74.
35 Letter from Hunter to Portland, 16 September 1795, HRNSW, vol. 2, p. 318.
36 Letter from Hunter to Portland, 21 December 1795, HRNSW, vol. 2, p. 346.
37 Letter from Hunter to Bentham, 20 May 1799, HRNSW, vol. 3, p. 674.
38 Hunter's Instructions, 23 June 1794, HRNSW, vol. 2, p. 227.
39 F.M. Bladen, 'Introduction', HRNSW, vol. 3, p. x.
40 Letter from Hunter to Paterson, 8 February 1796, HRNSW, vol. 3, p. 17.
41 Letter from Hunter to Paterson, 8 February 1796, HRNSW, vol. 3, p. 17.
42 Letter from Portland to Hunter, 31 August 1797, HRNSW, vol. 3, p. 294.

43 Letter from Hunter to Portland, 12 November 1796, HRNSW, vol. 3, p. 168.
44 Letter from Hunter to Portland, 1 June 1797, HRNSW, vol. 3, p. 212.
45 Letter from Portland to Hunter, 18 September 1797, HRNSW, vol. 3, p. 490.
46 John Hunter's Memorandum, HRNSW, vol. 3, p. 19.
47 J. Lawrence & C. Warne, *A Pictorial History of Balmain to Glebe*, Crows Nest: Kingsclear Books, c. 1995, p. 5.
48 Letter from Macarthur to Hunter, 24 February 1796, HRNSW, vol. 3, p. 26.
49 Letter from Macarthur to Portland, 15 September 1796, HRNSW, vol. 3, p. 132.
50 Letter from Macarthur to Portland, 15 September 1796, HRNSW, vol. 3, pp. 131–3.
51 Letter from Portland to Hunter, 30 August 1797, HRNSW, vol. 3, p. 293.
52 Letter from Banks to Hunter, 1 February 1799, HRNSW, vol. 3, p. 533.
53 May Meeting of Manly, Warringah and Pittwater Historical Society, Guest Speaker Captain C.W.T. Henderson of the Maritime Services Board.
54 Australian Bureau of Statistics, Year Book, Australia. No. 66, 1982. Catalogue 1301.0. Canberra: Australian Bureau of Statistics, p. 3.
55 *Report from the Select Committee on Transportation*, House of Commons, 10 July 1812.
56 M. Flinders, *A Voyage to Terra Australis, Volume 1*, London: W. Bulmer and Co., 1814, p. 67.
57 Hunter, *An Historic Journal of the Transactions at Port Jackson and Norfolk Island*, p. 125.
58 Letter from Hunter to Nepean, 2 September 1798, HRNSW, vol. 3, p. 474.
59 Flinders, *A Voyage to Terra Australis, Volume 2*, p. 82.
60 Flinders, *A Voyage to Terra Australis, Volume 1*, p. 93.
61 Flinders, *A Voyage to Terra Australis, Volume 1*, p. cxciii.
62 E. Scott, *The Life of Captain Flinders, RN*, Sydney: Angus & Robertson, 1914, p. 105.
63 Letter from Portland to Hunter, 26 February 1799, HRNSW, vol. 3, p. 636.
64 Letter from Portland to Hunter, 26 February 1799, HRNSW, vol. 3, p. 636.
65 Letter from Brownrigg to Paterson, 6 March 1799, HRNSW, vol. 3, p. 638.
66 Letter from Portland to Hunter, 5 November 1799, HRNSW, vol. 3, p. 734.
67 A.G.L. Shaw, 'Philip Gidley King (1758–1808)', *Australian Dictionary of Biography*, volume 2, Melbourne: Melbourne University Press, 1967, <http://adb.anu.edu.au/biography/king-philip-gidley-2309>.

68 Letter from Phillip to Dundas, 26 October 1793, HRNSW, vol. 2, p. 75.
69 Clark, *The Journal and Letters of Ralph Clark*, p. 161.
70 Letter from Hunter to King, 11 July 1800, HRNSW, vol. 4, p. 175.
71 Letter from King to Hunter, 11 July 1800, HRNSW, vol. 4, p. 177.
72 Letter from King to Banks, 3 May 1800, HRNSW, vol. 4, p. 82.
73 Letter from King to King, 3 May 1800, HRNSW, vol. 4, p. 84.
74 Letter from King to Portland, 29 September 1800, HRNSW, vol. 4, p. 179.
75 Shaw, 'Philip Gidley King (1758–1808)'.
76 Letter from King to Portland, 25 September 1801, HRNSW, vol. 4, p. 528.
77 Clark, *A History of Australia*, p. 39.
78 Letter from King to King, 8 November 1801, HRNSW, vol. 4, p. 612.
79 Letter from Camden to King, 24 October 1804, HRNSW, vol. 5, p. 480.
80 M. Steven, 'John Macarthur (1767–1834)'.
81 Duffy, *John Macarthur*, p. 215.
82 Letter from King to Banks, 21 July 1805, HRNSW, vol. 5, p. 672.
83 Letter from Hayes to Hobart, 6 May 1803, HRNSW, vol. 5, p. 104.
84 Letter from King to Banks, 2 October 1802, HRNSW, vol. 4, p. 846.
85 Letter from King to Hobart, 9 May 1803, HRNSW, vol. 5, p. 118.
86 Letter from King to Hobart, 30 November 1803, HRNSW, vol. 5, p. 130.
87 Letter from Hobart to King, 30 November 1803, HRNSW, vol. 5, p. 273.
88 Letter from Hobart to King, 30 November 1803, HRNSW, vol. 5, p. 273.
89 Shaw, 'Philip Gidley King (1758–1808)'.
90 Shaw, 'Philip Gidley King (1758–1808)'.

Chapter 9

1 Phillip's Instructions, 25 April 1787, HRNSW, vol. 1, pt. 2, p. 82.
2 Daily Universal Register, 11 November 1786.
3 J. Dunmore (ed.), *The Journal of Jean-Francois de Galaup de La Pérouse 1785–1789*, vol. 2, London: Hakluyt Society, 1995, pp. 442–3.
4 Phillip's Instructions to King, 12 February 1788, HRNSW, vol. 1, p. 137.
5 Letter from King to Banks, 9 May 1803, HRNSW, vol. 5, p. 134.
6 Van Diemen's Land did not become known as Tasmania until the 1850s. The first European discoverer was Abel Tasman in 1642, after a remarkable voyage that included the discovery of New Zealand. For 150 years after Tasman, it was thought that Van Diemen's Land was part of the south coast of New Holland,

later New South Wales; the circumnavigation of the island by George Bass and Matthew Flinders in 1798 confirmed it was an island.

7 Letter from King to Baudin, 23 December 1802, HRNSW, vol. 5, p. 830.

8 The British Arrowsmith maps were largely based on the chart Flinders had made when he circumnavigated Van Diemen's Land in 1798 with George Bass. As Baudin pointed out, the earlier and more extensive maps of southern Van Diemen's Land had been made by Charles-François Beautemps-Beaupré, who had sailed on the Bruni d'Entrecasteaux expedition six years earlier.

9 Letter from Baudin to King, 23 December 1802, HRNSW, vol. 5, p. 830.

10 Letter from King to Hobart, 9 May 1803, HRNSW, vol. 5, p. 131.

11 Clark, *A History of Australia*, vol. 1, p. 190.

12 Letter from King to Bowen, 28 March 1803, HRNSW, vol. 5, p. 76.

13 Letter from King to Bowen, 1 May 1803, HRNSW, vol. 5, p. 100.

14 Letter from Hobart to the Admiralty, 15 January 1803, HRNSW, vol. 5, p. 4.

15 Letter from Hobart to the Admiralty, 15 January 1803, HRNSW, vol. 5, p. 4.

16 Letter from Hobart to Collins, 7 February 1803, HRNSW, vol. 5, p. 16.

17 Letter from Hobart to Collins, 7 February 1803, HRNSW, vol. 5, p. 16.

18 J.H. Tuckey, *An Account of a Voyage to Establish a Colony at Port Phillip in Bass's Strait, on the South Coast of New South Wales, in his Majesty's Ship Calcutta, in the years 1802-3-4*, p. 14.

19 Letter from Hobart to Collins, 5 April 1803, HRNSW, vol. 5, p. 86.

20 A.G.L. Shaw, *A History of the Port Phillip District: Victoria before separation*, Melbourne: Melbourne University Press, 1999, p. 11.

21 Tuckey, *An Account of a Voyage*, p. 27.

22 Tuckey, *An Account of a Voyage*, p. 15.

23 Letter from Collins to Hobart, 15 July 1803, HRNSW, vol. 5, p. 171.

24 Tuckey, *An Account of a Voyage*, p. 153.

25 Tuckey, *An Account of a Voyage*, p. 154.

26 Tuckey, *An Account of a Voyage*, p. 174.

27 Letter from Collins to King, 5 November 1803, HRNSW, vol. 5, p. 248.

28 R. Knopwood, *The Diary of Rev. Robert Knopwood (1805–1808)*, 6 November 1803.

29 Tuckey, *An Account of a Voyage*, p. 153.

30 Knopwood, *The Diary of Rev. Robert Knopwood*, 6 November 1803.

31 Letter from King to Collins, 26 November 1803, HRNSW, vol. 5, p. 263.

32 Tuckey, *An Account of a Voyage*, p. 191.

33 Letter from Collins to King, 28 February 1804, HRNSW, vol. 5, p. 312.

34 Letter from Collins to King, 28 February 1804, HRNSW, vol. 5, p. 312.

35 Shaw, *A History of the Port Phillip District*, p. 11.

36 W. Buckley (introduced and edited by T. Flannery), *The Life and Adventures of William Buckley*, Melbourne: The Text Publishing Company, 2002, p. 144.

37 Knopwood, *The Diary of Rev. Robert Knopwood*, 16 February 1804.

38 E. McMahon, *Islands, Identity and the Literary Imagination*, London & New York: Anthem Press, 2016, p. 255.

39 Hughes, *The Fatal Shore*, p. 125.

40 'Collins, David (1756–1810)', *Australian Dictionary of Biography*, Melbourne University Press, volume 1, 1966, pp. 236–40.

41 R.W. Kirk, *Paradise Past: The transformation of the South Pacific, 1520–1920*, Jefferson, North Carolina & London: McFarland and Company Inc., 2012, p. 88.

42 State Library of New South Wales, 'Marking the Spanish Expedition to Sydney in 1793', State Library of New South Wales, 14 March 2018, <www.sl.nsw.gov.au/blogs/marking-spanish-expedition-sydney-1793>.

43 L. Olcelli, 'Alessandro Malaspina: An Italian-Spaniard at Port Jackson', *Sydney Journal*, vol. 4, no. 1, 2013, pp. 38–48.

44 Collins, *An Account of the English Colony of New South Wales, Vol. 1.*

45 Letter from Grose to Dundas, 19 April 1793, HRNSW, vol. 2, p. 24.

46 R.J. King & V. Ibáñez, 'A Letter from Thaddaeus Haenke to Sir Joseph Banks, Sydney Cove, 15 April 1793', *Archives of Natural History*, vol. 23, no. 2, 1996, pp. 255–9.

47 Collins, *An Account of the English Colony of New South Wales, Vol. 1*, p. 275.

48 Collins, *An Account of the English Colony of New South Wales, Vol. 1*, p. 275.

49 Collins, *An Account of the English Colony of New South Wales, Vol. 1*, p. 278.

50 Collins, *An Account of the English Colony of New South Wales, Vol. 1*, p. 279.

51 R.J. King, 'Francisco Muñoz y San Clemente and his Reflexions on the English Settlements of New Holland', *British Library Journal*, vol. 25, no. 1, 1999, pp. 55–76.

52 R.J. King, *The Secret History of the Convict Colony*, Sydney: Allen & Unwin, 1990, pp. 102–3.

53 L. Olcelli, 'Alessandro Malaspina, An Italian–Spaniard at Port Jackson,' *Sydney Journal*, vol. 4, no. 1, 2013, pp. 38–48.

54 Australian Association for Maritime History, 'Spanish "Allies" Had Sydney in Their Sights for Invasion', *AAMH Quarterly Newsletter*, issue 147, March 2018, p. 1, <https://aamh.asn.au/wp-content/uploads/2018/04/Issue-147-2018-03.pdf>.
55 R.J. King, *The Secret History of the Convict Colony*, pp. 102–3.

Chapter 10

1 W. Hirst, *Great Escapes by Convicts in Colonial Australia*, East Roseville: Kangaroo Press, 2003, p. 5.
2 Hirst, *Great Escapes by Convicts in Colonial Australia*, p. 43.
3 Heads of a Plan HRNSW, 18 August 1786, HRNSW, vol. 1, pt. 2, p. 17.
4 J. Easty, *Memorandum of Transactions of a Voyage from England to Botany Bay, 1787–1791: A First Fleet Journal*, Sydney: Trustees of the Public Library of New South Wales, 1965.
5 Letter from Phillip to Nepean, 5 June 1787, HRNSW, vol. 1, pt. 2, p. 108.
6 Hunter, *An Historical Journal*, p. 10.
7 Hunter, *An Historical Journal*. p. 10.
8 Letter from Captain Manning to Alderman Macaulay, 24 October 1791, HRNSW, vol. 1, pt. 2, p. 527.
9 Watling, *Letters from An Exile at Botany Bay*, 13 December 1791.
10 Watling, *Letters from An Exile at Botany Bay*, 13 December 1791.
11 Watling, *Letters from An Exile at Botany Bay*, 13 December 1791.
12 R. Rienits, 'Thomas Watling (1762–?)', *Australian Dictionary of Biography*, Volume 2, Melbourne: Melbourne University Press, 1967, <http://adb.anu.edu.au/biography/watling-thomas-2776>.
13 Most of Watling's surviving artworks are in the British Natural History Museum, with some at the Mitchell Library in Sydney.
14 White, *Journal of a Voyage to New South Wales*, January 1788.
15 White, *Journal of a Voyage to New South Wales*, January 1788.
16 Letter from Phillip to Nepean, 14 December 1791, HRNSW, vol. 1, pt. 2, p. 565.
17 Letter from Phillip to Nepean, 23 August 1790, HRNSW, vol. 1, pt. 2, p. 394.
18 Letter from Phillip to Nepean, 14 December 1791, HRNSW, vol. 1, pt. 2, p. 565.
19 Report of Captain Wilkinson on Convict Stowaways, HRNSW, vol. 2, p. 295.
20 Hunter, General Order, 19 October 1799, HRNSW, vol. 3, p. 725.

21 King, General Order, 31 March 1805, HRNSW, vol. 5, p. 588.

22 Letter from Bligh to Windham, 31 October 1807, HRNSW, vol. 6, p. 364.

23 C. Cunneen & M. Gillen, 'Caesar, John Black (1763–1796)', *Australian Dictionary of Biography*, Supplementary Volume, Melbourne: Melbourne University Press, 2005, <http://adb.anu.edu.au/biography/caesar-john-black-12829>.

24 Collins, *An Account of the English Colony in New South Wales, Vol. 1*, p. 58.

25 W. Bradley, *A Voyage to New South Wales: The journal of Lieutenant William Bradley RN on the HMS Sirius, 1786–1792*, Sydney: Trustees of the Public Library of New South Wales, in association with Ure Smith, 1968, <http://acms.sl.nsw.gov.au/_transcript/2015/D02131/a138.html>, 31 January 1790.

26 Collins, *An Account of the English Colony in New South Wales, Vol. 1*, p. 320.

27 Collins, *An Account of the English Colony in New South Wales, Vol. 1*, p. 320.

28 Hunter, *An Historical Journal*, 1 January 1793.

29 C. Cunneen & M. Gillen, 'Caesar, John Black (1763–1796)'.

30 Collins, *An Account of the English Colony in New South Wales,* vol. 1, p. 377.

31 In 1806 a number of convicts, including Ann Badger and Catherine Hagerty, with the support of the ship's crew, seized the *Venus* at Port Dalrymple in Van Diemen's Land and escaped to the Bay of Islands in New Zealand. In 1834 ten convicts seized the *Frederick* at Macquarie Island and escaped to Valdivia, Chile.

32 The eleven ships of the Third Fleet were the *Mary Ann*, the *Matilda*, the *Active*, the *Admiral Barrington*, the *Albemarle*, the *Atlantic*, the *Britannia*, the *Salamander*, the *William and Ann*, the *Queen* and HMS *Gorgon*.

33 Mutiny on the Albemarle (unsigned report believed to be written by Lieutenant Robert Parry Young), 24 April 1791, HRNSW, vol. 1, pt. 2, p. 487.

34 Mutiny on the Albemarle, 24 April 1791, HRNSW, vol. 1, pt. 2, p. 487.

35 Mutiny on the Albemarle, 24 April 1791, HRNSW, vol. 1, pt. 2, p. 487.

36 Mutiny on the Albemarle, 24 April 1791, HRNSW, vol. 1, pt. 2, p. 487.

37 Mutiny on the Albemarle, 24 April 1791, HRNSW, vol. 1, pt. 2, p. 487.

38 Letter from Phillip to Nepean, 18 November 1791, HRNSW, vol. 1 pt. 2, p. 556.

39 P. Cunningham, *Two Years in New South Wales*, London: Henry Colburn, 1827, p. 283.

40 Dann (ed.), *The Nagle Journal*, p. 179.

41 India Government Officials to Hunter (King papers), 11 November 1799, HRNSW, vol. 4, p. 111.

42 India Government Officials to Hunter (King papers), 11 November 1799, HRNSW, vol. 4, p. 111.

43 Public Office, Bow Street, 21 July 1792, HRNSW, vol. 2, p. 800.

44 Collins, *An Account of the English Colony in New South Wales, Vol. 1*, March 1791.

45 Public Office, Bow Street. Reprinted from the *Dublin Chronicle* of 28 May 1793, HRNSW, vol. 2, p. 809.

46 J. Martin, *James Martin's Memorandums: An astonishing escape from early New South Wales* (part of the Bentham papers held in the special collections of London University), republished in M. Walker, *A Long Way Home: The life and adventures of the convict Mary Bryant*, Chichester, West Sussex, England; Hoboken, NJ: Wiley, 2005, p. 27.

47 Kupang is located in the modern Indonesian province of East Nusa Tenggara, also known as West Timor.

48 Public Office, Bow Street, reprinted from the *Dublin Chronicle* of 28 May 1793, HRNSW, vol. 2, p. 801.

49 Public Office, Bow Street, reprinted from the *Dublin Chronicle* of 28 May 1793, HRNSW, vol. 2, p. 802.

50 Martin, *James Martin's Memorandums*, in Walker, *A Long Way Home*, p. 29.

51 Public Office, Bow Street, reprinted from the *Dublin Chronicle* of 28 May 1793, HRNSW, vol. 2, p. 802.

52 Collins, *An Account of the English Colony in New South Wales, Vol. 1*, March 1791.

53 Martin, *James Martin's Memorandums*, in Walker, *A Long Way Home*, p. 34.

54 Tench, *A Complete Account of the Settlement at Port Jackson*, footnote to p. 108.

55 Letter from Hunter to Portland, 10 January 1798, HRNSW, vol. 3, p. 345.

56 Letter from Hunter to Portland, 10 January 1798, HRNSW, vol. 3, p. 345.

57 Letter from Hunter to Portland, 10 January 1798, HRNSW, vol. 3, p. 345.

58 Letter from Hunter to Portland, 1 March 1798, HRNSW, vol. 3, p. 364.

59 Hunter, General Order, 6 November 1797, HRNSW, vol. 3, p. 306.

60 J. Earnshaw, 'Thomas Muir', *Australian Dictionary of Biography*, Volume 2, Melbourne: Melbourne University Press, 1967, <http://adb.anu.edu.au/biography/muir-thomas-2488>.

61 Earnshaw, 'Thomas Muir'.

62 F. Clune, *The Scottish Martyrs: Their trials and transportation to Botany Bay*. Sydney: Angus & Robertson, 1969, p. 6.

63 HRNSW, vol. 2, p. 827 (note).

64 Letter from Portland to Hunter, August 1796, HRNSW, vol. 3, p. 98.
65 Collins, *An Account of the English Colony in New South Wales, Vol. 1*, p. 333.
66 Hunter to a friend in Leith, 25 October 1795, HRNSW, vol. 3, p. 882.
67 Clune, *The Scottish Martyrs*, p. 112.
68 Clune, *The Scottish Martyrs*, p. 113.
69 Clune, *The Scottish Martyrs*, p. 112.
70 Clune, *The Scottish Martyrs*, p. 110.
71 Clune, *The Scottish Martyrs*, p. 119.
72 Clune, *The Scottish Martyrs*, p. 127.
73 Clune, *The Scottish Martyrs*, p. 127.
74 J. Earnshaw, 'Thomas Muir Scottish Martyr', Cremorne: Stone Copying Company, 1959, p. 19.
75 Clune, *The Scottish Martyrs*, p. 128.

Chapter 11

1 Parliament of Ireland, 15 February 1790, HRNSW, vol. 2, p. 754.
2 A.-M. Whitaker, *Unfinished Revolution: United Irishmen in New South Wales, 1800–1810*, Darlinghurst: Crossing Press, 2010, p. 18.
3 Whitaker, *Unfinished Revolution*, p. 23.
4 Whitaker, *Unfinished Revolution*, p. 32.
5 Marsden, *Essays Concerning New South Wales, 1807–18.*
6 Collins, *An Account of the English Colony of New South Wales, Vol. 1*, p. 380.
7 Letter from Hunter to Portland, 12 November 1796, HRNSW, vol. 3, p. 174.
8 Letter from Hunter to Portland, 12 November 1796, HRNSW, vol. 3, p. 175.
9 Letter from Hunter to Portland, 10 January 1798, HRNSW, vol. 3, p. 348.
10 Letter from Hunter to Portland, 15 February 1798, HRNSW, vol. 3, p. 359.
11 Whitaker, *Unfinished Revolution*, p. 5.
12 Whitaker, *Unfinished Revolution*, p. 17.
13 Whitaker, *Unfinished Revolution*, p. 17.
14 Whitaker, *Unfinished Revolution*, p. 23. The ships were the *Minerva*, the *Friendship II*, the *Anne I* (or *Anne Luz St Anne*), the *Hercules I*, the *Atlas I*, the *Rolla* and the *Tellicherry.*
15 Letter from King to Portland, 28 September 1800, HRNSW, vol. 4, p. 185.
16 Letter from King to Portland, 28 September 1800, HRNSW, vol. 4, p. 185.
17 Letter from King to Hobart, 9 May 1803, HRNSW, vol. 5, p. 117.
18 Letter from King to Portland, 21 May 1802, HRNSW, vol. 4, p. 765.

19 Letter from Hobart to King, 24 February 1803, HRNSW, vol. 5, p. 47.

20 R.W. Connell, 'The Convict Rebellion of 1804', *Melbourne Historical Journal*, vol. 5, no. 1, 1965, p. 28, <http://journal.mhj.net.au/index.php/mhj/article/view/1147>.

21 Connell, 'The Convict Rebellion of 1804', p. 28.

22 Connell, 'The Convict Rebellion of 1804', p. 28.

23 A. Moore, 'Phillip Cunningham: A forgotten Irish–Australian Rebel', paper delivered at 'Remembering Vinegar Hill', seminar, Blacktown City Council, 7 March 2004, <www.labourhistory.org.au/hummer/vol-4-no-2/cunningham>.

24 Letter from King to Portland, 10 March 1801, HRNSW, vol. 4, p. 326.

25 Whitaker, *Unfinished Revolution*, p. 17.

26 Whitaker, *Unfinished Revolution*, p. 17.

27 Marsden, *Essays Concerning New South Wales, 1807–18.*

28 Heney, *Dear Fanny*, p. 28.

29 Letter from King to Hobart, 12 March 1804, HRNSW, vol. 5, p. 355.

30 A.T. Yarwood, 'George Johnston (1764–1823)', *Australian Dictionary of Biography*, volume 2, Melbourne: Melbourne University Press, 1967, <http://adb.anu.edu.au/biography/johnston-george-2277>.

31 Letter from Johnston to Paterson, 9 March 1804, HRNSW, vol. 5, p. 348.

32 Letter from Johnston to Paterson, 9 March 1804, HRNSW, vol. 5, p. 348.

33 Proclamation by Governor King, 5 March 1804, HRNSW, vol. 5, p. 345.

34 Proclamation by Governor King, 5 March 1804, HRNSW, vol. 5, p. 345.

35 Letter from Johnston to Paterson, 9 March 1804, HRNSW, vol. 5, p. 348.

36 Letter from Johnston to Paterson, 9 March 1804, HRNSW, vol. 5, p. 348.

37 Letter from Johnston to Paterson, 9 March 1804, HRNSW, vol. 5, p. 348.

38 Letter from Johnston to Paterson, 9 March 1804, HRNSW, vol. 5, p. 348.

39 Letter from Johnston to Paterson, 9 March 1804, HRNSW, vol. 5, p. 348.

40 Letter from Johnston to Paterson, 9 March 1804, HRNSW, vol. 5, p. 348.

41 Letter from Johnston to Paterson, 9 March 1804, HRNSW, vol. 5, p. 348.

42 Letter from Johnston to Paterson, 9 March 1804, HRNSW, vol. 5, p. 348.

43 Letter from King to Hobart, 12 March 1804, HRNSW, vol. 5, p. 354.

Chapter 12

1 Letter from Bligh to Banks, 6 August 1787, HRNSW, vol. 1, pt. 2, p. 109.

2 C. Alexander, *The Bounty: The true story of the mutiny on the Bounty*, New York: Viking, 2003, pp. 154–6.

3 G.G.B. Byron, *The Island; or Christian and his Comrades*, volume 3, Second Edition, London: John Hunt, 1823, p. 92.
4 Byron, *The Island*, p. 91.
5 W. Bligh, *Bligh's Log*, Melbourne: Hutchison, 1979, p. 163.
6 G. Kennedy, *Captain Bligh: The Man and his Mutinies*, London: Duckworth, p. 287.
7 Letter from Bligh to Banks, 21 March 1805, State Library of New South Wales.
8 Bligh's Instructions, 20 May 1805, HRNSW, vol. 5, p. 637.
9 *Sydney Gazette*, 8 August 1806.
10 Kennedy, *Captain Bligh*, p. 287.
11 Letter from Bligh to Windham, 31 October 1807, HRNSW, vol. 6, p. 357.
12 Letter from Bligh to Windham, 31 October 1807, HRNSW, vol. 6, p. 353.
13 Letter from Bligh to Windham, 31 October 1807, HRNSW, vol. 6, p. 355.
14 Letter from Bligh to Windham, 31 October 1807, HRNSW, vol. 6, p. 356.
15 Letter from Bligh to Windham, 31 October 1807, HRNSW, vol. 6, p. 353.
16 Sydney settlers to Bligh, 22 September 1806, HRNSW, vol. 6, p. 188.
17 Kennedy, *Captain Bligh*, p. 289.
18 Kennedy, *Captain Bligh*, p. 289.
19 Heney, *Dear Fanny*, p. 35.
20 Letter from Johnston to Lt Colonel Gordon, 8 October 1808, HRNSW, vol. 6, p. 652.
21 Letter from Harris to King, 25 October 1807, HRNSW, vol. 6, p. 337.
22 Letter from Harris to King, 25 October 1807, HRNSW, vol. 6, p. 344.
23 Letter from Bligh to Castlereagh, 28 April 1808, HRNSW, vol. 6, p. 609.
24 Kennedy, *Captain Bligh*, p. 291.
25 Letter from Bligh to Windham, 31 October 1807, HRNSW, vol. 6, p. 355.
26 J.M. Bennett, 'Richard Atkins', *Australian Dictionary of Biography*, volume 1, Melbourne: Melbourne University Press, 1966, <http://adb.anu.edu.au/biography/atkins-richard-1723>.
27 Letter from Macarthur to Bligh, 22 January 1808, HRNSW, vol. 6, p. 420.
28 Letter from Bligh to Castlereagh, 30 April 1808, HRNSW, vol. 6, p. 611.
29 Letter from six officer judges to Bligh, 25 January 1808, HRNSW, vol. 6, p. 422.
30 H.V. Evatt, *Rum Rebellion: A study of the overthrow of Governor Bligh by John Macarthur and the New South Wales Corps*, Ayer Co. Pub., 1937.

31 Letter from Macarthur and others to Major Johnston, 26 January 1808, HRNSW, vol. 6, p. 434.
32 J. Richie, *A Charge of Mutiny*, Canberra: National Library of Australia, 1988, p. vii.
33 Eyewitness account quoted in Seale, 'Mary, Bligh, O'Connell'. <www.hawkesbury.history.net.au>. Accessed 2015.
34 Letter from Johnston to Bligh, 26 January 1808, vol. 6, p. 434.
35 Letter from Macarthur to his wife, 26 January 1808, HRNSW, vol. 6, p. 594.
36 Richie, *A Charge of Mutiny*, p. viii.
37 Letter from Johnston to Castlereagh, 11 April 1808, HRNSW, vol. 6, p. 576.
38 Letter from Johnston to Castlereagh, 11 April 1808, HRNSW, vol. 6, p. 576.
39 G. Johnston, *Proceedings of a General Court-Marshal at Chelsea Hospital. Taken in Shorthand by Mr Bartrum of Clement's Inn*, London: Sherwood, Neely and Jones, 1811, p. 423.
40 Letter from Bligh to Castlereagh, 30 April 1808, HRNSW, vol. 6, p. 607.
41 Letter from Bligh to Castlereagh, 30 April 1808, HRNSW, vol. 6, p. 607.
42 Letter from Bligh to Castlereagh, 30 April 1808, HRNSW, vol. 6, p. 609.
43 Richie, *A Charge of Mutiny*, p. ix.
44 Letter from settlers to Johnston, 18 April 1808, HRNSW, vol. 6, p. 596.
45 Letter from settlers to Johnston, 18 April 1808, HRNSW, vol. 6, p. 597.
46 Letter from Foveaux to Castlereagh, 4 September 1808, HRNSW, vol. 6, p. 729.
47 Letter from Foveaux to Castlereagh, 4 September 1808, HRNSW, vol. 6, p. 729.
48 *Mutiny; and the Trial of Lt. Col. Johnston: An outline of the Rum Rebellion. Taken in shorthand by Mr Bartrum of Clement's Inn*, London: Sherwood Neeley and Jones, 1811, <http://gutenberg.net.au/ebooks13/1300731h.html>.
49 Letter from Castlereagh to Macquarie, May 1809, HRNSW, vol. 7, p. 143.
50 Kennedy, *Captain Bligh*, p. 299.
51 Richie, *A Charge of Mutiny*, p. ix.
52 Richie, *A Charge of Mutiny*, pp. 1–2.
53 Richie, *A Charge of Mutiny*, p. 140.
54 Richie, *A Charge of Mutiny*, p. 152.
55 Richie, *A Charge of Mutiny*, p. 405.
56 Letter from Castlereagh to Macquarie, 14 May 1809, HRNSW, vol. 7, p. 144.

57 M. Steven, 'John Macarthur'.
58 Richie, *A Charge of Mutiny*, p. xvii.
59 Letter from Bligh to Elizabeth Bligh, 11 August 1810, Mitchell Library, State Library of New South Wales, ML MS 1/45.
60 A.G.L. Shaw, 'William Bligh (1754–1817)', *Australian Dictionary of Biography*, volume 1, Melbourne: Melbourne University Press, 1966, <http://adb.anu.edu.au/biography/bligh-william-1797>.

Chapter 13

1 Nightingall was not permanently disabled by his illness. After pulling out of the New South Wales governorship, he resumed active army duty, was wounded in the Peninsular War in 1811, was knighted in 1814 and served in Java in 1813 and 1815, and then as lieutenant governor in Bombay from 1816 to 1819. He became a member of parliament from 1820 until he died in 1829.
2 Ellis, *John Macarthur*, p. 166.
3 Macquarie's journal, 26 March 1805.
4 *Report from the Select Committee on Transportation*, House of Commons, 10 July 1812.
5 *Report from the Select Committee on Transportation*, House of Commons, 10 July 1812.
6 L. Macquarie, *Proclamation: His Majesty having felt the utmost regret and displeasure on account of the late tumultuous proceedings in this his colony and the mutinous conduct of certain persons therein towards his late representative William Bligh*, Sydney: Government Press, 1810.
7 *Sydney Gazette*, 28 April 1810.
8 Letter from Macquarie to Castlereagh, 30 April 1810, HRNSW, vol. 7, p. 335.
9 Letter from Macquarie to Castlereagh, 30 April 1810, HRNSW, vol. 7, p. 336.
10 Letter from Macquarie to Castlereagh, 30 April 1810, HRNSW, vol. 7, p. 337.
11 Letter from Macquarie to Castlereagh, 30 April 1810, HRNSW, vol. 7, p. 335.
12 Letter from Macquarie to Castlereagh, 30 April 1810, HRNSW, vol. 7, p. 337.
13 Macquarie, Proclamation, 24 February 1810, HRNSW, vol. 7, p. 292.
14 Macquarie, General Order, 16 February 1810, HRNSW, vol. 7, p. 289.
15 Macquarie, General Order, 16 February 1810, HRNSW, vol. 7, p. 289.
16 Letter from Macquarie to Castlereagh, 30 April 1810, HRNSW, vol. 7, p. 338.
17 Letter from Macquarie to Castlereagh, 30 April 1810, HRNSW, vol. 7, p. 357.
18 Letter from Macquarie to Castlereagh, 30 April 1810, HRNSW, vol. 7, p. 357.

19 Letter from Macquarie to Castlereagh, 30 April 1810, HRNSW, vol. 7, p. 357.

20 J.V. Byrnes, 'Andrew Thompson (1773–1810)', *Australian Dictionary of Biography*, volume 2, Melbourne: Melbourne University Press, 1967, <http://adb.anu.edu.au/biography/thompson-andrew-2728>.

21 D.R. Hainsworth, 'Simeon Lord (1771–1840)', *Australian Dictionary of Biography*, volume 2, Melbourne: Melbourne University Press, 1967, <http://adb.anu.edu.au/biography/lord-simeon-2371>.

22 D.R. Hainsworth, 'Simeon Lord (1771–1840)'.

23 Letter from Liverpool to Macquarie, 4 May 1812, HRA series 1, vol. VII, pp. 447–8.

24 F.M. Bladen, 'Introduction', HRNSW, vol. 7, p. liii.

25 J.J. Auchmuty, 'D'Arcy Wentworth (1762–1827)', *Australian Dictionary of Biography*, volume 2, Melbourne: Melbourne University Press, 1967, <http://adb.anu.edu.au/biography/wentworth-darcy-1545>.

26 E.W. Dunlop, 'Garnham Blaxcell (1778–1817)', *Australian Dictionary of Biography*, volume 1, Melbourne: Melbourne University Press, 1966, <http://adb.anu.edu.au/biography/blaxcell-garnham-1794>.

27 J. Conway, 'Riley, Alexander (1778–1833)', *Australian Dictionary of Biography*, volume 2, Melbourne: Melbourne University Press, 1967, <http://adb.anu.edu.au/biography/riley-alexander-2591>. Alexander Riley's two sisters married Captains Ralph Wilson and Anthony Kemp.

28 F.M. Bladen, 'Introduction', HRNSW, vol. 7, p. liv.

29 Letter from Macquarie to Liverpool, 18 October 1811, HRNSW, vol. 7, p. 606.

30 Letter from Macquarie to Liverpool, 18 October 1811, HRNSW, vol. 7, p. 604.

31 Letter from Macquarie to Liverpool, 18 October 1811, HRNSW, vol. 7, p. 606.

32 Letter from Liverpool to Macquarie, 4 May 1812, HRA series 1, vol. VII, p. 477.

33 Letter from Liverpool to Macquarie, 19 May 1812, HRA series 1, vol. VII, pp. 486–8.

34 Letter from Macquarie to Liverpool, 9 November 1812, HRA series 1, vol. VII, p. 525.

35 Ellis, *John Macarthur*, p. 220.

36 Macquarie's journal, 23 November 1811.

37 Macquarie's journal, 25 December 1811.

38 State Library of New South Wales, 'Crossing the Blue Mountains', State Library of New South Wales, <www.sl.nsw.gov.au/stories/crossing-blue-mountains>.

39 J. King, *Great Moments in Australian History*, Sydney: Allen & Unwin, 2009, p. 128.

40 King, *Great Moments in Australian History*, p. 128.

41 V. Parsons, 'Barrallier, Francis Louis (1773–1853)', *Australian Dictionary of Biography*, volume 1, Melbourne: Melbourne University Press, 1966, <http://adb.anu.edu.au/biography/barrallier-francis-louis-1745>.

42 King, *Great Moments in Australian History*, p. 128.

43 Parsons, 'Barrallier, Francis Louis (1773–1853)'.

44 King, Extracts, 2 November 1805, HRNSW, vol. 5, p. 726.

45 *Report from the Select Committee on Transportation,* House of Commons, 10 July 1812.

46 Australian Museum, 'Gregory Blaxland, William Charles Wentworth, William Lawson', Australian Museum, 13 November 2018, <https://australianmuseum.net.au/Gregory-blaxland-william-charles-wentworth-william-lawson>.

47 W.C. Wentworth, *Journal of an Expedition Across the Blue Mountains, 11 May–6 June 1813*, State Library of New South Wales, <www.sl.nsw.gov.au/stories/crossing-blue-mountains/journals>.

48 G. Blaxland, *The Journal of Gregory Blaxland, 1813*, State Library of New South Wales, <http://gutenberg.net.au/ebooks02/0200411h.html>.

49 Letter from Macquarie to Bathurst, 19 January 1814, HRA series 1, vol. VIII, pp. 123–4.

50 Macquarie, Government Order, 12 February 1814.

51 E. Hickson, 'William Cox (1764–1837)', *Australian Dictionary of Biography*, Melbourne: Melbourne University Press, <http://adb.anu.edu.au/biography/cox-william-1934>.

52 *Report of Parliamentary Select Committee on Aboriginal Tribes British Settlements*, London: William Ball, Aldine Chambers, Pasternoster Row, and Hatchard and Son, 1837, pp. 3–4, <https://archive.org/details/reportparliamen00britgoog/page/n6>.

53 *Report of Parliamentary Select Committee on Aboriginal Tribes British Settlements*, pp. 3–4.

54 *Report of Parliamentary Select Committee on Aboriginal Tribes British Settlements*, p. vi.

55 *Report of Parliamentary Select Committee on Aboriginal Tribes British Settlements*, pp. 3–4.
56 Letter from Macquarie to Bigge, 6 November 1819, HRA series 1, vol. X, p. 222.
57 A.T. Yarwood, 'Samuel Marsden (1765–1838)', *Australian Dictionary of Biography*, volume 2, Melbourne: Melbourne University Press, 1967, <http://adb.anu.edu.au/biography/marsden-samuel-2433>.
58 Yarwood, 'Samuel Marsden (1765–1838)'.
59 M.H. Ellis, *Lachlan Macquarie: His life, adventures and times,* Sydney: Angus & Robertson, 1978, p. 337.
60 Ellis, *Lachlan Macquarie*, p. 325.
61 Letter from Macquarie to Bathurst, 4 December 1817, HRA series 1, vol. IX, p. 502.
62 Letter from Macquarie to Marsden, 8 January 1818.
63 J. Spigelman & D.A. Roberts, 'The Macquarie Bicentennial: A reappraisal of the Bigge Reports', Sydney: History Council of NSW, 2009.
64 Letter from Bathurst to Bigge, 6 January 1819, HRA series 1, vol. X, p. 7.

Bibliography

C. Alexander, *The Bounty: The true story of the mutiny on the Bounty*, New York: Viking, 2003.

The Atheneum; or Spirit of the English Magazines, vol. V, *Memoirs of the First Thirty-Two Years of the Life of James Hardy Vaux, a Swindler and a Pickpocket, now transported to New South Wales for the second time, and for life. Written by Himself. London 1819 in 2 Volumes.* From the Literary Gazette. Boston: Munroe and Francis, 1819.

J.J. Auchmuty, 'D'Arcy Wentworth (1762–1827)', *Australian Dictionary of Biography*, volume 2, Melbourne: Melbourne University Press, 1967, <http://adb.anu.edu.au/biography/wentworth-darcy-1545>.

Australian Association for Maritime History, 'Spanish "Allies" Had Sydney in Their Sights for Invasion', *AAMH Quarterly Newsletter*, issue 147, March 2018, p. 1, <https://aamh.asn.au/wp-content/uploads/2018/04/Issue-147-2018-03.pdf>.

Australian Royalty, 'Simon Mould', *Australian Royalty: A family tree of colonial Australians, their forbears and descendants*, <https://australianroyalty.net.au/individual.php?pid=I253&ged=purnellmccord.ged>.

C. Bateson, *The Convict Ships*, Glasgow: Brown and Son, 1959.

J.C. Beaglehole (ed.), *The Endeavour Journal of Joseph Banks: 1768–1771*, Sydney: The Trustees of the Public Library of New South Wales, in association with Angus & Robertson, 1963.

L. Becke & W. Jeffery, *Admiral Phillip: The founding of New South Wales*, London: T. Fisher Unwin, 1899.

L. Becke & W. Jeffery, *The Naval Pioneers of Australia*, London: John Murray, 1899.

G. Blaxland, *The Journal of Gregory Blaxland, 1813*, State Library of New South Wales, <http://gutenberg.net.au/ebooks02/0200411h.html>.

W. Bligh, *Bligh's Log*, Melbourne: Hutchison, 1979.

A. Bowes Smyth, *A Journal of a Voyage from Portsmouth to New South Wales and China—in the Lady Penrhyn, Merchantman—William Cropton Sever, Commander by Arthur Bowes Smyth, Surgeon—1787-1788-1789*, April 1787, <http://archival-classic.sl.nsw.gov.au/_transcript/2017/D36405/a1085.html>.

W. Bradley, *A Voyage to New South Wales: The journal of Lieutenant William Bradley RN on the HMS Sirius, 1786–1792*, Sydney: Trustees of the Public Library of New South Wales, in association with Ure Smith, 1968, <http://acms.sl.nsw.gov.au/_transcript/2015/D02131/a138.html>.

B. Bubacz, 'The Female and Male Orphan Schools in New South Wales 1801–1850', PhD thesis submitted to the University of Western Sydney, 2007, <www.westernsydney.edu.au/__data/assets/pdf_file/0007/926188/FOS_Website_text_with_footnotes_UPDATED_19_Aug_15.pdf>.

W. Buckley (introduced and edited by T. Flannery), *The Life and Adventures of William Buckley*, Melbourne: The Text Publishing Company, 2002.

J.V. Byrnes, 'Andrew Thompson (1773–1810)', *Australian Dictionary of Biography*, volume 2, Melbourne: Melbourne University Press, 1967, <http://adb.anu.edu.au/biography/thompson-andrew-2728>.

G.G.B. Byron, *The Island; or Christian and his Comrades*, volume 3, Second Edition, London: John Hunt, 1823.

M. Clark, *A History of Australia, Vol. 1, From the Earliest Times to the Age of Macquarie*, Melbourne: Melbourne University Press, 1962.

R. Clark, *The Journal and Letters of Lieutenant Ralph Clark 1787–1792*, Sydney: Australian Documents Library in association with the Library of Australian History Pty Ltd, University of Sydney, 1981.

T. Clements, *Guardian: A Journal of Proceedings on Board the Above Ship, Lieutenant Riou, Commander; as Delivered into the Admiralty Board by Mr. Clements*, London: Charles Stalker, 1790.

F. Clune, *The Scottish Martyrs: Their trials and transportation to Botany Bay*, Sydney: Angus & Robertson, 1969.

J. Cobley, *The Crimes of the First Fleet Convicts*, Sydney: Angus & Robertson, 1970.

D. Collins, *An Account of the English Colony of New South Wales, Vol. 1*, London: T. Cadell Jun. and W. Davies, 1798.

D. Collins, *An Account of the English Colony of New South Wales, Vol. 2*, London: T. Cadell Jun. and W. Davies, 1802.

'Collins, David (1756–1810)', *Australian Dictionary of Biography*, volume 1, Melbourne: Melbourne University Press, 1966, <http://adb.anu.edu.au/biography/collins-david-1912/text2269>.

P. Colquhoun, *A Treatise on Police of Metropolitan London*, London: Gillet, 1805.

R.W. Connell, 'The Convict Rebellion of 1804', *Melbourne Historical Journal*, vol. 5, no. 1, 1965, p. 28, <http://journal.mhj.net.au/index.php/mhj/article/view/1147>.

J. Conway, 'Elizabeth Macarthur (1766–1850)', *Australian Dictionary of Biography*, volume 2, Melbourne: Melbourne University Press, 1967, <http://adb.anu.edu.au/biography/macarthur-elizabeth-2387>.

J. Cook, *Captain Cook's Journal During His First Voyage Round the World Made in H.M. Bark Endeavour 1768–1771*, London: Elliot Stock, 1893.

J. Cook, *The Journal of HMS Endeavour 1768–1771*, Adelaide: Rigby, 1977.

P. Cunningham, *Two Years in New South Wales*, London: Henry Colburn, 1827.

T. Dalton & E. Lobbecke, 'Part 4. Day of Destiny. First Fleet—A Graphic Journal', *Weekend Australian*, 23 January 2018.

W. Dampier, *A New Voyage Round the World*, London: Argonaut Press, 1927.

J.C. Dann (ed.), *The Nagle Journal: A Diary of the Life of Jacob Nagle, Sailor, from the Year 1775 to 1841*, New York: Weidenfeld & Nicolson, 1988.

Lord Dover (ed.), *Letters of Sir Horace Walpole, Earl of Orford to Sir Horace Mann, British Envoy at the Court of Tuscany*, London: Richard Bentley, 1833.

M. Duffy, *John Macarthur: Man of honour*, Sydney: Pan Macmillan, 2003.

E.W. Dunlop, 'Garnham Blaxcell (1778–1817)', *Australian Dictionary of Biography*, volume 1, Melbourne: Melbourne University Press, 1966, <http://adb.anu.edu.au/biography/blaxcell-garnham-1794>.

J. Dunmore (ed.), *The Journal of Jean-Francois de Galaup de La Pérouse 1785–1789*, vol. 2, London: Hukluyt Society, 1995.

J. Earnshaw, 'Thomas Muir', *Australian Dictionary of Biography*, volume 2, Melbourne: Melbourne University Press, 1967, <http://adb.anu.edu.au/biography/muir-thomas-2488>.

J. Earnshaw, 'Thomas Muir Scottish Martyr', Cremorne: Stone Copying Company, 1959.

J. Easty, *Journal, November 1786—May 1793.*

J. Easty, *Memorandum of Transactions of a Voyage from England to Botany Bay, 1787–1791: A First Fleet Journal*, Sydney: Trustees of the Public Library of New South Wales, 1965.

M.H. Ellis, *John Macarthur*, Sydney: Angus & Robertson, 1955.

M.H. Ellis, *Lachlan Macquarie: His life, adventures and times*, Sydney: Angus & Roertson, 1978.

H.V. Evatt, *Rum Rebellion: A study of the overthrow of Governor Bligh by John Macarthur and the New South Wales Corps*, Ayer Co. Pub., 1937.

B. Field (ed.), *Memoirs of James Hardy Vaux: A Swindler and a Thief. Now Transported to New South Wales for the second time, and for life. Written by himself and signed 18 May 1817*, London: Whittaker, Treacher, and Arnot, 1830.

B.H. Fletcher, 'Francis Grose (1758–1814)', *Australian Dictionary of Biography*, volume 1, Melbourne: Melbourne University Press, 1966, <http://adb.anu.edu.au/biography/grose-francis>.

M. Flinders, *A Voyage to Terra Australis, volume 1*, London: W. Bulmer and Co., 1814.

A. Frost, *The First Fleet: The real story*, Collingwood: Black Inc., c. 2011.

J.L. Guy, 'Building Construction Practice in the Colony of New South Wales from the Arrival of the First Fleet to the End of the Primitive Era and Its Influence in Later Time', paper presented to the Second International Congress on Construction History, Queens College, Cambridge University, 2006, <www.arct.cam.ac.uk/Downloads/ichs/vol-2-1475-1500-guy.pdf>.

D.R. Hainsworth, 'Simeon Lord (1771–1840)', *Australian Dictionary of Biography*, volume 2, Melbourne: Melbourne University Press, 1967, <http://adb.anu.edu.au/biography/lord-simeon-2371>.

J. Hall, *Theft, Law and Society*, Michigan: Little, Brown, 1937.

H. Heney, *Dear Fanny: Women's letters to and from New South Wales 1788–1857.* Canberra: Australian National University Press, 1985.

W. Hirst, *Great Escapes by Convicts in Colonial Australia*, East Roseville: Kangaroo Press, 2003.

R. Holden, *Orphans of History: The forgotten children of the First Fleet*, Melbourne: Text Publishing, 2000.

J. Howard, *The State of Prisons in England and Wales: With preliminary observations, and an account of some foreign prisons and hospitals*, Warrington: William Eyres, 1777.

R. Hughes, *The Fatal Shore: The epic of Australia's founding*, New York: Vintage Books, 1986.

J. Hunter, *An Historical Journal of the Transactions at Port Jackson and Norfolk Island with the Discoveries which have been made in New South Wales and the Southern*

Ocean since the Publication of Phillip's Voyage compiled from the official papers, including the Journals of Governors Phillip and King and Lieut. Ball and the Voyages of the first sailing of the Sirius in 1787 to the return of that Ship's Company to England in 1792, Piccadilly: John Stockdale, 1793.

J. Hunter, *Journal Kept on Board the Sirius During a Voyage to New South Wales, May 1787–March 1791*, State Library of New South Wales, <http://acms.sl.nsw.gov.au/_transcript/2015/D06318/a1518.html>.

G. Johnston, *Proceedings of a General Court-Marshal at Chelsea Hospital. Taken in Shorthand by Mr Bartrum of Clement's Inn*, London: Sherwood, Neely and Jones, 1811.

H. King, *Elizabeth Macarthur and Her World*, Sydney: Sydney University Press, 1980.

J. King, *Great Moments in Australian History*, Sydney: Allen & Unwin, 2009.

P. King, *The Journal of Philip Gidley King, Lieutenant R.N. 1787–1790*, Sydney: Australian Documents Library, 1980.

R.J. King, 'Francisco Muñoz y San Clemente and his Reflexions on the English Settlements of New Holland', *British Library Journal*, vol. 25, no. 1, 1999, pp. 55–76.

R.J. King, *The Secret History of the Convict Colony*, Sydney: Allen & Unwin, 1990.

R.J. King & V. Ibáñez, 'A Letter from Thaddaeus Haenke to Sir Joseph Banks, Sydney Cove, 15 April 1793', *Archives of Natural History*, vol. 23, no. 2, 1996, pp. 255–59.

R.W. Kirk, *Paradise Past: The transformation of the South Pacific, 1520–1920*, Jefferson, North Carolina & London: McFarland and Company Inc., 2012.

R. Knopwood, *The Diary of Rev. Robert Knopwood (1805–1808)*.

J.L. Kohen, 'Pemulwuy', *Australian Dictionary of Biography*, Supplementary Volume, Melbourne: Melbourne University Press, 2005, <http://adb.anu.edu.au/biography/Pemulwuy-13147>.

J. Lawrence & C. Warne, *A Pictorial History of Balmain to Glebe*, Crows Nest: Kingsclear Books, c. 1995.

J. Lynravn, 'Margaret Catchpole (1762–1819)', *Australian Dictionary of Biography*, volume 1, Melbourne: Melbourne University Press, 1966, <http://adb.anu.edu.au/biography/catchpole-margaret-1886>.

D.S. Macmillan, 'Robert Ross', *Australian Dictionary of Biography*, volume 2, Melbourne: Melbourne University Press, 1967.

L. Macquarie, *Proclamation: His Majesty having felt the utmost regret and displeasure on account of the late tumultuous proceedings in this his colony and the mutinous conduct of certain persons therein towards his late representative William Bligh*, Sydney: Government Press, 1810.

S. Marsden, *Essays Concerning New South Wales, 1807–18*, Mitchell Library, State Library of New South Wales, MLMSS 18, <http://acms.sl.nsw.gov.au/_transcript/2015/D06597/a2105.html>.

C. McDowall, 'Fantastic Flora in Australia—First Fleet to Federation', *The Culture Concept Circle*, 31 May 2014, <www.thecultureconcept.com/fantastic-flora-in-australia-first-fleet-to-federation>.

E. McMahon, *Islands, Identity and the Literary Imagination*, London & New York: Anthem Press, 2016.

G. Menzies, *1421: The year China discovered the world*, London: Bantam, 2003.

J. Nicol, *The Life and Adventures of John Nicol, Mariner*, Edinburgh & London: W. Blackwood & T. Cadell, 1822.

L. Olcelli, 'Alessandro Malaspina: An Italian-Spaniard at Port Jackson', *Sydney Journal*, vol. 4, no. 1, 2013, pp. 38–48.

V. Parsons, 'Barrallier, Francis Louis (1773–1853)', *Australian Dictionary of Biography*, volume 1, Melbourne: Melbourne University Press, 1966, <http://adb.anu.edu.au/biography/barrallier-francis-louis-1745>.

A. Phillip, *The Voyage of Governor Phillip to Botany Bay with an Account of the Establishment of the Colonies*, London: Stockdale Piccadilly, 1789.

L. Radzinowicz, *A History of the English Criminal Law and Its Administration from 1750, Vol. 1*, London: Stevens and Sons, 1948–50.

J. Ramsland, 'Children's Institutions in Nineteenth-century Sydney', *The Dictionary of Sydney*, 2011, <https://dictionaryofsydney.org/entry/childrens_institutions_in_nineteenth_century_sydney>.

J. Richie, *A Charge of Mutiny*, Canberra: National Library of Australia, 1988.

R. Rienits, 'Thomas Watling (1762–?)', *Australian Dictionary of Biography*, volume 2, Melbourne: Melbourne University Press, 1967, <http://adb.anu.edu.au/biography/watling-thomas-2776>.

E. Riou, *The Journal of the Proceedings on Board His Majesty's Ship the Guardian, Commanded by Lieutenant Riou, Bound for Botany Bay from 22 December 1789 to the 15th of January, 1790*, London: Ridgeway, 1790.

E. Scott, *The Life of Captain Flinders, RN*, Sydney: Angus & Robertson, 1914.

A.G.L. Shaw, *A History of the Port Phillip District: Victoria before separation*, Melbourne: Melbourne University Press, 1999.

A.G.L. Shaw (ed.), *Gipps–La Trobe Correspondence 1839–1846, Melbourne:* Miegunyah Press, 1989.

A.G.L. Shaw, 'Philip Gidley King (1758–1808)', *Australian Dictionary of Biography*, volume 2, Melbourne: Melbourne University Press, 1967, <http://adb.anu.edu.au/biography/king-philip-gidley-2309>.

A.G.L. Shaw, 'William Bligh (1754–1817)', *Australian Dictionary of Biography*, volume 1, Melbourne: Melbourne University Press, 1966, <http://adb.anu.edu.au/biography/bligh-william-1797>.

D. Southwell, *Journal and Letters of Daniel Southwell*, Sydney: Charles Potter, 1893, <http://gutenberg.net.au/ebooks12/1204411h.html>.

J. Spigelman & D.A. Roberts, 'The Macquarie Bicentennial: A reappraisal of the Bigge Reports', Sydney: History Council of NSW, 2009.

State Library of New South Wales, 'Crossing the Blue Mountains', State Library of New South Wales, <www.sl.nsw.gov.au/stories/crossing-blue-mountains>.

State Library of New South Wales, 'Marking the Spanish Expedition to Sydney in 1793', State Library of New South Wales, 14 March 2018, <www.sl.nsw.gov.au/blogs/marking-spanish-expedition-sydney-1793>.

M. Steven, 'John Macarthur (1767–1834)', *Australian Dictionary of Biography*, volume 2, Melbourne: Melbourne University Press, 1967, <http://adb.anu.edu.au/biography/macarthur-john-2390>.

M. Steven, 'John Palmer', *Australian Dictionary of Biography*, volume 2, Melbourne: Melbourne University Press, 1967, <http://adb.anu.edu.au/biography/palmer-john-2533>.

A. Summers, *Damned Whores and God's Police: The colonization of women in Australia*, Melbourne: Pelican, 2002.

Tanner & Associates, *Female Orphan School, Rydalmere: Conservation management plan, prepared for University of Western Sydney*, Surry Hills: Tanner & Associates, 2000.

W. Tench, *A Complete Account of the Settlement at Port Jackson, in New South Wales, concluding an Accurate Description of the Situation of the Colony*, London: G. Nicol and J. Sewell, 1793.

W. Tench, *A Narrative of the Expedition to Botany Bay: With an Account of New South Wales. Its Productions, Inhabitants, Etc: to which is Subjoined a List of Civil and Military Establishments at Port Jackson*, London: Debrett, 1789 (reprinted by Angus & Robertson, in association with the Royal Australian Historical Society, Sydney, 1961).

J.H. Tuckey, *An Account of a Voyage to Establish a Colony at Port Phillip in Bass's Strait, on the South Coast of New South Wales, in his Majesty's Ship Calcutta, in the years 1802-3-4.*

P. Turbet, *The First Frontier: The occupation of the Sydney region 1788–1816*, Sydney: Rosenberg Publishing, 2011.

M. Walker, *A Long Way Home: The life and adventures of the convict Mary Bryant*, Chichester, West Sussex, England; Hoboken, NJ: Wiley, 2005.

T. Watling, *Letters from an Exile at Botany Bay to his Aunt in Dumfries, 1784*, with an Introduction by George Mackaness, Australia: Review Publications, 1976.

F. Watson (ed.), *Historical Records of Australia* (37 volumes), Sydney: Library Committee of the Commonwealth Parliament.

W.C. Wentworth, *Journal of an Expedition Across the Blue Mountains, 11 May–6 June 1813*, State Library of New South Wales, <www.sl.nsw.gov.au/stories/crossing-blue-mountains/journals>.

A.-M. Whitaker, *Unfinished Revolution: United Irishmen in New South Wales, 1800–1810*, Darlinghurst: Crossing Press, 2010.

J. White, *Journal of a Voyage to New South Wales*, Piccadilly: J. Debrett, 1790.

G.B. Worgan, *Journal of a First Fleet Surgeon*, Sydney: Library Council of New South Wales in association with the Library of Australian History, 1978.

A.T. Yarwood, 'Samuel Marsden (1765–1838)', *Australian Dictionary of Biography*, volume 2, Melbourne: Melbourne University Press, 1967, <http://adb.anu.edu.au/biography/marsden-samuel-2433>.

List of Illustrations

Samuel John Neele's engraving of James Grant's painting, *Pimbloy: Native of New Holland in a canoe of that country*, 1804. State Library of Victoria.

Fernando Brambila, *View of Sydney*, 1793. British Library.

Robert Dighton, *Philip Gidley and Anna Josepha King with Their Children*, 1799. Mitchell Library, State Library of New South Wales.

Artist unknown, *John Macarthur*. Dixson Galleries, State Library of New South Wales.

Artist unknown, *Elizabeth Macarthur*. State Library of New South Wales.

François Bonneville, *Thomas Muir*, 1800. Musée de la Révolution française, Domaine de Vizille, Inv. MRF 1984.439.

John T. Barber, portrait miniature of David Collins, c. 1797–c. 1803. Mitchell Library, State Library of New South Wales.

Frederick Woodhouse, *The First Settlers Discover Buckley*, 1861. State Library of Victoria.

Bill Lacey, *They Rowed to Freedom*, 1966. Look and Learn History Picture Library.

George Gordon McCrae, *Sullivan Bay, Port Phillip*, 1803. State Library of Victoria.

Water casks sunk by Collins's expedition, Sorrento, Victoria, 1803. Rose Stereograph Co, ca. 1940. State Library of Victoria's Pictures Collection. Accession number: H32492/3839. http://handle.slv.vic.gov.au/10381/209302

Artist unknown, *Convict Uprising at Castle Hill*, 1804. National Library of Australia.

Hobart Town, 1805, probably by George Prideaux Harris. National Library of Australia.

New South Wales Government Printer—Arrest of Governor Bligh January 26, 1808. Copy of the original manuscript documents. Call number: PX*D 332-IE1014984-FL1015021. State Library of New South Wales. http://archival.sl.nsw.gov.au/Details/archive/110322228

Artist unknown, *Lachlan Macquarie*, c. 1819. Mitchell Library, State Library of New South Wales.

Artist unknown, *Elizabeth Macquarie*, c. 1819. Mitchell Library, State Library of New South Wales.

Panoramic views of Port Jackson, c. 1821, drawn by Major James Taylor, engraved by R. Havell & Sons. State Library of New South Wales, FL863898.

Index